C000244065

THE RING

THE RING

AN ILLUSTRATED HISTORY OF WAGNER'S RING AT THE ROYAL OPERA HOUSE

by John Snelson

OBERON BOOKS

LONDON

First published in 2006 by the Royal Opera House in association with Oberon Books

Oberon Books Ltd
521 Caledonian Road, London N7 9RH
Tel: 020 7607 3637/Fax: 020 7607 3629
info@oberonbooks.com / www.oberonbooks.com

A catalogue record for this book is available from the British Library.

ISBN: 1 84002 602 2
Book design: Jeff Willis
Printed in Great Britain by Antony Rowe Ltd, Chippenham.

Image Credits
Images have been sourced from the Royal Opera House Collections; we are grateful to the specific collections and additional copyright holders for permission to reproduce them.

Derek Allen: 77 (left), 79
Catherine Ashmore: 140 (right), 141 (above)
Clive Barda: 150–63
A. Console: 62
Zoë Dominic: 128 (right), 129, 133, 134 (below), 135, 137–9, 140 (left)
The Lady de Grey Albums at the Royal Opera House Collections: 14 (left), 15 (right), 20 (right), 21, 27, 29, 34 (above)
Houston Rogers, Theatre Museum, Victoria & Albert Museum: 74, 77 (right), 80 (above right and below), 86
Richard Holttum: 127
Richard H. Smith: 134 (above), 136 (above), 141 (centre and below)
The Donald Southern Collection at the Royal Opera House Collections: 83 (below), 85, 87–9, 97–102, 104–8, 110, 111 (left, above and below), 112–14, 115 (left), 116–17, 118 (above and centre), 119
Reg Wilson: 103

Every effort has been made to trace the copyright holders of all images reprinted in this book. Acknowledgement is made in all cases where the image source is available.

CONTENTS

ACKNOWLEDGEMENTS

Despite the single authorial name, a book such as this is essentially collaborative. Almost the entire staff of the Royal Opera House Collections have been drawn in at some point– whether digging out material or giving up desk space – ever-willing to help amid their dizzying programme of exhibitions, curating, cataloguing and publishing. Consequently, I am greatly indebted to Francesca Franchi, Archivist, for her support from the outset; Julia Creed, Assistant Archivist, was endlessly patient with my ever-increasing demands as I plundered the vaults week after week. Samya Waked, Archive Projects Assistant, quietly and efficiently arranged for the all-important photography of original materials, while Tom Tansey, Archive Projects Assistant, helped in particular with the partly unknown territory of the thousands of negatives in the Donald Southern Collection. First Sue Whyte, Archive Officer, and later Rachel Hayes, Archive Assistant, dealt with various administrative nuts and bolts, while Jane High and Katherine Rose, Cataloguers, guided me through the contents of original poster, set and costume design collections. A special mention must be made of Margaret Nicholson, who has worked for almost forty years on archival material at the Royal Opera House; her ongoing meticulous logging of the essential casting details of performances has been invaluable to anyone researching the who/what/when of those appearing on the main stage. I am also most grateful to my colleague in Publications, Anna Papaeti, who set up the administrative necessities of the project and also prepared the initial formats of the appendices, proving that patience is indeed a virtue.

Rosamund Bartlett, Patrick Carnegy, Eduardo Bennaroch and Helen Bishoprick were most encouraging in their words on the draft text. Maria Lord and Sarah Lenton readily brought their enthusiasm, operatic knowledge, writing and editing skills to bear on the material – as they are always so willing to do. Stewart Spencer, generous of his time and expertise in matters Wagnerian, provided valuable suggestions and additional information to the undoubted benefit of the reader. I am most appreciative of those who have allowed us to reproduce their work, and to Judith Vickers for her negotiations of this. The project began at the Royal Opera House under then Finance Director Anne Bulford who, with Katie Town, arranged the administrative niceties of publication with Oberon Books. For the publishers, James Hogan believed from the outset in the value of the project, while Ian Higham and my editor Dan Steward have in different ways ensured that the book would get into print! Jeff Willis has produced for us all an elegant design to display the results of my researches. Finally, Henry Wilson has been – yet again – supportive and patient from initial thoughts through to completion.

John Snelson

FOREWORD

When Wagner brought to life his operatic cycle *Der Ring des Nibelungen* he created not just an entire world on stage through its four linked operas, but a visionary cultural event. From the first performance of a full cycle at Bayreuth in August 1876 right through to our time, the *Ring* has been woven ever tighter into the fabric of the operatic world to the extent that it colours any view we have on what opera is. Composers and theatre practitioners have had some 130 years to react to Wagner's concepts, and as each successive generation has embraced, rejected or manipulated Wagner's intentions, new layers of interpretation have been added. Now, each time an opera company presents the cycle, it provokes almost as many responses to it as there are audience members – perhaps a showcase for singers and orchestra, a reflection of the philosophical and political zeitgeist, a celebratory event of the art form itself, or even a weather vane for the artistic vitality of the company presenting it. No opera lover today can escape the influence of the *Ring*, and no opera house can – or should – avoid it.

Beyond the saga of gods and mortals, dwarfs and giants told on the stage, the *Ring*'s own production history now makes for quite a tale, one to which the Royal Opera House has added its own plots and characters since that first *Siegfried* and single cycle in 1892. Some of the personalities in our story are the greatest Wagnerians of their times, household names during their lives and beyond; others provide a sense of intriguing local detail by virtue of their near-anonymity today. Early imagery from Royal Opera House *Rings* illustrates how strong the ties could be between the experiences of opera lovers in different countries and on different continents; this was the time when the dramatic and visual interpretation established a shared understanding of Wagner's tetralogy. Later developments in production illustrate how individuality increasingly came to the fore, so that each new production of the cycle was especially distinctive.

Seeing more than a century of Royal Opera House *Rings* celebrated in one volume brings home this dual focus of the global and the local. We can be excited by our vibrant and resonant contribution to the shared history worldwide of a work at the core of the operatic repertory. But we can also be proud of what the Royal Opera House has uniquely brought to the phenomenon of *Der Ring des Nibelungen*.

Tony Hall
Chief Executive
Royal Opera House

THEATRE ROYAL

COVENT GARDEN.

LESSEE - - SIR AUGUSTUS HARRIS.

German Opera

(1892.)

MR. BASIL TREE begs to announce that he has made arrangements with SIR AUGUSTUS HARRIS, by which he is empowered to receive Subscriptions for the Series of purely GERMAN OPERA which will take place at COVENT GARDEN, on the following Wednesdays:

Wednesday, June 8th.
Wednesday, June 15th.
Wednesday, June 22nd.
Wednesday, June 29th.
Wednesday, July 6th.
Wednesday, July 13th.
Wednesday, July 20th.

The Series is to comprise the following Works:

Das Rheingold. **Siegfried.**

Die Walküre. **Die Götterdämmerung.**

(These FOUR PERFORMANCES constitute the entire "NIBELUNGEN RING.")

Tristan und Isolde. **Fidelio.**

Some of the most eminent German Artists are to take part in the Performances. Full particulars will be given in due course; in the meantime some information which appeared in *The Daily Telegraph*, of *February 23rd*, is reprinted on the other side.

Mr. BASIL TREE is prepared to receive Subscriptions at the following rates, for the

SERIES of SEVEN PERFORMANCES;

PIT and GRAND TIER BOXES,	£42.
FIRST TIER BOXES, -	£14 14s.
SECOND TIER BOXES, -	£8 8s.
STALLS, - -	£7.
BALCONY STALLS, - -	£4 18s.
AMPHITHEATRE STALLS (First Two Rows) -	£3 10s.
(Remaining Rows) -	£1 11s. 6d.

☞ *In ordering please fill in the annexed Form.*

J. MILES & CO., PRINTERS, WARDOUR ST., W.

Annotated booking form listing the performances of the 1892 German Opera Season at the Royal Opera House

CHAPTER ONE

THE EARLY RINGS

1892–1914

When the great theatrical impresario Sir Augustus Harris began to present Seasons at the Royal Italian Opera (Covent Garden) in 1888 he also began to move towards the performance of operas in their original languages. This was a time when Italian was the principal language for opera in London, and anything not Italian was likely to be made so. French works were the first to receive Harris's linguistic rectification, with *Roméo et Juliette* in 1889 followed in the next two years by operas including *Hamlet, Carmen* and *Faust.* Wagner's operas – *Lohengrin, Tannhäuser* and *Die Meistersinger von Nürnberg* – were still sung in Italian.

For his 1892 Season, Harris decided to make a substantial foray into German repertory by presenting Wagner's *Ring* cycle. It was not to be the first London cycle – that had been given ten years earlier by the impresario Angelo Neumann at Her Majesty's Theatre – but it would be the first time on the Covent Garden stage. Harris's pursuit of original-language performances meant that the cycle would also be sung in German, and thus a small problem became that much larger: the title Royal Italian Opera would no longer do, and as a consequence the institution was renamed the Royal Opera House. Next, Harris needed to employ singers and conductors already familiar with the operas in German, and so he looked not to London but to Hamburg, where a former business partner of his, Pollini (an Italianized version of his real name, Bernhard Pohl), was Intendant. Consequently, the entire Hamburg opera – singers, chorus, orchestral players and the company's newly appointed conductor, Gustav Mahler – came to London to present the first *Ring* cycle at Covent Garden, in its original language, using sets and costumes advertised as copied from Bayreuth.

Not surprisingly, this was a financially risky venture, so the chosen timing ensured that performances took place when the social calendar had London at its most populated and the potential high-society audience for opera at its greatest. The *Daily Telegraph* (23 February) seemed confident, and Harris was happy to use its remarks in his own publicity: 'It need scarcely be added that the expenses of the entire undertaking are enormous. Inasmuch as good performances are assured, the readiness of the public to make successful so plucky an enterprise should be proportionately great.' Tickets were available through a subscription to all of a series of seven performances of German opera on Wednesday evenings to include *Der Ring des Nibelungen, Fidelio* and *Tristan und Isolde;* Pit Tier and Grand Tier box seats were the most expensive, at £42 for all performances, while Amphitheatre seats from the third row back were the cheapest at £1/11/6. The *Ring* performances were *Das Rheingold* on 22 June, *Die Walküre* on 29 June, *Siegfried* on 6 July and *Götterdämmerung* on 13 July. To begin, however, a single performance of *Siegfried* was given on 8 June so that the leading Heldentenor Max Alvary could make his London debut in the title role, one for which he was particularly noted.

That first *Siegfried* opened the German Opera Season at Covent Garden at eight o'clock on 8 June with Alvary's Siegfried garnering praise; the critic for *The Times* noted Alvary's 'manly beauty, expressive features, dramatic power, and a remarkably fine voice, which he employs admirably'. Critics also admired the carrying power of Julius Lieban's Mime who 'as the only comedian in the cast, contributed greatly to the success which was achieved' and the voice of Rosa Sucher proved 'charming as ever' as Brünnhilde. The orchestra under Mahler was supplemented by German musicians who had the benefit of experience with the score. In the event, subscription to the performances was so popular that a second performance of *Siegfried* by the same cast was arranged for 13 June at the Theatre Royal, Drury Lane – also under Harris's management – and a second complete cycle followed with an instalment each week from 27 June.

The printed reviews reveal the sometimes wary attitudes towards Wagner at a time when French and Italian works dominated the repertory. As the Wanderer, in *Siegfried,* Karl Grengg 'sang with all possible effect the fatiguing, and for the most part, thankless, utterances with which his *rôle* abounded', so *The Times* reported of the opening performance. With *Die Walküre* the sentiment was expanded, for the whole cast 'sang and acted remarkably well. They had little chance of distinguishing themselves as vocalists; seeing they had solely to declaim passages devoid of melody; passages sometimes forty and fifty lines in length. They did their work well, but their fine voices were, to a great extent, wasted. They were simply engaged in affording clues to the orchestration, and this was admirable; full of colouring, and from beginning to end obviously the work of a master.' That this was not solely a *Ring* concern was shown in response to *Tristan und Isolde* in the same subscription series:

> The orchestral music (the most valuable portion of the score) was satisfactorily played; the opera was well 'mounted', and has seldom, if ever, been better performed in this country. That it will ever become popular here is unlikely. The tedious harangues of the leading personages, rarely relieved by melodious composition of any length, become irksome to all but Wagner's inveterate admirers; the plot is uninteresting, and in some respects absurd, and it is a pity to waste time on such a work as *Tristan und Isolde,* when much better works are available.

However, such complaints were overshadowed by the public response, as the *Times* reviewer noted in his concluding remarks on that first performance of *Siegfried*: 'An enormous audience received the work and the performance with an amount of enthusiasm quite beyond the average, and evidently quite sincere.'

On stage, the sets were naturalistic, interpreting literally such locations as the rocky mountain top of the Valkyries, the forest lair of the dragon Fafner and the pillared hall of the Gibichungs, with its view over the Rhine. Costumes adopted a similar vein, with a concatenation of Nordic and Celtic imagery – long cloaks for gods and rulers, fur for Siegfried and the now much-parodied war dress of breastplates and helmets for the Valkyries. There were some omissions (no chariot drawn by rams for Fricka, for example), but the presentation of the *Ring* for the most part followed Bayreuth practice, even to the extent that in 1892, the newly electrified house lights were dimmed during the performances enough to enhance noticeably the picture on stage, although the orchestra pit lights remained visible. And if the annoyance from those society figures who preferred to be seen rather than see appears petty to us today, a more significant complaint came from those who were accustomed to buying copies of opera librettos to refer to during the performance: many found themselves faced with a long and complicated work they did not know, and were unable to see the texts they had bought (similar complaints were to persist for over twenty years). At the end of the first cycle, *The Times* concluded that

> the houses have been filled from floor to ceiling with enthusiastic audiences drawn less from the circle of Wagner's professed admirers than from the great public, and this despite, not in consequence, of the influence of fashion. It is a favourite sneer of the less intelligent opponents of musical progress that the *Ring* depends for the attraction which it exercises upon the arts of stage management and its novelties of stage effect. It is a little strange to see that this sneer has been revived in a season when the work has been presented with as few as possible of these additions. From this point of view the mounting of the cycle will not bear comparison with that of the performance given ten years ago at Her Majesty's; but happily, the cutting down of the stage effects has not gone hand in hand with the more important process of cutting down the music. With very few exceptions, such as some regrettable excisions from the second act of *Die Walküre* and the... omission of the [Norns'] prologue to the final drama, the four works have been presented as Wagner wrote them, with infinite advantage to their general effect, for it is a paradox of which the truth is confirmed as much by the maimed second act of the Italian *Lohengrin* as by the result of the unreduced scenes of the trilogy that these works only become tedious when they are shortened.

Although the presentation of the *Ring* caught the ticket-buying public's imagination and the houses for the originally scheduled performances and the extra ones at Drury Lane were packed out, the experience was not immediately repeated, and a complete cycle was not given again at Covent Garden for several years. There were, however, individual performances of two of the operas. *Siegfried* was presented in 1893 for a single performance that again included Alvary in the title role. *Die Walküre* made more regular appearances, first in 1893, but then most notably in the 1895 Grand English Opera Season as *The Valkyrie* – the first performances of the opera in English. The direction was by the Canadian tenor Charles Hedmont, who also sang Siegmund, while the American performer David Bispham played Wotan for the first time at Covent Garden, returning in following years' *Rings* to repeat that role and also to play Alberich and Hunding. Susan Strong as Sieglinde provoked particular praise not just for fine singing but for effective acting ('Gifted with a fine physique and an unusually dignified stage presence, her command of beautiful and appropriate gesture is such as the most experienced singers rarely attain'). George Henschel, moving from his more usual popular orchestral repertory into opera, was the conductor of 'an augmented orchestra of 90 performers'. A change of language also marked two performances of *Die Walküre* in 1896, sung this time in French, but in 1897 German returned for more performances of *Die Walküre* and *Siegfried.*

It was in 1898 that the *Ring* was presented as a cycle again, and not surprisingly this became the major event of the Royal Opera Season. To mark it, a souvenir in two volumes was produced. The first volume described the operas and their stories and was accompanied by beautiful art nouveau illustrations, while the second featured information on and photographs of the singers and conductors. From today's perspective, the tone adopted by Louis N. Parker in his scene-setting essay in volume one is that of hyperbole. However, his reverential presentation of the thoughts of Wagner is revealing of how the spotlight of operatic attention was beginning to shift towards the German repertory, increasingly displacing French operatic perennials (only *Carmen, Faust* and *Roméo et Juliette* made regular appearances into the first decade of the 1900s). As Parker portrays it – with the benefit of hindsight – Wagner

> sat down and said to himself: I, the refugee; I the failure; I whom people come to see on the sly, and whose books they circulate under the mantle, I, whose works have not been played in my native country these many days; I, who am nobody, living nowhere – I will now write a drama for the performance of which a special theatre must be built. I will have it built in the furthermost corner of the world. My drama shall last four nights, no living artists shall have the skill to play therein until they have gone to school again, unlearnt all they now know, and learnt all I can teach them. I will write my music for an orchestra such as does not exist. I will write for instruments that have not been invented. I will invent them. For my poem I will take all heaven and all earth and the waters that are under the earth, and I will write it in a new tongue. My scenery shall be the unrepresentable: rainbows, fire, and the depths of the rivers. My characters shall be gods, toads, heroes and birds of the air. All this I will do with my own hand, and without any man's help. I will build my theatre, teach my artists, design my scenery, stage-manage, conduct my orchestra, invent my scenarios, write my poems, and compose my music. Moreover, I will create my public. To-day nobody knows me. If anybody knows me he suppresses the fact. To-morrow they shall come from England, from America, from the Indies, from China and Japan, stream in their thousands up the hill where my theatre stands and fight for the privilege of entry. Emperors and kings shall come tedious journeys to sit in my house. The town where I build shall be unheard of one day, and the next it shall be the capital of a new art, and from it a new influence shall radiate into all the world. This I, Wagner, the exile, will do.

The language is that of myth with the fairly heavy resonance of Biblical overtones; and in one sense the caricature of 'Today Bayreuth. Tomorrow the World!' is not so far from the truth, as Parker continues:

> the world saw [*Parsifal*], understood, and acclaimed, and in the following February the Titan was able to lay his weary limbs to rest, knowing that his work was done; that henceforward, day by day, it would be better understood, would sink gradually into the heart, not of his own ungrateful nation only, but of all the peoples of the world, north and south, east and west.
>
> The subsequent history of the *Ring* is without any great interest. It has become the great stock-piece in all the theatres of the Continent, and has been mangled and mauled in the process. Here and there, at Dresden, at Vienna, at Munich, and at Carlsruhe, it has found a worthy home; it has been revived with great splendour at Bayreuth; it has eaten up its detractors, and at last it has come to London. We have to be thankful that we live near enough to its origins to profit by the teachings of Wagner's own personal pupils and those most deeply in his confidence: Richter, Mottl, Seidl, and, above all, the woman [Cosima Wagner] who all through Wagner's later life was his good angel, and since his death has

become the guardian and propagator of his fame.

The link with Bayreuth is an important one, for the 'official seal of approval' bestowed on anyone who had worked there gave an added impact to the 1898 Covent Garden performances. Wotan was sung by Anton van Rooy, who had made his acclaimed debut in the role at Bayreuth in 1897, and who was to be the leading Royal Opera Wotan right through to 1913; while Hans Breuer, who sang Mime, was the regular Bayreuth performer of the role from 1896 to 1914. Ernestine Schumann-Heink, who had been in that first Covent Garden *Ring* of 1892 (Flosshilde, Fricka, Siegrune, Erda and Waltraute) began in 1896 nearly two decades as a regular performer at Bayreuth. Marie Brema, who returned as Brünnhilde, had been the first singer born in Britain to take a leading role at Bayreuth (as Ortrud) in 1894, the same year that Lillian Nordica (a well-established member of Harris's troupe of singers), made her first appearance there as Elsa. Ernest Van Dyck, one of the two Siegmunds (the other was Jean de Reszke), had first appeared on the Bayreuth stage in 1888. Also, behind the proscenium arch, Bayreuth's stage machinist had been brought over to supervise some of the technical aspects of the production.

But there was one particularly strong connection between the Bayreuth 'tradition' and London *Ring* performances up until the start of World War I: the conductors. Felix Mottl, Anton Seidl, Hermann Zumpe and Hans Richter provided a direct link from the very first Bayreuth Festival. When Mottl took up the baton for the *Ring* in London in 1898, he was firmly established at the forefront of Bayreuth conductors (he had given the premieres there of *Tristan und Isolde, Tannhäuser* and *Lohengrin,* with that of *Der fliegende Holländer* to follow in 1901). Hans Richter, whose career was inextricably bound up with Wagner's works and who had conducted at nearly every Bayreuth Festival for some 25 years (in 1888 for the first time, in 1912 for the last), brought his first-hand experience to London as the most frequent interpreter of the *Ring*, conducting its operas at Covent Garden in 1903, 1905, 1906, 1907, 1908, 1909 and 1910. With the addition of Karl Muck, Franz Schalk, Emil Steinbach, Otto Lohse and Arthur Nikisch, the first decades of the Covent Garden conducting roster for individual *Ring* operas or complete cycles set a pattern for the future, drawn as they were from the top Wagnerian interpreters of the day.

Richter was not only the conductor for what were seen as ground-breaking performances of the cycle in 1908, but also provided the impetus for them.

> The performances of Wagner's *Der Ring des Nibelungen* given in German at Covent Garden Theatre during the past Grand Seasons under the direction of Dr Hans Richter have proved an important factor in musical life and have done much to acquaint the public with Wagner's masterpiece. The Directors of the Grand Opera Syndicate have now decided to give, at the suggestion of Dr Richter, the whole of *The Ring of the Nibelung* in English, for the *first time,* being of the opinion that it would appeal to a much wider circle when sung in the National language.

The adoption of Frederick Jameson's translation was very successful, but one of the biggest changes that could instantly be seen was in the different casting – obviously some foreign performers were not as keen or able as others to learn an entirely new translation. Consequently, English-speaking performers figure more prominently on the cast lists, as with Clarence Whitehill, who was already established as a regular Wotan alongside Van Rooy. In 1908 Whitehill sang in the English-language performances, while Van Rooy took the part in later performances that same year in the original German. Whereas in 1907 *Das Rheingold* (in German) featured in its cast Herr Knüpfer, Herr Raboth and Herr Nietan as Fasolt, Fafner and Froh, in *The Rhinegold* of 1908 the same roles were taken by Mr Radford, Mr Harford and Mr Hyde.

Other changes were happening in the early 1900s with the very gradual replacement of the original Bayreuth copies of scenery and costumes, in part required by changes to the theatre's stage itself (history was to repeat itself a hundred years later, when another stage rebuilding was to make similar demands). In 1903, under the scenic director Harry Brooke, new stage images began to be introduced for some of the scenes. *Das Rheingold* was the first to receive such a reworking, on 27 April 1903 (as *The Times* reported): 'A very special attention has to be paid to the scenery and stage-management, which on this occasion have been undertaken from the very beginning. The three scenes of the prelude have been painted by Mr Harry Brooke, and all three are altogether admirable, and none the less so because they differ here and there from the conventional pattern set by Wagner. The scene of Walhall and the Rhine is a magnificent piece of stage landscape, and the rainbow bridge surpasses even that of Bayreuth.' While we are now used to the preparation of a completely new interpretation by a single designer, carried through all operas, for several of the opening decades of Covent Garden *Ring* performances, changes were introduced bit by bit. 'From time to time new scenes are added – as was the case last night', reported the *Daily Express* on the opening of the first cycle of 1914, 'and new experiments attempted with more or less obsolete mechanical devices and lighting apparatus, but the result falls painfully short of modern requirements.' For this *Rheingold* the 'rugged grandeur and the inaccessiblity of the rocky stronghold reared by the giants for the gods, forms a most effective background for the weighty happenings of this scene, and, as the whole gradually came into view, while the splendid Walhalla motive is intoned by the orchestra, the total result was exceedingly fine'. *Die Walküre* also garnered praise for a new setting for Act III to complement one for Act II introduced the previous year: both were 'admirably in keeping with the heroic spirit of Wagner's work, and an immense improvement on the old style of staging the opera'.

What was especially to distinguish the final *Rings* of 1914 before the commencement of World War I was the conducting of Arthur Nikisch, returning after his great success with the cycle at the Royal Opera House the previous year. Through the benefit of a succession of *Ring* performances now spanning over thirty years in London (going back to Neumann's 1882 cycles), there was a more mature awareness of the possibilities open to the performance of Wagner. Nikisch's interpretation was 'based on tradition read by modern lights' (*Morning Post*), and his performances brought out 'the difference between his conception of the music and that of the older school of conductors'. Comparison with Hans Richter was inevitable, as summarized in this extract from a review in *The Standard* for *Die Walküre:*

> Dr Richter's readings were largely concerned with what may be called the dynamics of the *Ring*. Herr Nikisch seems far more intent on exploiting the aesthetics. Singers who failed to hold their own with the orchestra or lagged behind Dr Richter's rigid tempi received short-shrift at his hands. Herr Nikisch is not only more lenient, rhythmically speaking, but he moderates the composer's transports so successfully that it is possible to hear the words in the most strenuous passages.

The 1914 cycles were widely acclaimed for casting, musical presentation and (with a few exceptions, such as the *Rheingold* rainbow, which failed to impress this time round) its developing staging. The seriousness with which Wagner was approached is illuminated by one observation made in the *News of the World* on the change in the Opera Season itself in May 1914.

> With the conclusion of the German opera, the season at Covent Garden enters upon its second and more social phase. The lights have gone up and there will now be some object in the ladies wearing their jewels. A pitch dark auditorium has, as usual, been the rigid rule during the two cycles of the *Ring*, *Parsifal*, and the other Wagner works, with the result that it has been hopeless for anyone ignorant of the stories to follow the books. The month has been a striking success, especially in view of the fact that the recent winter season, which only ended a month or so before the beginning of the present season, was almost entirely devoted to Wagner.

However, the outbreak of World War I prevented any immediate intentions to build on the 1914 success, and it would not be until October 1921 that any of the *Ring* operas returned to the Covent Garden stage.

Sir Augustus Harris, who instigated the first *Ring* cycle at Covent Garden, in 1892. Underneath this image of him in her photograph album, Lady de Grey described Harris as 'the most enterprising of impresarios'.

Felix Mottl, conductor for *Ring* cycles at Covent Garden in 1898 and 1900.

Max Alvary chose to make his London debut in the title role of *Siegfried,* 8 June 1892 at Covent Garden. According to *The Times*, Alvary 'proved himself worthy of the high reputation he has earned on the continent as a vocalist and actor of the first rank. He has much in his favour; manly beauty, expressive features, dramatic power, and a remarkably fine voice, which he employs admirably. He at once made himself a favourite of the metropolitan public, and will henceforth be regarded as one of the chief attractions – if not the absolute chief – of the German Opera Company engaged by Sir Augustus Harris.' In the same Season, Alvary also appeared as Loge, Siegmund, Tristan and Tannhäuser (the last two roles he had sung at Bayreuth the previous year). He returned to Covent Garden as Siegmund and Siegfried on, respectively, 5 and 19 July 1893.

Autographed portrait of Max Alvary, Munich 1893. Alongside the image in her album, Lady de Grey described him as 'one of the best German tenors'.

A photograph of the stage set for *Siegfried* Act II at Covent Garden in 1892, along with a reconstruction made by the Opera House Model Room.

Photographs of *Siegfried* Act I and Act III scene 1, 1892. The *Times* reviewer noted:

The orchestra, greatly augmented in size, is of very fine quality, and it is pleasant to see certain excellent German practices adopted. For example, Herr Mahler, the admirable conductor, sits, or rather stands, not close to the stage, but in the middle of his players. The effect of the beautiful scenery was immensely enhanced by the absence of all light in the auditorium during the acts. As a rule the elaborate effects demanded by Wagner were realized; the dragon was not more ridiculous than usual, and the forging of the sword was realistically accomplished. It would have been difficult, however, for the ignorant spectator to grasp the fact that Siegfried's ascent of Brünnhilde's rock was a dangerous adventure, since scarcely any fire was used at all, and no actual flames appeared.

Photographs of the stage settings for *Götterdämmerung* at Covent Garden in 1892: Act I 'Gunther's Hall', Act II 'outside Gunther's dwelling' and the conclusion of Act III. These designs were to influence future stage settings for half a century, and the effects of their style and detailing can be seen in such later Covent Garden developments as those by Gabriel Volkoff in 1934–5.

The Dutch baritone Anton van Rooy made his Bayreuth debut as Wotan in 1897 and appeared for the first time at Covent Garden in the same part the following year, on 11 May in *Die Walküre.* In her photograph album, Lady de Grey described Van Rooy as 'the great Bass – Wotan, Kurwenal, Hans Sachs, all wonderful + satisfying'. He returned to Covent Garden in the role in 1899 and appeared as Wotan every year up to 1913 except in 1904, a Season in which the *Ring* operas were not performed, and 1909, when the cycle was given only in English.

Jean de Reszke as Siegfried (1898).

'Jean & Edouard de Reszke – a perfect duo', so Lady de Grey inscribed in her photograph album. They were internationally at the top of their profession, each with large repertories and regular appearances – frequently together – on both sides of the Atlantic. Their voice types, Jean the tenor (after an initial career as the baritone Giovanni di Reschi) and Edouard the baritone, often put them in complementary roles, such as Gounod's Faust and Méphistophélès, and hence Jean was Siegfried to Edouard's Wanderer in London in 1898. These London *Ring* appearances also saw the debut of Jean as Siegfried in *Götterdämmerung* (with brother Edouard as Hagen) although he had already played the character in the third opera of the cycle in 1897, a year after his local role debut as Tristan. Edouard was also known for Wagnerian roles – Hans Sachs, King Mark and Hagen – although he did not entirely please his audience this time as the Wanderer when, through illness, both he and his brother sang edited versions of their roles. Complaints from those in the audience who now preferred their Wagner 'complete and unmutilated', as one reviewer put it, made such an impact that

> The moment that [Jean de Reszke] learned how serious a point had been made on the subject of the cuts by those self-constituted guardians of art to whom the words protest and hysteria are synonymous terms, he, doubtless, seeing the essential justice of the objection, which we also found it impossible to overlook, made immediate arrangements to sing the whole part of Siegfried, while M. Eduoard de Reszke, with a graciousness rare indeed among artists, stood aside to make way for Herr [Anton] Van Rooy, who has studied the part of the Wanderer in its totality.

Programmes for the first English-language *Valkyrie* and for *The Rhinegold,* the opening night of the first English *Ring*. The *Valkyrie* performances were part of the Moody-Manners Autumn Opera Season at Covent Garden in 1895. A quick scan of the names of the performers – including David Bispham, Susan Strong, Lilian Tree, Alex Bevan and Charles [E.C.] Hedmont (who was also the director) – reveals that native-language performance also meant native-language casting, from Britain and North America. It took a further 12 years before the entire cycle was given in English, in 1908, when Richter conducted. Hedmont, who was by birth a Canadian, but had been established as a singer and director in England since the early 1890s, again directed and also sang Loge. The 1908 programme also shows a change in the formalities of the Royal Opera House: 'Herr' is replaced in print for all the men singers of whatever nationality by 'Mr'. For the cycles that began on 1 May 1908, the language returned to German and the printed titles to 'Herr'; titles were finally dropped from early in May 1914, the change happening between a 'titled' programme of *Das Rheingold* on 4 May and an 'untitled' one for *Die Walküre* the following night.

NO CHARGE FOR THIS PROGRAMME.

Theatre Royal Covent Garden

Sole Lessee and Manager · Sir AUGUSTUS HARRIS.

Sir Augustus Harris has made arrangements with Mr. E C. Hedmondt for a

GRAND ENGLISH OPERA SEASON 1895

SATURDAY, OCTOBER 12th, at 7.45

Wagner's Opera,

TANNHÄUSER.

Tannhäuser ... Mr. E. C. HEDMONDT
Wolfram von Eshinbach — Minstrel Knights — Mr. DAVID BISPHAM
Walther von der Vogelweide — Mr. REGINALD BROPHY
Biterolf ... ... Mr. WM. LLEWELYN
Heinrich ... ... Mr. ROBERT EADIE
Reinmar von Zwetter Mr. WHITNEY TEW
Venus ... ... Miss L. RECOSCHEWITZ
A Young Shepherd ... Miss CLARE ADDISON
Hermann (Landgrave of Thuringia) Mr. ALEX. BEVAN
AND
Elizabeth (Landgrave's Niece) Miss ALICE ESTY

Four Noble Pages,
Mesdames McCUSKER, RUSSELL, GRAY, and SHORTLAND.

Act I. Interior of the Horselberg or Temple of Venus, and the Valley of Wartburg.
Act II. The Castle of Wartburg.
Act III. The Valley of Wartburg.

The action takes place in the beginning of the 13th century.

Conductor ... Mr. FELD

MONDAY, OCTOBER 14th, at 7.45

Wagner's Opera,

LOHENGRIN.

Lohengrin (Knight of the Holy Grail) Mr. E. C. HEDMONDT
Henry I. (King of Germany) Mr. FRANKLIN CLIVE
Frederick Telramund (A Noble of Brabant) Mr. WINFRED GOFF
The Royal Herald ... Mr. WILSON SHEFFIELD
Gottfried (Elsa's Brother) Miss CLARE ROTHWELL
Ortrud (Wife of Telramund) Miss ROSA OLITZKA
AND
Elsa of Brabant ... Miss ALICE ESTY

Four Pages,
Mesdames RUSSELL, McCUSKER, GRAY, ADDISON.

Conductor ... Mr. FELD

TUESDAY, OCTOBER 15th, at 7.45

Gounod's Opera,

FAUST.

Faust ... ... Mr. PHILIP BROZEL (For the First Time in English)
AND
Mephistopheles ... Mr. CHARLES MANNERS
Valentine ... ... Mr. WINFRED GOFF
Wagner ... ... Mr. ARTHUR WELTON
Siebel ... ... Miss ROSA OLITZKA
Martha ... ... Miss KATE LEE
AND
Marguerite ... ... Madame FANNY MOODY

Act I. Faust's Study.
Act II. The Fair.
Act III. Marguerite's Garden.
Act IV. Scene 1.—A Room in Marguerite's House. Scene 2.—Exterior of a Church.
Act V. The Prison.

Conductor ... Mr. J. M. GLOVER.

WEDNESDAY, OCTOBER 16th, at 7.45

Grand Production of Wagner's Music Drama

Under the Direction of Mr. E. C. Hedmondt

THE VALKYRIE

English Version by H. & F. Corder.

FOR THE FIRST TIME IN ENGLISH.

Siegmund ... ... Mr. E. C. HEDMONDT
Hunding ... ... Mr. ALEX. BEVAN
Wotan ... ... Mr. DAVID BISPHAM
Fricka ... ... Miss ROSA OLITZKA
Sieglinde ... ... Miss SUSAN STRONG
AND
Brunnhilde ... ... Madame LILIAN TREE

The Valkyries,
Mesdames RUSSELL, SINICO, GRAY, TREFELYN, LEE, ADDISON, McCUSKER, OLITZKA.

Conductor ... Mr. HENSCHEL

THURSDAY, OCTOBER 17th, at 7.45

Sir AUGUSTUS HARRIS'S COMPANY
IN
Bizet's Opera,

CARMEN.

Don Jose ... ... Mr. PHILIP BROZEL
AND
Michaela ... ... Miss ALICE ESTY
Frasquita ... ... Miss KATE LEE
Mercedes ... ... Miss CLARE ADDISON
Escamillo ... ... Mr. WINFRED GOFF
Dancairo ... ... Mr. WILSON SHEFFIELD
Remendado ... ... Mr. WILFRED ESMOND
Zuniga ... ... Mr. WM. LLEWELYN
Morales ... ... Mr. ROBERT EADIE
AND
Carmen ... ... Miss AGNES JANSON

Conductor, ... Mr. FELD

FRIDAY, OCTOBER 18th, at 7.45,

A POPULAR OPERA.

MORNING PERFORMANCE.

SATURDAY, OCTOBER 19th, at 1.45

ONLY MORNING PERFORMANCE OF
Gounod's Opera,

FAUST

Marguerite ... ... Madame FANNY MOODY
Faust ... ... Mr. PHILIP BROZEL
Mephistopheles ... Mr. CHARLES MANNERS

SATURDAY EVENING, OCTOBER 19th, at 7.45

Wagner's Opera,

TANNHÄUSER.

50th ANNIVERSARY OF THE PRODUCTION OF TANNHAUSER.

Elizabeth (Landgrave's Niece) Miss MARGUERITE MACINTYRE
Wolfram von Eshinbach ... Mr. DAVID BISPHAM
Tannhäuser ... ... Mr. E. C. HEDMONDT

Doors Open Half-an-Hour before the Performance commences.

Private Boxes, One Guinea to Five Guineas.
Orchestra Stalls, Reserved, 10s. 6d. Grand Circle, Reserved, 7s. 6d.
Back Stalls, Reserved, 6s. Balcony Stalls, Reserved, 4s.
Amphitheatre Stalls, Unreserved, 2s. 6d.
Amphitheatre, Admission, 1s.

Box Office open from 10 a.m. to 5 p.m. for future Booking, and all day long for the Sale of Seats for the same evening.

The Pianofortes supplied by Steinway.
Conductor's Piano by Bechstein.

Theatre Royal Drury Lane.

Sole Lessee and Manager · · Sir Augustus Harris.

EVERY EVENING AT 7.30

A New and Original Drama, entitled,

Cheer Boys Cheer!

WRITTEN BY
SIR AUGUSTUS HARRIS,
CECIL RALEIGH and
HENRY HAMILTON.
(AUTHORS OF "THE DERBY WINNER.")

Matinee Every Saturday at 1.30

Prices of Admission

Private Boxes, Grand Tier, to hold Four, £2 12s. 6d.
Double Boxes, to hold Eight, £5 5s.
First Tier Boxes, to hold Four, £2 2s. Second Tier, £1 1s.
Stalls, 10s. 6d. Grand Circle, 1st Two Rows, 7s.; Other Rows, 6s.
First Circle, 1st Two Rows, 5s.; Other Rows, 4s. Balcony, Admission, 3s.
Pit, Admission, 2s. 6d. Amphitheatre, Admission, 1s. 6d.
Gallery, Admission, 1s.

BOX OFFICE OPEN FROM 10 ALL DAY.

IN ACTIVE PREPARATION

Sir Augustus Harris's

SEVENTEENTH ANNUAL GRAND

Christmas Pantomime, 1895-6,

CINDERELLA

In consequence of so many applications, the

BOX OFFICE IS NOW OPEN.

All Communications should be addressed to Sir Augustus Harris. Assistant Acting Manager Mr. Neil Forsyth.

G. ADAM & CO.,
FLORISTS & FRUITERERS
NEW BOND STREET, W.
Telephone
THE LONDON SHOE COMY.
H.R.H. THE DUCHESS OF YORK.
H.R.H. THE CROWN PRINCE OF GREECE
45a, CHEAPSIDE, E.C.
116 & 117, NEW BOND STREET, W.
READ
THE SUNDAY TIMES
THE BEST SUNDAY PAPER
POLITICS, ART, LITERATURE,
FINANCE and SATURDAY'S SPORTS.
SPECIAL ARTICLES ON MUSIC AND THE DRAMA
PRICE ONE PENNY.
Offices: 46, Fleet Street, E.C.
ANGLO HUNGARIAN BAND
WHITE HUNGARIAN BAND
LACON & OLLIER,
Theatre Royal Covent Garden
GRAND
OPERA IN ENGLISH
Commencing SATURDAY, OCTOBER 12.
GRAND CHORUS OF EIGHTY VOICES.
ORCHESTRA OF 70 PERFORMERS.
MORNING PERFORMANCE EVERY SATURDAY, at 1.45.
EDWIN S. HILL & CO.,
Hairdressers and Perfumers,
MANICURE & CHIROPODY.
LONDON FUR COMPANY.
M. B. FOSTER & SONS,
Pure Mineral Water Manufacturers,
RESTAURANT.
THE NEW
PERSIAN ROOM
CAFE VERREY
DINING AND LUNCHING.
"Johannis"
THE ONLY NATURAL TABLE WATER
SUPPLIED TO THE THEATRE ROYAL COVENT GARDEN.
FINEST CYCLE SCHOOL IN LONDON.
Rudge Whitworth, Ltd.
AN EFFICIENT STAFF OF INSTRUCTORS.
THE BUGLE BAND.
E. B. FOSTER & SONS, LTD.
Ale and Beer Merchants,
BASS'S ALE AND GUINNESS'S STOUT.

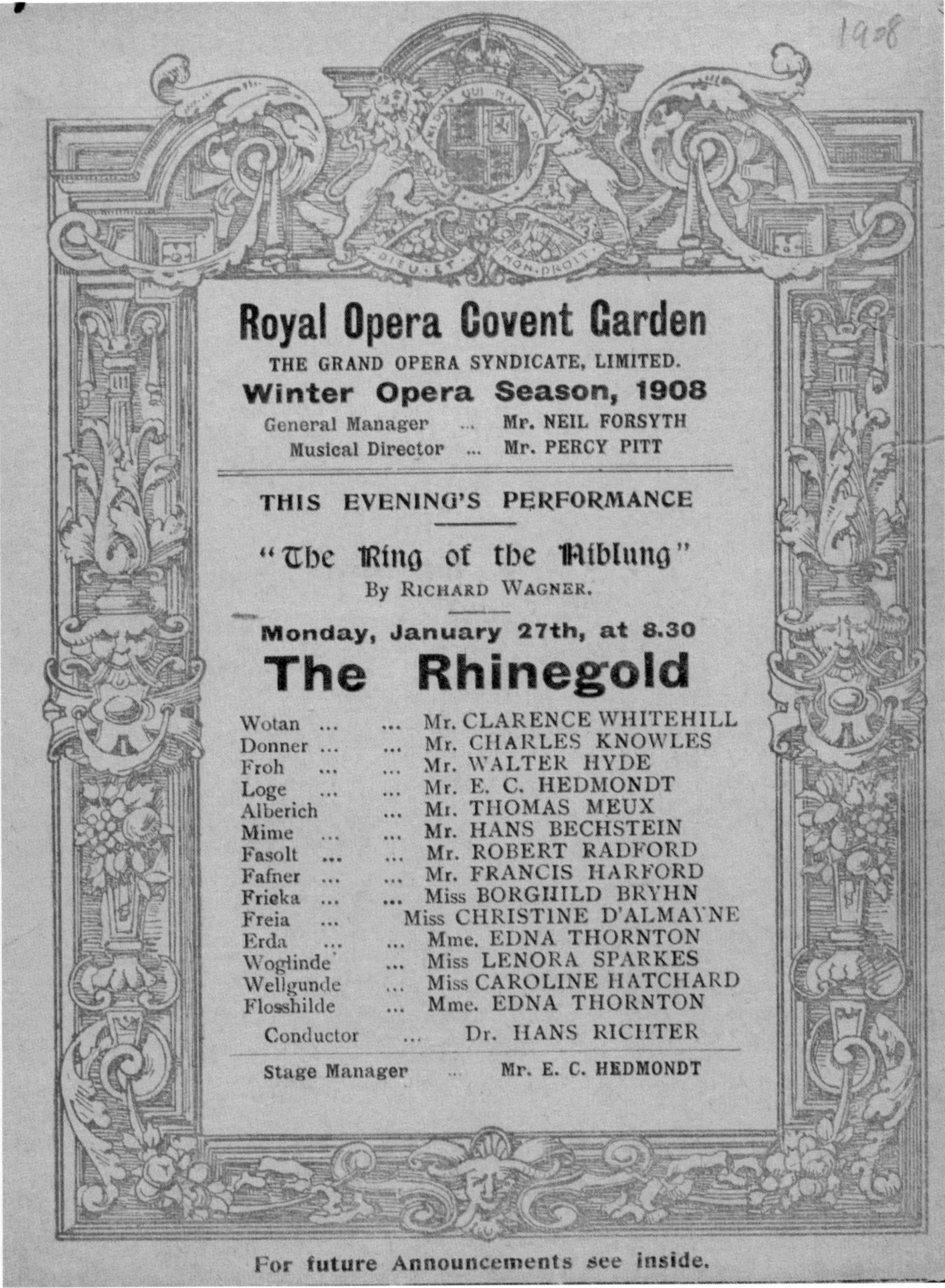
1908

Royal Opera Covent Garden
THE GRAND OPERA SYNDICATE, LIMITED.
Winter Opera Season, 1908
General Manager ... Mr. NEIL FORSYTH
Musical Director ... Mr. PERCY PITT

THIS EVENING'S PERFORMANCE

"The Ring of the Niblung"
By RICHARD WAGNER.

Monday, January 27th, at 8.30
The Rhinegold

Wotan ...	... Mr. CLARENCE WHITEHILL
Donner ...	... Mr. CHARLES KNOWLES
Froh ...	... Mr. WALTER HYDE
Loge ...	... Mr. E. C. HEDMONDT
Alberich	... Mr. THOMAS MEUX
Mime ...	... Mr. HANS BECHSTEIN
Fasolt ...	... Mr. ROBERT RADFORD
Fafner ...	... Mr. FRANCIS HARFORD
Frieka ...	... Miss BORGHILD BRYHN
Freia ...	Miss CHRISTINE D'ALMAYNE
Erda ...	... Mme. EDNA THORNTON
Woglinde	... Miss LENORA SPARKES
Wellgunde	... Miss CAROLINE HATCHARD
Flosshilde	... Mme. EDNA THORNTON

Conductor ... Dr. HANS RICHTER

Stage Manager ... Mr. E. C. HEDMONDT

For future Announcements see inside.

A souvenir album in two volumes was produced to accompany the 1898 *Ring* cycles. The first volume contained a history of the work's creation and the stories of the operas, written by Louis N. Parker (he was active in the London Wagner Society and in 1910 became the first President of the Wagner Association). The text was illustrated with intricate borders by P.J. Billinghurst and plates by Charles Robinson depicting the principal characters and scenes from the opera. The combination of the hyperbolic text by Parker and beautifully stylized illustrations that draw on the sensuality of art nouveau heighten the romanticization of the mythic elements in the *Ring*. The second volume featured photographs of the conductor, Mottl, and the performers.

THE RHINE

WOTAN SEES WALHALL.

SIEGFRIED & BRUNNHILDE.

WALTRAUTE.

Marie Brema made her first appearance at the Royal Opera House as Brünnhilde on 12 June 1897 (she had been the Valkyrie Siegrune in 1893) and went on to sing Fricka the following year having sung the part at Bayreuth. She was, in fact, the first singer born in Britain to appear at Bayreuth (in 1894), had already established herself in the Wagner repertory in America and had sung Ortrud and Brangäne at Covent Garden the year before her first Brünnhilde there. The photograph for Lady de Grey was inscribed and signed by Brema; the image of the recumbent Brünnhilde doll has been also inscribed by her, with 'The rest is silence!'.

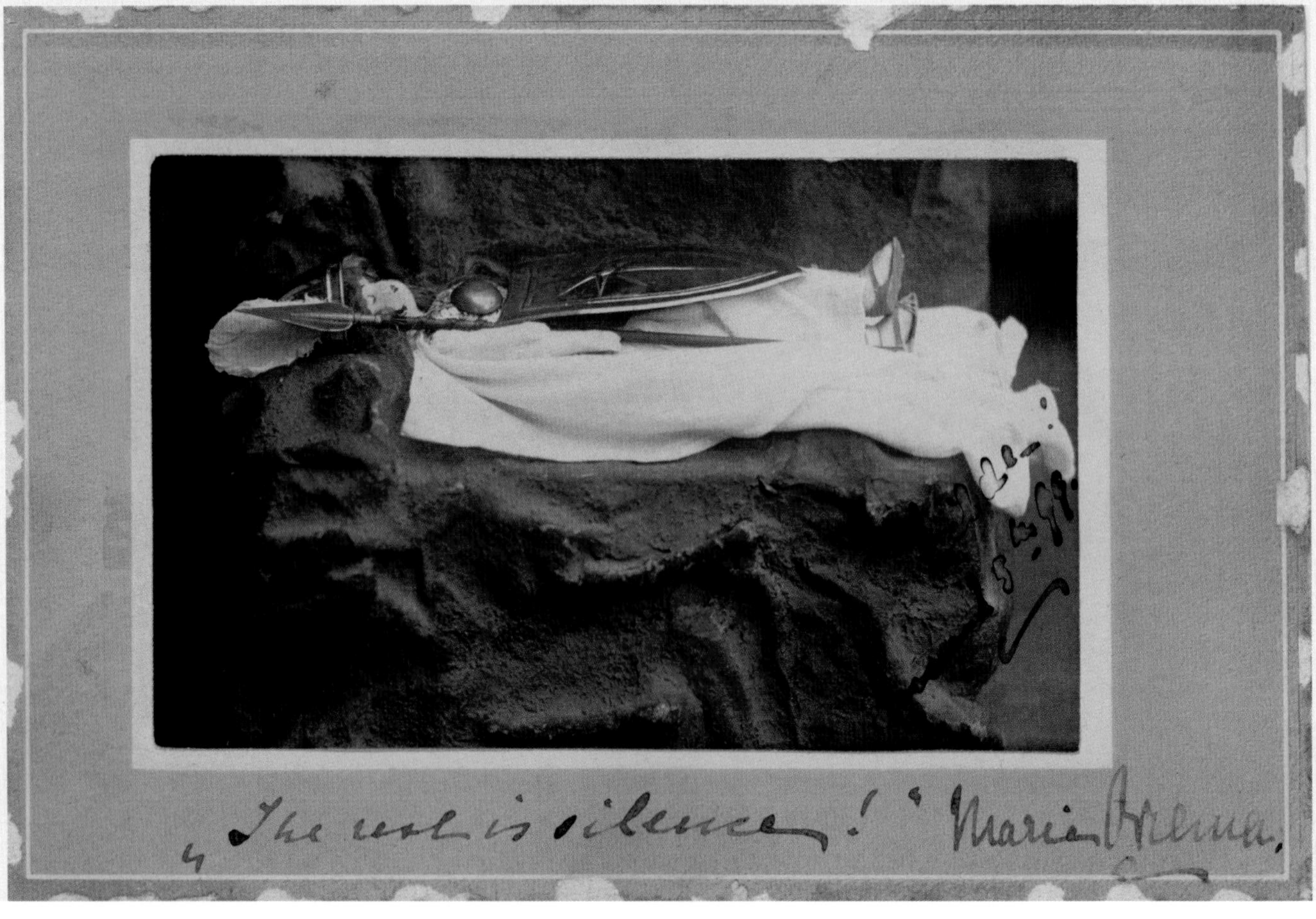

„The rest is silence!" Marie Brema.

Lillian Nordica had appeared in several roles (including Carmen, Aida, Marguerite and Selika) in Augustus Harris's first Season at Covent Garden, in 1888. After attending a performance of *Die Meistersinger von Nürnberg* at Bayreuth in the same year she began to bring the Wagnerian roles into her repertory, singing Elsa at Covent Garden the following year. She shared Brünnhilde in the 1898 *Ring* cycles with Marie Brema and Milka Ternina. She was ill for the planned performance of *Götterdämmerung* on 24 June, which was initially postponed until Tuesday 5 July, but brought forward to Monday 4 July. She returned as Brünnhilde in 1899 (*Die Walküre*) and 1902 (*Die Walküre* and *Siegfried*).

The early years of the Covent Garden *Rings* drew a fine set of performers as Brünnhilde. Pictured here are Rosa Sucher and Minnie Saltzmann-Stevens. Sucher had appeared at the Theatre Royal, Drury Lane, in 1882 as Elsa, Senta, Eva and Isolde (she was to be the first Bayreuth Isolde four years later), and sang Brünnhilde in the first *Siegfried* performance under Mahler at Covent Garden in 1892. Minnie Saltzmann-Stevens was an American singer who came to Covent Garden through the connection of her teacher, Jean de Reszke. After taking the part of Brünnhilde in all three of the 1909 cycles in English she then became the principal Covent Garden performer in the role for several years. For *Die Walküre* in 1912 and 1913 she was Sieglinde (a role she also took at Bayreuth), with Gertrud Kappel as Brünnhilde.

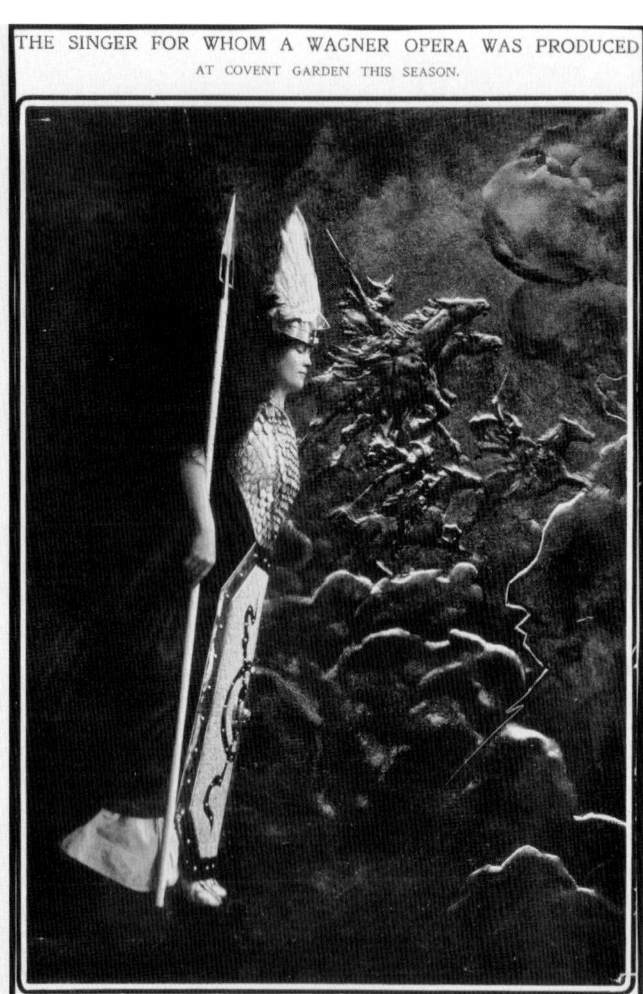

THE SINGER FOR WHOM A WAGNER OPERA WAS PRODUCED
AT COVENT GARDEN THIS SEASON.

'Hans Richter the colossal conductor of Wagner.' The inscription with the photograph in Lady de Grey's album reflects the status of Richter both in Britain and in the wider musical world. His career was closely involved with the music of Wagner: at the age of 23 he had assisted Wagner in preparing the score of *Die Meistersinger von Nürnberg* and later in musical preparations for the first Bayreuth Festival, at which he conducted. As well as becoming one of the regular Bayreuth conductors, he held influential posts in Vienna, ran more than two decades of his 'Richter Concerts' in London (the first in 1879) and later was conductor of the Hallé orchestra. He made his first conducting appearance with the *Ring* at Covent Garden in 1903 (for three cycles), and was to appear with the operas each year from 1905 to 1910, including the performances sung in English in 1908 and 1909.

Costume designs by Attilio Comelli for the *Ring*. From 1899 on, the stage and its mechanisms at Covent Garden were gradually updated and improved, requiring the redesign and replacement of much of the old scenery. The opportunity was taken to extend the overhaul of productions to include costume, to which end Comelli was appointed as designer in 1903. His designs for the *Ring* characters included the Valkyrie costumes shown here for Gerhilde (Louisa Sobrino) and Ortlinde (Marie Knüpfer-Egli).

Costume designs by Attilio Comelli. The design for Gutrune shows the delicacy and detail of Comelli's style, while the *Götterdämmerung* vassal draws on a typical Nordic archetype.

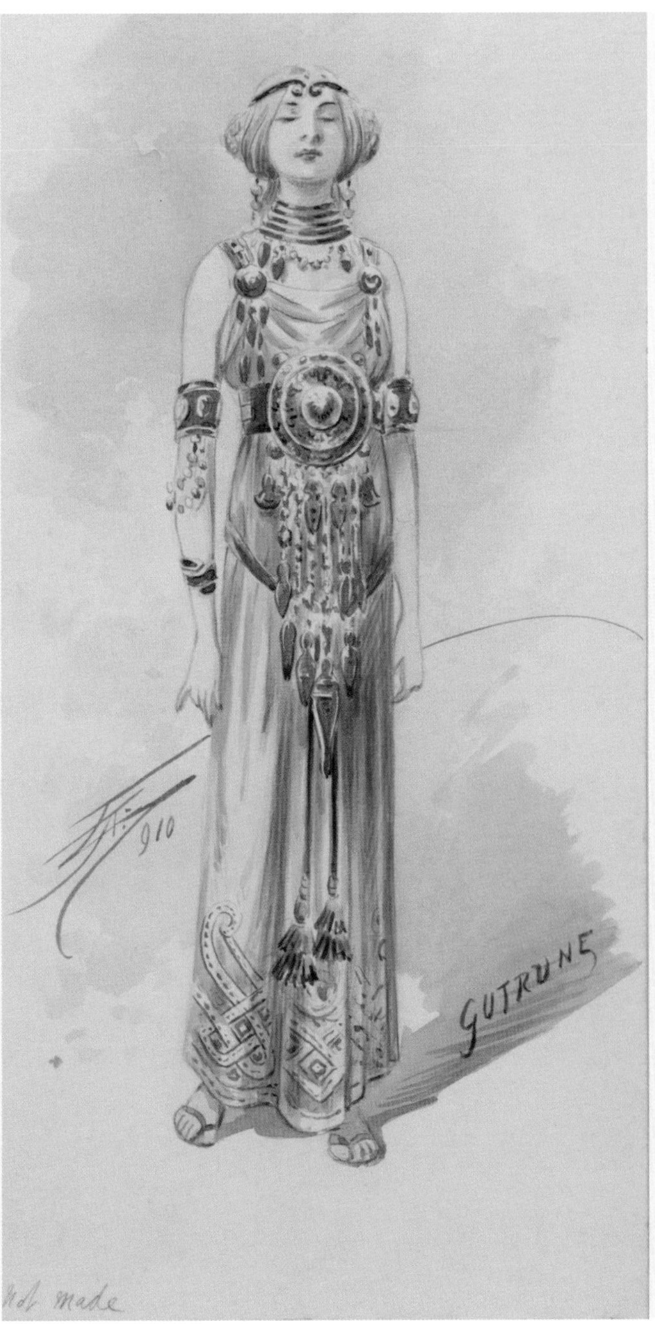

The opening scene of *Das Rheingold,* 1892.

'How the Rhine Maidens Swim', illustration (1903).

A naturalistic staging of Wagner has to rely on the ingenuity of stage machinery and its operators, not least for the opening scene of the whole cycle. The following description of a rehearsal for the 1898 staging at the Royal Opera House gives some idea of the effort involved to make the Rhinedaughters' swimming seem effortless:

> Six men holding on to one end of a line, at the other a mermaid swinging in mid-air, for all the world like a mighty fish about to be landed by stalwart anglers. And yet a mermaid of curious appearance – in bonnet and blue and tailor-made skirt, she swims in the 'green twilight' and 'flowing water' of the Rhine of Wagner's fancy, singing the while more like a bird than a half human fish, and protesting in the intervals that it is trying work dangling up there while Herr. Mottle [*sic*] barks back with his orchestra, and shouting admonitions to the brass and muttering injunctions to the strings, hears again the motive of the 'primeval element', while the organist in a hole in the wall puts a tired foot on a pedal note and seems to hold it indefinitely for the opened pipe to growl out a rumbling sound like elephants at feeding time. …
>
> To the spectator in the wings it is only a jumble of trestles and boxes, of cardboard and canvas, with three ladies of some weight suspended in air by almost invisible wires and six sturdy men holding like grim death to the end of a rope. But a good deal has happened before the perfect picture is evolved and the Rhine daughters are in a position to sing in their playfulness the motive of Happiness. First of all, Woglinde and Flosshilde need fixing on their aerial pedestals tilted at an angle to suggest the forward attitude for swimming. Next the men on the ropes have to learn as best they can from German instruction which is which, when to lower no.3 and raise no.1 (numbers they persistently jumbled up to the discomfort of the singing maidens and the annoyance of the Teutonic commander); when to drop the maidens in the water, when to 'land them', when and how, in fact, to obey these many injunctions which the 'Master' left as a legacy to his apostles who have come all the way from Beyreuth [sic] to show how the thing should be done. Now the *Rheintöchter* are ready for the ascent; the six men pull on the ropes, up near the 'flies' and the day light, little wheels run noiselessly, and a dozen feet from the stage swim, or swing, the mermaids, while below each a man holds on to a guiding line, and in his efforts to check the violence of these saltatory motions is swayed from side to side, hitting boxes and knocking scenery in his enforced vagaries. …
>
> At last the Rhine daughters pass satisfactorily through the ordeal of singing and swimming, not, however, without many a bump against the Rhinegold rock, and now the crafty Alberich, in fashionable tweed suit, looking anything but the 'beginning of Evil' comes creeping along… The mermaids must here dive deeper, says Wagner, and a Bayreuth expert shouts to the men at the end of the line, the order is misunderstood, one Rhine daughter suddenly sinks to the bottom of the river, another takes an upward leap like salmon jumping a stream, and the third remains poised in mid-air, i.e. swimming in the middle of the Rhine. One more wait while the deep dive is perfected, and then on again to the end of the scene, when Alberich steals the gold and joyous song of the water nymphs turns into lamentations.

Design by Attilio Comelli for the Rhinedaughters. This costume design was introduced in 1903. Further improvements to the swimming mechanism were made in 1913, with the critic for *The Globe* wryly noting in 1914: 'Since the first scene now creates a real illusion it would be worth while to perfect it by concealing the wires by which the maidens are suspended. At present they gleam almost as brightly as the gold.'

Some fifty years after the event, Agnes Nicholls recalled what the experience was like in one of the first of these 'swimming' contraptions from the perspective of a performer:

> When I first went to Covent Garden in 1905, one of my roles was the first Rhinemaiden [Woglinde in *Götterdämmerung*], and to my horror we were put on what were called the 'machines'; enormous things, I don't know how high, and we stepped out from a platform into an iron bodyholder, high in the air and supported on a sort of wooden truck. An iron band went round our waists, things like stirrups were for our feet, there were two things round our knees – and we were strapped tight. There were four men below who pushed us about, and we had to sing swaying high above the stage. The machines were draped in green material to look like water. One girl refused to get on to the machine once she discovered what she was in for.

Julius Lieban (below) made a strong impression as Mime in the 1892 *Ring;* alongside his photograph in her album, Lady de Grey described him as 'The best Mime in *Siegfried*'. Lieban returned to Covent Garden for the same role in the four performances of *Siegfried* in 1897, in 1903 for a single performance in *Siegfried,* and only took the part in a full cycle again in 1906. In between times, Hans Breuer played the part as, in one description from 1898, 'a peculiarly grimy and grotesque little gnome, [who] emphasized the malignity of the character with a profusion of felicitous touches in gesture, accent and facial expression'. Albert Reiss also took the part (in 1901, 1902, 1903 and 1905) as did Payne Clarke for a single performance in 1903 in the Moody-Manners Autumn Opera Season. In 1907 Hans Bechstein made his first appearance as Mime, a role which was to remain his own at the Royal Opera House in every subsequent performance in every year (excepting a single *Rheingold* in the 1909 third cycle, with Denis Byndon-Ayres) through to the outbreak of war.

DIEU ET MON DROIT

1906

Royal Opera Covent Garden

THE GRAND OPERA SYNDICATE, LIMITED.
Manager .. .. .. M. ANDRE MESSAGER
Secretary and Business Manager, Mr. NEIL FORSYTH

THIS EVENING'S PERFORMANCE.

"Der Ring des Nibelungen"
By RICHARD WAGNER.
First Performance of 1st Cycle.

Friday, May 4th, at 8.30

DAS RHEINGOLD

Wotan	Herr BRAUN
Donner	Herr HÜPEDEN
Froh	Herr NIETAN
Loge	Herr JÖRN
Alberich	Herr ZADOR
Mime	Herr LIEBAN
Fasolt	Herr KNÜPFER
Fafner	Herr RABOTH
Fricka	Frau REINL
Freia	Frau KNÜPFER-EGLI
Erda	Mme. KIRKBY LUNN
Woglinde	Mme. AGNES NICHOLLS
Wellgunde	Frl. BURCHARDT
Flosshilde	Frl. GRIMM
Conductor ...	Dr. HANS RICHTER

Stage Manager .. .. .. Herr WIRK

For future Announcements see inside.

1906

DIEU ET MON DROIT

1906

Royal Opera Covent Garden

THE GRAND OPERA SYNDICATE, LIMITED.
Manager .. .. .. M. ANDRE MESSAGER
Secretary and Business Manager, Mr. NEIL FORSYTH

THIS EVENING'S PERFORMANCE.

"Der Ring des Nibelungen"
By RICHARD WAGNER.
Third Performance of 1st Cycle.

Monday, May 7th, at 5

SIEGFRIED

Brünnhilde	Frau WITTICH
Erda	Frl. GRIMM
Waldvogel	Mme. AGNES NICHOLLS
Mime	Herr LIEBAN
Der Wanderer ...	Herr WHITEHILL
Fafner	Herr RABOTH
Alberich	Herr ZADOR
Siegfried	Herr KONRAD
Conductor ...	Dr. HANS RICHTER

Stage Manager .. .. .. Herr WIRK

For future Announcements see inside.

Sets for *Das Rheingold* scenes 2 and 3, and *Die Walküre* from 1892. Although many of the cycle designs were retained through many revivals, for 1903 Bruce Smith designed new settings for *Die Walküre* Acts I and III, and the settings for *Götterdämmerung* Act II and Act III scene 2 were also new, by (respectively) Hawes Craven and W. Telbin. In general, the sets both from 1892 and in the following few decades followed the contemporary practice of a naturalistic interpretation of Wagner's descriptions, with their mountains and forests, huts and halls. What can be seen is a technique that leads the eye simultaneously towards the centre front of the stage through the coincidence of entrances down steps from the sides or back, and also creates the effect of recession towards a distant point (misty mountain tops, the far bank of a river) through a painted backcloth, with trees or rocks tipping in at the sides or arching right over the top. It is a perpetual conceit in such naturalistic representations of the *Ring* settings that the most artifcially enclosed of spaces – the proscenium-framed stage – is constantly called upon to portray landscapes that lack finite boundaries.

The edition of *Madame* for 16 May 1908 included a special feature on the three performances of *Die Walküre* and the two of *Götterdämmerung* that had taken place earlier that month at the Royal Opera House. They were conducted by Hans Richter, who had also conducted the cycles in English at the start of the year, but these performances reverted back to German. Sets reproduced in the magazine included the 'Wooded Place on the Rhine' of *Götterdämmerung* Act III scene 2; a drawing by F.R. Skelton depicted Act III of *Die Walküre*.

1912

ROYAL OPERA

COVENT  GARDEN

PROPRIETORS ... ... THE GRAND OPERA SYNDICATE, LIMITED

General Manager - - Mr. NEIL FORSYTH
Musical Director - - Mr. PERCY PITT

1912

Der Ring des Nibelungen

By RICHARD WAGNER

TUESDAY, APRIL 23 at 8.30

FIRST SERIES. FIRST PERFORMANCE.

DAS RHEINGOLD

(IN GERMAN)

Wotan	.	Herr ANTON VAN ROOY
Donner	.	Herr FRANZ KRONEN
Froh	.	Mr. MAURICE D'OISLY
Loge	.	Herr HEINRICH HENSEL
Alberich	.	Herr AUGUST KIESS
Mime	.	Herr HANS BECHSTEIN
Fasolt	.	Mr. JAMES H. GODDARD
Fafner	.	Herr JOHANNES FÖNSS
Fricka	.	Mme. KIRKBY LUNN
Freia	.	Frau MARIA KNÜPFER-EGLI
Erda	.	Miss GWLADYS ROBERTS
Woglinde	.	Mlle. VON GLEHN
Wellgunde	.	Mlle. KACEROWSKA
Flosshilde	.	Mlle. BOBERG

Conductor . Dr. ROTTENBERG

To commence at 8.30 and finish at 11 p.m. There will be no interval.

A few Seats left at the following Prices:
Boxes, 8, 4, 3 and 2½ Guineas. Orchestra Stalls, £1 10s. Balcony Stalls, £1. Amphitheatre Stalls, 14s., 10s. 6d. and 7s. 6d. Gallery (Reserved), 6s.

Applications for Tickets to be made to the Box Office, from 10 to 6 Telephone Nos. 463—464 Gerrard.

DOORS OPEN HALF-AN-HOUR BEFORE THE PERFORMANCE COMMENCES

MILES, 68-70, Wardour Street, W.

Poster for *Das Rheingold* on 23 April 1912, the first opera of the first of two cycles of that year, sung in German and conducted by Ludwig Rottenberg.

Booking form for the 1913 cycles, conducted for the first time in London by Arthur Nikisch; two cycles had originally been announced, but an extra one was added in response to public demand.

ROYAL OPERA
COVENT GARDEN

Proprietors - The Grand Opera Syndicate, Limited
General Manager - Mr. NEIL FORSYTH
Musical Director - Mr. PERCY PITT

GRAND OPERA SEASON
1913

Monday, April 21st
to Monday, July 28th

(vi)

"DER RING DES NIBELUNGEN"

THE Works will be presented in their entirety, without cuts, in the same manner as at Bayreuth, and as at Covent Garden in previous seasons. All the Operas of the "RING," except "DAS RHEINGOLD," will commence in the afternoon and terminate at about eleven o'clock, with an interval, after the second act, of an hour and a-half for dinner. This arrangement, which has proved so successful in connection with the "RING" performances on former occasions, has the further advantage of allowing the Theatre to be thoroughly ventilated during this interval, and of allowing the audience to hear the first and last acts in comfort.

Each act will commence punctually at the time mentioned, and as the doors will be closed during the acts, the greatest punctuality is enjoined; visitors should time themselves to arrive in their seats ten minutes in advance of the actual commencement.

No restriction will be made as regards dress at the "RING" performances. The only rule that will be rigorously enforced is: that ladies must remove hats, bonnets, or any headgear whatsoever, and the Management relies on the co-operation of the public to strictly enforce this rule.

Every effort is being made by the DIRECTORS OF THE ROYAL OPERA to render the performances again artistically complete.

The Prices, for each Complete Cycle of Four Performances, are as follows:

Pit-Tier and Grand-Tier Boxes
(Subscription for entire Season only)

		£	s.	d.
First-Tier Boxes (for 4 persons)	£12 12 0 and	16	16	0
Second-Tier Boxes (for 4 persons)		8	8	0
Orchestra Stalls		5	10	0
Gallery Slips (Reserved)		1	1	0

All other seats are sold

Tickets are now being issued for Single Performances of either Cycle at the following prices:

		£	s.	d.
Boxes	£4 4 0, £3 3 0 and	2	12	6
Orchestra Stalls		1	10	0
Gallery Slips (Reserved)		0	6	0

All other seats are sold

Proprietors - The Grand Opera Syndicate, Limited
General Manager - Mr. NEIL FORSYTH
Musical Director - Mr. PERCY PITT

SEASON OF GRAND OPERA, 1913

FOR A PERIOD OF FOURTEEN WEEKS
Commencing on MONDAY, APRIL 21st

APPLICATION FORM

'o the Manager, Box Office,
Royal Opera, Covent Garden.

I WISH to reserve for the complete Cycle of "DER RING DES NIBELUNGEN"

st Cycle (April 22nd, 23rd, 25th and 28th)
nd ,, (April 30th, May 1st, 3rd and 6th)

	Per Cycle of Four Performances £ s. d.
..........Pit- and Grand-Tier Boxes (Subscriptions for Season only)	
..........First-Tier Boxes	12 12 0 / 16 16 0
..........Second-Tier Boxes	8 8 0
..........Orchestra Stalls	5 10 0
..........Gallery Slips (Reserved)	1 1 0

All other seats are sold

SUBSCRIPTION FOR THE SEASON
(Monday, April 21 to Monday, July 28)

I WISH to reserve the following Seats on the MONDAYS, TUESDAYS, WEDNESDAYS, THURSDAYS, FRIDAYS, SATURDAYS throughout the Season at the following prices:

	Per Night £ s. d.
............Pit- and Grand-Tier Boxes	7 0 0
............First-Tier Boxes	4 0 0 / 3 0 0
............Second-Tier Boxes	2 10 0
............Orchestra Stalls	1 0 0
............Balcony Stalls	0 15 0
Amphitheatre Stalls	
.... 1st & 2nd Rows	0 10 6
.... 3rd & 4th Rows	0 7 6
.... Other Rows	0 5 0

¶ PLEASE STRIKE THROUGH THE PERFORMANCES YOU DO NOT WISH TO ATTEND

Name..

Address..

ate.................................. ....

SEATING PLAN
OF
ROYAL OPERA COVENT GARDEN

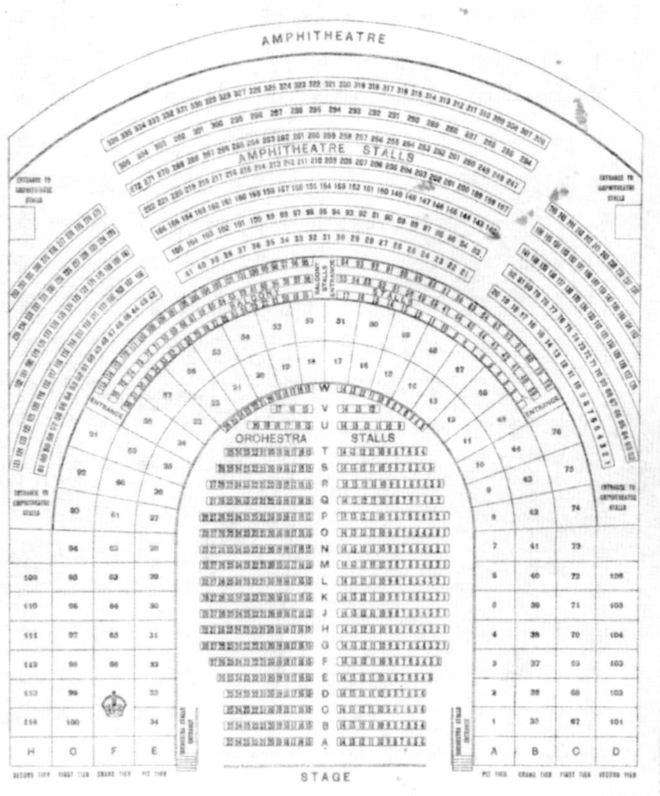

ROYAL  OPERA

COVENT GARDEN

LESSEES ... ... COVENT GARDEN OPERA SYNDICATE (1930), LTD.

COVENT GARDEN OPERA SYNDICATE (1930) L^TD. SEASON

TWO COMPLETE CYCLES

OF

DER RING DES NIBELUNGEN

	First Cycle	Second Cycle
DAS RHEINGOLD 8.30 to 11 p.m.	**Wed., APRIL 29**	**Fri., MAY 15**
DIE WALKÜRE ACT 1. 5.45 to 6.45 ACT 2. 8.15 to 9.45 ACT 3. 10.15 to 11.15	**Thurs., APRIL 30**	**Tues., MAY 19**
SIEGFRIED ACT 1. 5.45 to 7.0 ACT 2. 8.15 to 9.30 ACT 3. 10.0 to 11.15	**Mon., MAY 4**	**Fri., MAY 22**
GÖTTERDÄMMERUNG ACT 1. 5.15 to 7.15 ACT 2. 8.30 to 9.35 ACT 3. 10.5 to 11.25	**Fri., MAY 8**	**Mon., MAY 25**

(Please note Revised Times which are approximate)

J. MILES & CO., Ltd., Printers, Wardour Street, W.

Poster for the 1931 *Ring* cycle performances

CHAPTER TWO

BETWEEN THE WARS

1921–1939

In the immediate aftermath of World War I there was a keenness to bolster a sense of national identity, and this was as evident in opera as in other parts of British life: there was a desire for a specifically British operatic identity – not Italian, not German – which meant British singers using the national language. As a consequence, opera in English quickly became widely accepted; for example, *Parsifal* received its first performance in English in the UK in Sir Thomas Beecham's 1919/20 Season. It was against this background that, in 1921, the first of the *Ring* operas after World War I at the Royal Opera House were sung in English: two performances each of *The Rhinegold, The Valkyrie* and *Siegfried* by the Carl Rosa company, with Eva Turner as Fricka in the first opera and Brünnhilde in the following two.

The next year, the whole cycle was given for the first time after World War I, and also in English for the first time since the 1908/9 cycles under Richter. So, on Monday 15 May (at what seems today the somewhat late time of 8.30pm), *The Rhinegold* opened with Albert Coates conducting. *The Morning Post* described the venture in appreciative terms: 'A definite note of individuality was established from the first in the opening production of the representation of Wagner's *Nibelung's Ring* at Covent Garden last night by the British National Opera Company, a feature of that individuality is clear enunciation of the words, well marked vocal phrasing, and illustrative acting. Thus the large audience had every reason to congratulate itself, for one of the most important offices of the whole duty of giving opera in the vernacular is fulfilled; the piece can be understood.'

The casting provided a clear link with pre-war performances, for several of the singers had appeared in the same roles in the first 1908 English *Ring*: Clarence Whitehill (Wotan), Edna Thornton (*Siegfried* Erda and the second cycle *Götterdämmerung* Waltraute; in 1922 she also sang Fricka), Robert Radford (Fasolt and Hunding), Walter Hyde (Siegmund) and Agnes Nicholls (Sieglinde). Of the newer names, Florence Austral was a Brünnhilde whose singing with Arthur Jordan in the last scene of the last act of *Siegfried* was picked out for praise, while Norman Allin's Fafner gave him his first appearances of what were to become some fifteen years of Fafners and Hundings at the Royal Opera House. Indeed, there was appreciation all round for the cast – from Sydney Russell's Mime through to the Valkyrie ensemble – and for Albert Coates's interpretation in the pit.

There was an understanding of the breadth of the interpretative potential in this 'red-hot Allegory and the most glorious pamphlet ever written; the greatest because it extends beyond the frontiers of nationality, its application for all time'. As the *Daily Telegraph* continued in 1922, 'Dwarfs, giants and gods are here, but we have their universal type in our social complex as surely to-day as in 1850, and 1950 is unlikely to see much alteration in the parable. The fact that Wagner took the main incidents of this drama from the old sagas of the Norsemen does not make the inherent logic of the Wagner story less relentless, its philosophy less vital and impelling in the 20th century. We have our Alberichs, our Wotans, and our Loges as forces strong and permanent even if they cannot always be recognised as individuals in the street. In the street they are for certain; if not in our street, then in our neighbour's.' But if the contemporary resonance of the themes was apparent, mythic distancing through such imagery as helmets with horns was also to be around for a little while longer.

There were changes, however, and 1923 saw the introduction of some new stage settings by Oliver Bernard that continued a slow move away from as near a literal interpretation of Wagner's stage instructions as was possible towards something more interpretative and, here, impressionistic and colourful. The differences were sufficiently marked to prompt several detailed descriptions. The opening of *The Rhinegold* 'leaves a good deal to the imagination, the lighting of the foreshortened stage making deliberately for a certain vagueness, which gives an almost spectral suggestion to the figures of the swaying nymphs, and even to the rock that bears the magic gold'. The same *Daily Telegraph* reviewer waxed lyrical about *The Valkyrie.*

> Long ago the feeble cinematographic expedient was abandoned, and in its place we were given merely a background showing effects as of scudding clouds. All that has now been changed, and the ride of the Valkyries is left to the spectator's imagination. And why not, indeed, seeing that Wagner himself has described the scene for us so graphically in the orchestra? Hunding's rough-hewn dwelling, in Mr Bernard's representation of it, is a less homely place than the old familiar one, though it appears to be

warmed on one side by what looks suspiciously like an anthracite stove – a very necessary precaution, one imagines, in a habitation that seems to be exposed to all the winds of heaven. And when, at the appointed moment, double doors at the back of the dwelling swing open to let in the moonlight they reveal the pale blue and green tints of a forest that obviously is somewhere on the borders of fairyland.

For the second act, the designer has devised a simple setting, with a background which at once strikes the imagination and lends itself admirably to some singularly beautiful effects of lighting, particularly during and after the fight between Hunding and Siegmund. There is real imaginative beauty, too, combined with perfect simplicity, in the scheme designed for the final scene of all. Banished are all the theatrical devices of old for the illusion of flames leaping up around Brünnhilde's rocky couch. Instead, the encircling fires are suggested on the backcloth by means of lighting effects that illumine the skies with a brilliant, yet soft, roseate glow, and make a sufficiently vivid appeal to the imagination. Wagner's music is rightly trusted to do the rest.

For a different, and less complimentary, angle the *Daily Mail* reported that Act II of *The Valkyrie* was 'composed of monstrous stalagmites, and Mr Bernard suggests that the men of that age spent their time making staircases amid the relics of the glacial epoch. And the new fire effect at the very end was not a great success, though we liked the impression of Wotan's silhouette against the incarnadined sky'. What was important, however, was that old habits were being broken for at least some elements of Royal Opera *Rings*.

When the 1924 Grand Opera Season opened on 5 May with *Das Rheingold,* there were further changes through the contribution of Charles Moor as the new Stage Manager (a role that was then nearer to that of today's director). Originally from Edinburgh, he had worked as a singer and conductor, especially in German opera houses, and from that had eventually moved into stage management and by 1924 was based in Bremen. Moor recognized that Wagner's own ideas on staging had been the product of his time; but times had changed and stage techniques had moved with them. His approach, as described in an interview for the *Yorkshire Observer* before the season began, attempted to balance naturalism and stage pragmatism.

When you enter the realm of myth you encounter phenomena quite incapable of being adequately staged. The size of gianthood and the dignity of godhead, the wrigglesomeness of serpents, the dreadfulness of dragons, the Etruscan massiveness of a Valhalla and the insubstantial dependability of a rainbow bridge are only a few examples of qualities of phenomena easier to be imagined by the dramatist than to be realised by the stage manager.

One method of evading difficulty is to cut out all naturalism. This, in my judgement, is a mistake. Wagner meant to be naturalistic. Some things we can now do better than Wagner could, at all events in the early days. (For instance, his stage lighting began with gas, and at the end of his life he had but a crude form of control over his electric light.) Other things remain to this day impossible.

Take, for instance, his steam-curtain at the end of scene II of *Rhinegold.* With an ideal installation, clay piping, and so forth, it may be possible to carry out this effect properly, but I have personally never come across this ideal installation, and my experience is that an intolerable hissing here always drowns out the music. And the music is the thing. In this passage it describes quite adequately (and very beautifully) the descent of Wotan and Loge to the caverns of Nibelheim. Nothing beyond the music is here needed, and I shall simply darken the stage, drop a cloud or two and change the scenery invisibly (and I hope silently!) in that way.

Take another example – the end of *The Dusk of the Gods.* Hundreds of stage managers have tried to carry out Wagner's detailed instructions, and all have failed. Houses cannot be burnt down on stages. It is against all plausibility, to say nothing of the London County Council regulations. My plan is to have Brünnhilde's pile out of sight. One or two attendants passing toward it with logs, and Brünnhilde herself approaching it with her torch, are quite enough as 'pointers' for the imagination of the spectators. A factor to be taken into

> account is the increased education of the present-day Wagnerites. They know the stories, they have imagination, and they do not need to have everything brought actually before their eyes. …
>
> The general aim of my staging is (a) perfect lighting and (b) as much naturalistic effect as is possible without degenerating into (let us use the word boldly) the comic. I hope I shall obtain the effects I have in mind. If so, I believe that London Wagner-lovers will be content.

Some of his changes were welcome, especially the disappearance from view of the Norns in *Götterdämmerung,* where the by-then conventional descent through a trap door was replaced by a gradual darkness surrounding the stooping figures. Other changes were either not always successful or not appreciated, and the frequent ineptitude of the execution of staging and lighting at Covent Garden – a recurring issue over decades of Royal Opera House reviews – was not immediately solved. Of the fight with the dragon Fafner in *Siegfried,* George Bernard Shaw wrote: 'For all the audience could tell it might have been a night-watchman's glowing brazier that Siegfried playfully poked with his sword. Like most of these big fights it was hopelessly one-sided.' And while the end of the whole cycle followed Moor's intentions as he described them, it was not as effective for the audience as he had hoped. There were problems with shadows of stage-hands on the sunset backcloth, Grane 'misbehaved' and an offstage pyre was considered by some anti-climactic (there had also been no rainbow in *Das Rheingold*).

There were other changes in 1924, with a return to a pre-war sense of social style (evening dress, supper intervals) and most importantly to pre-war language: the *Ring* was sung in German again. There was a German conductor – Bruno Walter – and the return of a preponderance of foreign singers. A certain bitterness was in evidence over this, even before the event, with the *Daily Mail* commentator finding it difficult to sound even-handed:

> To-night at Covent Garden German singers and the German language reappear for the first time since the war. Since 1914 a new generation of German singers has arisen, and hence the names of the new company are unfamiliar. They are, of course, assured of a fair hearing, while at the same time it must be noted that Londoners are not so ready as they once were to accept obediently all that comes with a foreign reputation. The new Wotans, Isoldes and Siegfrieds will be heard critically, but real eminence will be thankfully acknowledged.

Not surprisingly, much was made of the British contingent in the cast, including Nellie Jaffary as Freia, Margaret Duff and Edith Furmedge as two of the Rhinemaidens, and a bevy of British Valkyries with Duff, May Busby, Kathleen Burton, Furmedge and Evelyn Arden; but, in the process, this only made it more evident how the major roles were dominated by non-British singers. After the performances, *The Times* reported: 'The cast of singers was a thoroughly competent one, but not all its members excelled in vocal quality. A German cast rarely does. It may have been some comfort to those who are distressed by the return of the foreigners to Covent Garden to reflect that there were many passages which we have heard sung with greater beauty of tone in the years of the foreigners' absence.' The *Daily Sketch* commentator was also keen to provide a bit of nationalistic distance, with a sideswipe of his own: 'The long love duet which forms most of the first act of *Die Wälküre* (for the moment they are not being called 'Valkyries') has surely never been better sung than it was at Covent Garden somewhere about tea-time yesterday afternoon. It was sung, too, by a Dutch tenor Jacques Urlus and a Swedish soprano Göta Ljungberg to the accompaniment of a British orchestra, so, in spite of the reversion to the original language of Wagner, this was by no means an exclusively German triumph.'

Yet a 'triumph' it was widely accepted to be. This description from the *Saturday Review* of the effectiveness of Bruno Walter's interpretation from the pit, if more florid in its literary style than many of its contemporaries, is nonetheless in line with the broad consensus:

> Walter takes the pace, as a rule, rather slower than we have been accustomed to of late. But this does not mean that the music drags; rather it enables the players and singers to give to the phrases their full sonority. He is able to do this, first because he has singers who can be relied on to hold their notes steadily for the requisite length

> of time, and secondly because he has the complete Wagnerian orchestra necessary to give the volume of sound. He has, incidentally, almost all our best players of their respective instruments under his command. So the music flowed on in a steady sweep from the first deep E flat of the Prelude, growing always in weight, volume, and complexity. But while there is this feeling of unity, the details are beautifully modelled. Phrases rise clear-cut out of the surface of the music and merge into it again, like goddesses of beauty born successively from the seething foam. I cannot see the conductor from my stall, but I fancy that he must have the same method as Weingartner, and that he is always accompanying the soloist, whether vocal or instrumental, with the rest of the orchestra. The result is, anyhow, that the important part of the moment is always audible. Although, so far as the singers are concerned, he has not to temper the wind to the shorn lamb, this is a marvellous achievement. For it amounts to his getting a perfect balance of all his forces without any sacrifice of the rich texture of the music.

The cast throughout was a striking one, with several first appearances in Covent Garden *Rings* of singers who already were, or for some considerable time after would be, considered leading exponents of their roles and return repeatedly to the Royal Opera House: Friedrich Schorr (Wotan), Maria Olczewska (Fricka), Eduard Habich (Alberich) and Frida Leider (Brünnhilde). In addition, in the second cycle, Lauritz Melchior made his debut as Siegmund. There was an eleventh-hour crisis in the last two operas of the first cycle, when Nicolai Reinfeld (Siegfried) sprained an ankle in rehearsals and was taken off to Charing Cross Hospital only hours before the start of the performance; consequently, at two hours notice for *Siegfried,* the German tenor Fritz Soot sang the role in the first cycle, so making his Covent Garden debut. (As a bonus for the audience, on the nights after the second cycle performances of *Siegfried* and *Götterdämmerung*, the Siegfried-Brünnhilde conclusion to *Siegfried*'s Act III was given on the same bill as performances of Strauss's *Salome;* on both occasions Karl Alwin conducted Florence Austral and Walter Kirchhoff.)

The opera Seasons of 1924 may have had artistic success, but financially it was a different matter. Losses incurred led to observations and suggestions on what had happened and what could be changed to help in future; several make salutary connections with today. For example, the London Opera Syndicate 'could possibly restrict its losses by building up a season of certain old favourites which always draw fairly well and are very little trouble to produce. This is not its object, and it intends to rely upon the musical interest of its repertoire and highest obtainable level of performance to securing increasing public support'. The structuring of the Season, formerly into a German section, an Italian section and so on, could be altered so that the repertory 'will be continuous, so that we may have Wagner one night, Verdi the next, and a French opera the next. That is a delightful idea, and incidentally, an expensive one!'. And what were then the not-so-old favourites still made their impact on the balance sheet: 'The most popular, and most profitable, opera of the season last June was *Tosca,* which will be prominent in next year's repertory.'

In any event, the 1925 Season included no *Ring* cycle, but instead three performances of *Die Walküre,* in the charge of the German conductor Robert Heger. He was making his first Wagner appearances at the Royal Opera House and also shared performances of *Der fliegende Holländer, Tristan und Isolde* and *Die Meistersinger von Nürnberg* with Bruno Walter. Heger and Walter went on to share Wagner performances, especially those of the *Ring* for the next several years, often alternating on cycles – Walter with the first, Heger with the second. Walter conducted his last *Rings* for the Royal Opera House in the 1931 Season, Heger in 1933, while in 1932 Beecham conducted *Götterdämmerung* and Heger conducted the rest. Consequently, it was not until 1934, with Sir Thomas Beecham, that a Covent Garden *Ring* did not include at all Walter or Heger. Thereafter, it was Beecham with two cycles in 1935 and 1936, then one in 1939, and Wilhelm Furtwängler with two each in 1937 and 1938. The rest of the *Ring* conductors beween 1924 and 1939 are rounded up with three *Walküres* under Sir Adrian Boult ('by kind permission of the BBC') and one under Albert Coates, who also conducted two *Siegfrieds*.

Such musical continuity was further helped with the casting. As a result, the list of longest-serving performers, many of whose appearances continued through the 1920s and into the 30s, is long: Norman Allin (Fafner and Hunding, spanning 1922 to 1938); Eduard Habich (Alberich in all but one year, 1924–36); Friedrich Schorr (a regular Wotan/Wanderer, 1924–33); Maria Olczewska (Waltraute and/or Fricka, 1924–33); Frida Leider (Brünnhilde every year, 1924–38); Lauritz Melchior (Siegfried or Siegmund – mostly both – each year but one from 1924 to 1939); Lotte Lehmann (Sieglinde in 1924, then every year from 1926 to 1935, mostly opposite Melchior's Siegmund); Herbert Janssen (Gunther, 1926–39); Otto Helgers (ranging through Fafner, Fasolt, Hunding and Hagen, 1926–33); Rudolf Bockelmann (from 1929, Wotan/Wanderer in seven Seasons); Josephine Wray (a decade of Freias, 1929–39); and Fritz Wolff (Loge in the 1930s).

Others appeared enough to become familiar faces and voices. They included: Florence Austral, Nanny Larsén-Todsen and latterly Kirsten Flagstad (Brünnhilde); Rudolf Laubenthal (Siegfried); Hans Clemens (Loge); Ivar Andrésen and Ludwig Weber (Hagen, Fafner and Hunding); Kerstin Thorborg (Fricka and Waltraute); Viktor Madin (Alberich and Donner); and Emil Schipper (Wotan/Wanderer). And if Albert Reiss wins a mention for longevity – Mime in 1901–05 as well as in 1924–9, then another regular, Odette de Foras, deserves notice for versatility: Sieglinde, Gutrune, Woglinde, Helmwige and a Norn.

Some major changes were made to the staging of the *Ring* in 1934 with new direction by Otto Erhardt (then a leading producer in Germany) and sets by Gabriel Volkoff. (Erhardt's involvement in planning the whole opera Season did not meet with complete approval from some of the Covent Garden staff stalwarts who felt they were being inappropriately overlooked.) Volkoff's design allied with new stage direction by Erhardt met with a generally good response, although the stage at times appeared to some overcrowded and underlit. As usual, it was the difficulty of balancing the naturalistic representation of Wagner's demands with the pragmatism of the theatre (the mechanics and the rehearsal time) that caused the problems, described here in *The Times:*

> The last scene of all [of *Götterdämmerung*] was not played in the hall of the Gibichungs but outside it (the same scene as Act II), and though this makes for effective grouping of the figures round the bier of Siegfried and allows the Rhinemaidens to come right to the front of the stage in the finale, it is an evasion of the difficulties of Wagner's stage requirements. Neither Grane nor the funeral-pyre is seen, and Brünnhilde's final exit is robbed of any special significance. She might be merely running away while the house on one side of the stage tumbles down and flames envelop the sky. But the problems of *Götterdämmerung* lie deeper than effects of the stage, and they are only to be solved by a close understanding between the participants hardly to be expected in the conditions of this season.

This proved to be the only opportunity to see this staging for the end of the cycle, as the previous conclusion was restored for the second cycle. Problems with the staging were still evident in the 1935 performances. Technical difficulties in 1934 with the cyclorama (that helped give the illusion of dissolving one scene into another) continued, and the breaking down of this cyclorama mechanism caused the *Rheingold* that opened the cycle (on 3 May) to be halted, with the house lights raised, between the first and second scenes. Although the performance was restarted, the staging problems continued, with scene 2 completed behind a curtain that had been lowered a bit too eagerly; the scene 3 gauze made the voices muffled (in the opinion of *The Times*) and the scene 'ineffective…, and the gyrations of Alberich's serpent were scarcely visible. Of the minor deities, Mr Henry Wendon's Froh was the most distinguished, but Miss Edith Furmedge was so awkwardly placed right at the back of the stage, with Wotan peering at her round the corner of a rock, that it was scarcely wonderful if she failed to make Erda's intervention the compelling factor in the situation that it ought to be'.

Nineteen-thirty-six was a Season that played to Beecham's particular interest in the German repertory, and introduced first Kirsten Flagstad's Isolde and then her Brünnhilde in the second of the two cycles (Frida Leider, of course, had sung the first). Flagstad was suffering from a cold for Isolde, but had recovered for the *Ring*; unfortunately Wotan then proved all-too-human, and her debut in *Die Walküre* on Monday 25 May was hampered, as an insert in the programme explained: 'The Management request the kind indulgence of the audience on behalf of Herr Rudolf Bocklemann, who is suffering from a cold.' At the end of the performance he collapsed, so Max Roth hastily had to be brought over from the Continent for the *Siegfried* performance on the Wednesday. One other notable debut in this *Ring* was made by Kerstin Thorborg – considered as fine an actress as she was a singer – as Fricka and Waltraute in the first cycle; she returned to play the same roles in 1937 and 1938 Seasons. 1938 was the last year of both Leider's Brünnhilde and Bockelmann's Wotan/Wanderer.

The 1939 *Ring* cycle took place under Beecham in the latter part of that year's Grand Opera Season. *Götterdämmerung,* on 14 June, was the final opera of what had been some 31 cycles since 1922 (mostly with two per year), and the Season itself ended two days later. War was declared less than three months after, and opera did not return to the Royal Opera House stage until 1947.

Programme listings for the first Covent Garden *Ring* cycle after World War I and the first cycle in English since 1909. In all respects, the performances were widely lauded.

Cast page of the programme for *The Rhinegold,* 15 May 1922.

The outstanding figure of Loge was admirably done by Mr Walter Hyde, who made the fiery god a genial and appropriately comforting kind of person, whose aims and objects we could all understand. (*Morning Post*)

PRICE OF PROGRAMME, 6d.

Eve
The Lady's Pictorial
THE TRIPLE ALLIANCE OF WIT, WORTH AND WISDOM
EVERY WEDNESDAY, 1/-

Dancing in the Palm Court of the Hotel Cecil every Evening 9 to 12.30

CHOCOLATS
On Sale in this Theatre

DANCING AT THE WALDORF HOTEL
Every TUESDAY, WEDNESDAY, FRIDAY and SATURDAY
Exhibition Dances by Miss DOROTHY RAYMOND and GEORGE SANDERS
DINNER in the newly decorated Restaurant (inclusive of Dance) . 10/6
Afternoon Tea in the Palm Court . 2/-
Theatre Suppers till 12.30
Orchestra plays till 12.15 — E. LUCARINI, *General Manager.*

Savoy Restaurant for Luncheon and Dinner
DANCING EVERY NIGHT FROM 9.30 P.M.

THE MASTER MUSICIANS
who record only for
Columbia Records
include
Dame CLARA BUTT
FRANK MULLINGS
NORMAN ALLIN
ARTHUR JORDAN
etc., ONLY on
Columbia RECORDS
For all gramophones. Lists from Columbia, 102 Clerkenwell Rd. E.C.1

Royal Opera House, Covent Garden
Proprietors: The Grand Opera Syndicate, Ltd.

1922
British National Opera Company's Season

Monday, May 15th, at 8.30

WAGNER'S OPERA

THE RHINEGOLD

Wotan	CLARENCE WHITEHILL
Donner	FREDERIC COLLIER
Froh	TUDOR DAVIES
Loge	WALTER HYDE
Alberich	WILLIAM MICHAEL
Mime	SYDNEY RUSSELL
Fasolt	ROBERT RADFORD
Fafner	NORMAN ALLIN
Fricka	EDNA THORNTON
Freia	ANNA LINDSEY
Erda	PHYLLIS ARCHIBALD
Woglinde	GERTRUDE JOHNSON
Wellgunde	MAY BLYTH
Flosshilde	EDITH FURMEDGE
Conductor	ALBERT COATES

For future Announcements see inside

BERKELEY RESTAURANT
DANCING AFTER DINNER
DURING THE SEASON

SCHWEPPE'S TABLE WATERS
Ask for
"*Whisky* & SCHWEPPE"

Told in English Verse
"The Ring of the Nibelung"
("RHINEGOLD," "VALKYRIE," "SIEGFRIED" and "TWILIGHT OF THE GODS")
By RANDLE FYNES. 2s. 6d.
"PARSIFAL," by RANDLE FYNES, and "TRISTAN," by LOUIS N. PARKER. 2s. 6d.
Of all Booksellers
JOHN MURRAY

"THE PRETTIEST SPOT IN TOWN"
CAFÉ MARGUERITE
171 Oxford St., W.1
Gerrard 2375
Licensed until Midnight

Imperial Restaurant for Dinner and Supper

Not to be excelled for TONE, TOUCH and DURABILITY
CHAPPELL PIANOS
50 New Bond St., London, W.1
Exclusively used at this Theatre

Boots
TOILET SPECIALISTS AND PERFUMERS
Chief London Branches:
182 Regent Street, W.1
112-118 Edgware Road, W.2
15 New Bond Street, W.1
Boots Pure Drug Co., Ltd.

BY APPOINTMENT
Apollinaris
The Fashionable Mineral Water for Private Entertaining

BY APPOINTMENT TO HIS MAJESTY THE KING
GILL & REIGATE
FURNITURE DECORATION
73-77 OXFORD ST. LONDON, W.1.

Finden Brown & Co. Ltd., Craven Street, Strand

Cast page of the programme for *The Valkyrie,* 16 May 1922.

The present representatives of Sieglinde, Fricka, Siegmund, Hunding, and Wotan have already won their spurs, but the statement does not mean that there was any suggestion of the conventional. Far from it. There was all the individuality, all the personality, and all the vocal resource that make these performances so distinctive, and since they also have a new degree of animation, the understanding is helped largely. Both Miss Nicholls and Mr Hyde sang superbly in the first scene, to which the churlishness of Mr Radford's Hunding made an excellent contrast. Next, the passages between Wotan and Fricka had a fresh appeal, because of the fine emphasis with which, through Miss Thornton, the goddess's reproaches were uttered. Miss Florence Austral, a new-comer, gave of her best as Brünnhilde, with an uncommonly effective delivery of the Valkyries' cry. The other members of Wotan's numerous family were well up to their work, and the famous Ride produced its wonted thrill, thanks to the remarkably fine playing of the orchestra as conducted by Mr Albert Coates, even though his attitude to the rest was more orchestral than operatic. (*Morning Post*)

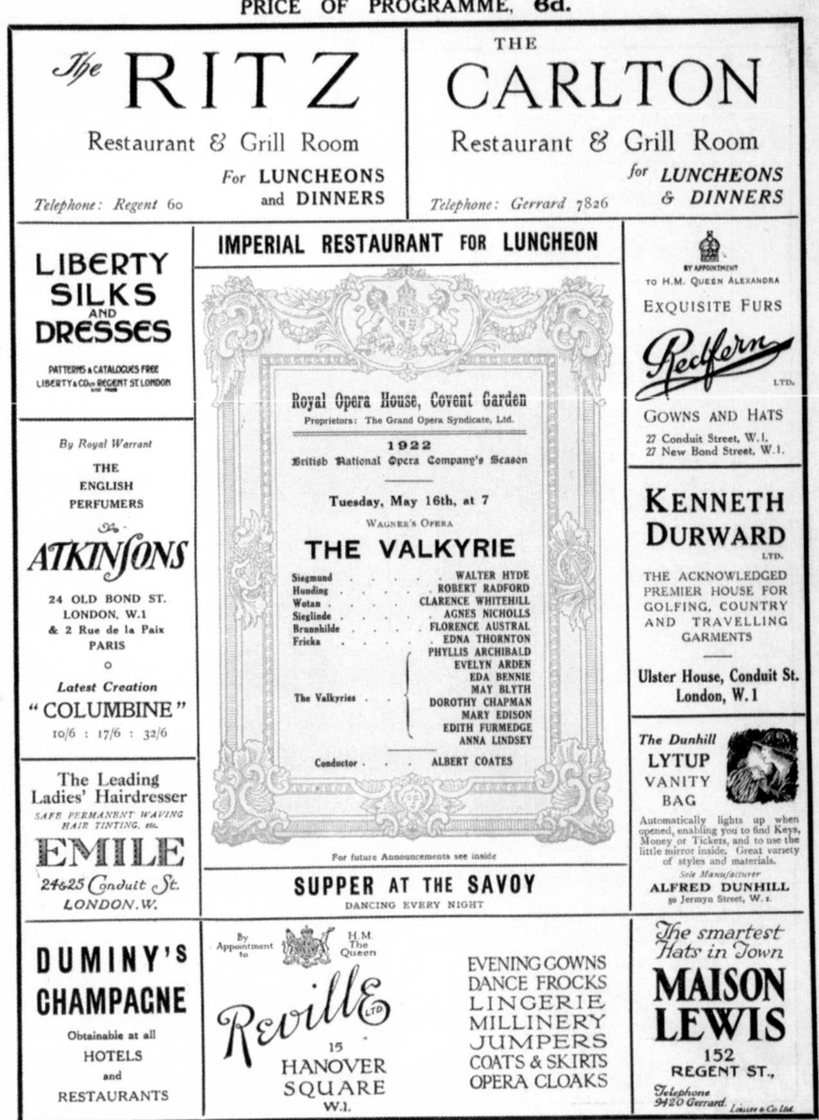

PRICE OF PROGRAMME, 6d.

The RITZ
Restaurant & Grill Room
For LUNCHEONS and DINNERS
Telephone: Regent 60

THE CARLTON
Restaurant & Grill Room
for LUNCHEONS & DINNERS
Telephone: Gerrard 7826

LIBERTY SILKS AND DRESSES
PATTERNS & CATALOGUES FREE
LIBERTY & CO. REGENT ST. LONDON

IMPERIAL RESTAURANT FOR LUNCHEON

Royal Opera House, Covent Garden
Proprietors: The Grand Opera Syndicate, Ltd.

1922
British National Opera Company's Season

Tuesday, May 16th, at 7

WAGNER'S OPERA

THE VALKYRIE

Siegmund	WALTER HYDE
Hunding	ROBERT RADFORD
Wotan	CLARENCE WHITEHILL
Sieglinde	AGNES NICHOLLS
Brunnhilde	FLORENCE AUSTRAL
Fricka	EDNA THORNTON
The Valkyries	PHYLLIS ARCHIBALD EVELYN ARDEN EDA BENNIE MAY BLYTH DOROTHY CHAPMAN MARY EDISON EDITH FURMEDGE ANNA LINDSEY
Conductor	ALBERT COATES

For future Announcements see inside

BY APPOINTMENT TO H.M. QUEEN ALEXANDRA
EXQUISITE FURS
Redfern LTD.
GOWNS AND HATS
27 Conduit Street, W.1.
27 New Bond Street, W.1.

By Royal Warrant
THE ENGLISH PERFUMERS
ATKINSONS
24 OLD BOND ST. LONDON, W.1
& 2 Rue de la Paix PARIS
Latest Creation
"COLUMBINE"
10/6 : 17/6 : 32/6

KENNETH DURWARD LTD.
THE ACKNOWLEDGED PREMIER HOUSE FOR GOLFING, COUNTRY AND TRAVELLING GARMENTS
Ulster House, Conduit St. London, W.1

The Leading Ladies' Hairdresser
SAFE PERMANENT WAVING
HAIR TINTING, etc.
EMILE
24 & 25 Conduit St.
LONDON. W.

SUPPER AT THE SAVOY
DANCING EVERY NIGHT

The Dunhill
LYTUP
VANITY
BAG
Automatically lights up when opened, enabling you to find Keys, Money or Tickets, and to use the little mirror inside. Great variety of styles and materials.
Sole Manufacturer
ALFRED DUNHILL
30 Jermyn Street, W.1.

DUMINY'S CHAMPAGNE
Obtainable at all HOTELS and RESTAURANTS

By Appointment to H.M. The Queen
Reville LTD
15 HANOVER SQUARE W.1.
EVENING GOWNS
DANCE FROCKS
LINGERIE
MILLINERY
JUMPERS
COATS & SKIRTS
OPERA CLOAKS

The smartest Hats in Town
MAISON LEWIS
152 REGENT ST.,
Telephone 9420 Gerrard.

Cast and Season list pages from the programme for *Siegfried,* 18 May 1922.

Mr Sydney Russell as Mime gave a really notable performance. In the first place, practically every word was clearly audible, and his acting of the character was extraordinarily vivacious and very rarely if ever too much so. It was he who kept the action of the first act alive, while Mr Coates looked after the music and Mr Whitehill's voice and presence supplied this contrast of dignity.
(*The Times*)

The voice of the Woodbird was uncredited, which prompted several critics to play detective, and to the *Times* writer 'it seemed as though the spirit of Sieglinde (of Tuesday night's performance) was giving the advice which directed the destiny of her son. Was it so?' He was not alone in thinking the Woodbird was Agnes Nicholls (she had sung the role in the 1906 and 1907 cycles).

PRICE OF PROGRAMME, 6d.

ROYAL OPERA HOUSE
COVENT GARDEN

Proprietors: THE GRAND OPERA SYNDICATE, Ltd.
Secretary & Business Manager - P. C. EALES

Under the direction of THE BRITISH NATIONAL OPERA CO., Ltd.
Artistic Director - PERCY PITT

British National Opera Company's Season, 1922

The RITZ

Restaurant *and* Grill Room

For Luncheons *and* Dinners

Telephone: REGENT 60

SPECIAL NOTICE.—For the convenience of all attending the performances, the Management earnestly request that everyone will attend punctually, and arrange to arrive in their seats *at least five minutes before the commencement of each Act.* Those who are unable to remain until the close of the last Act are requested to leave during the interval immediately preceding it, and thus *avoid disturbing the Artistes and the Audience* while the performance is actually proceeding.

"THE RING OF THE NIBELUNG"

Third Performance, First Cycle

Thursday, May 18th, at 6.15

SIEGFRIED

In Three Acts

By RICHARD WAGNER

Siegfried	ARTHUR JORDAN
Mime	SYDNEY RUSSELL
The Wanderer	CLARENCE WHITEHILL
Alberich	WILLIAM MICHAEL
Fafner	NORMAN ALLIN
Erda	EDNA THORNTON
Brunnhilde	FLORENCE AUSTRAL
Conductor	ALBERT COATES

Synopsis of Scenery

ACT I. A Cave in the Forest.
ACT II. The Depths of the Forest.
ACT III. Scene 1. A Wild Region in the Forest.
Scene 2. The Summit of the Valkyrie's Rock.

*** CONSOMME and SANDWICHES (*supplied by the* RITZ HOTEL, *Piccadilly*) are on sale in the Theatre.

Pianos supplied exclusively by CHAPPELL.

Friday, May 19th, at 7
THE MASTERSINGERS
By RICHARD WAGNER
Mmes. MIRIAM LICETTE, EDITH CLEGG.
Messrs. ARTHUR JORDAN, ANDREW SHANKS, ROBERT RADFORD, SYDNEY RUSSELL, TUDOR DAVIES, FREDERIC COLLIER.
Conductor - AYLMER BUESST

Saturday Matinee, May 20th, at 2
SAMSON AND DELILAH
By CAMILLE SAINT-SAËNS

Saturday Evening, May 20th, at 8
THE GOLDSMITH OF TOLEDO
By JACQUES OFFENBACH

Monday, May 22nd, at 6
THE TWILIGHT OF THE GODS

Tuesday, May 23rd, at 7.45
AÏDA

Wednesday, May 24th, at 7
TRISTAN AND ISOLDE

Thursday, May 25th, at 8.30
LA BOHÈME

Friday, May 26th, at 8
THE MAGIC FLUTE

Saturday Matinee, May 27th, at 1.15
PARSIFAL

Saturday Evening, May 27th, at 8.30
Command Performance
LA BOHÈME

May
29 Monday, at 8.30 . . . THE RHINEGOLD
30 Tuesday, at 7 . . . THE VALKYRIE
31 Wednesday, at 8 . . . CARMEN
June
1 Thursday, at 6.15 . . . SIEGFRIED
2 Friday, at 7 . . . THE MASTERSINGERS
3 Saturday (Matinée), at 2.15 . MADAM BUTTERFLY
" (Evening), at 7.45 . . . FAUST

5 Monday, at 6 . THE TWILIGHT OF THE GODS
6 Tuesday, at 8 . . . THE MAGIC FLUTE
7 Wednesday, at 7.30 . . . LOUISE
8 Thursday, at 7 . . TRISTAN AND ISOLDE
9 Friday, at 8.30 . . . TOSCA
10 Saturday (Matinée), at 2.30 . . LA BOHEME
" (Evening), at 7.45 . . TANNHAUSER

For THE BRITISH NATIONAL OPERA CO., LTD.

Stage Director - GEORGE KING
Business Manager - W. D. HUNT
Leader of Orchestra - BERNARD REILLIE
Dances arranged by ETHEL KING
Registered Offices: 18, Adam Street, Adelphi, London, W.C. 2.
Secretary - JOHN CUNINGHAME
Stage Director for "The Ring of the Nibelung" - CHARLES MOOR

PRICES OF ADMISSION (*including Tax*)

	Single Performances, except for the "Ring" and "Parsifal." £ s. d.	Special Prices for the "Ring" Operas and "Parsifal." £ s. d.	Complete Cycle of the "Ring" (Four Operas). £ s. d.
BOXES			
Pit and Grand-Tier	5 0 0	6 10 0	[illegible]
Balcony-Tier	[illegible]	[illegible]	[illegible]
ORCHESTRA STALLS	[illegible]	[illegible]	[illegible]
	[illegible]	[illegible]	[illegible]
GRAND CIRCLE			
Front Row	[illegible]	[illegible]	[illegible]
2nd and 3rd Rows	[illegible]	[illegible]	[illegible]
BALCONY STALLS			
Front Row, Centre	[illegible]	[illegible]	[illegible]
Other Seats	[illegible]	[illegible]	[illegible]
AMPHITHEATRE STALLS			
Row 1, Centre	[illegible]	[illegible]	[illegible]
Rows 1 (side), 2, 3, 4	[illegible]	[illegible]	[illegible]
Rows 5, 6, 7	[illegible]	[illegible]	[illegible]
GALLERY (unreserved)	[illegible]	[illegible]	—

Box Office open from [illegible] — Telephone: Gerrard [illegible]

THE CARLTON

Restaurant *and* Grill Room

For Luncheons *and* Dinners

Telephone: GERRARD 7826

T. VASCO, LTD.
16 Dover Street, Piccadilly, W.
World-celebrated Fi…
WAVING. MAKER…
HAIR TINTERS…

GUILDHALL S…

All Lov…
The New
"OPERA…
Price…
Printed on the fine… bound in blue clo… contains 384 page… illustrations, full … many full page p…
Obtainable from …
The Gramophon…

THE RIGHT…

HELENA…
Scientific…
24 Grafton St…

After the Opera, theatre or dance—
a gas fire provides comfort;
a gas cooker hot food; and
a gas water-heater a hot bath—
without making trouble, work or dirt and with a minimum of expense.
Gas is at once a Luxury and a Necessity.
It has risen less in cost than any other household commodity.
THE GAS LIGHT AND COKE C…
Horseferry Road, Westminster, S.W.

PRICE OF PROGRAMME, 6d.

EVE
The Lady's Pictorial
THE TRIPLE ALLIANCE OF WIT, WORTH AND WISDOM
EVERY WEDNESDAY, 1/-

Dancing in the Palm Court of the Hotel Cecil every Evening 9 to 12.30

CHOCOLATS
De Bry (de Paris)
On Sale in this Theatre

DANCING AT THE WALDORF HOTEL
Every TUESDAY, WEDNESDAY, FRIDAY and SATURDAY
Exhibition Dances by Miss DOROTHY RAYMOND and GEORGE SANDERS
DINNER in the newly decorated Restaurant (inclusive of Dance) . 10/6
Afternoon Tea in the Palm Court . 2/-
Theatre Suppers till 12.30
Orchestra plays till 12.30 — E. LUCARINI, *General Manager.*

Savoy Restaurant for Luncheon and Dinner
DANCING EVERY NIGHT FROM 9.30 P.M.

Royal Opera House, Covent Garden
Proprietors: The Grand Opera Syndicate, Ltd.
1922
British National Opera Company's Season
Thursday, May 18th, at 6.15
WAGNER'S OPERA
SIEGFRIED

Siegfried	ARTHUR JORDAN
Mime	SYDNEY RUSSELL
The Wanderer	CLARENCE WHITEHILL
Alberich	WILLIAM MICHAEL
Fafner	NORMAN ALLIN
Erda	EDNA THORNTON
Brunnhilde	FLORENCE AUSTRAL
Conductor	ALBERT COATES

For future Announcements see inside

THE MASTER MUSICIANS
who record only for
Columbia Records
include
Dame CLARA BUTT
FRANK MULLINGS
NORMAN ALLIN
ARTHUR JORDAN
etc., ONLY on
Columbia RECORDS
For all gramophones. Lists from Columbia, 102 Clerkenwell Rd. E.C.1

BERKELEY RESTAURANT
DANCING AFTER DINNER
DURING THE SEASON

SCHWEPPE'S TABLE WATERS
Ask for "*Whisky & Schweppe*"

Told in English Verse
"The Ring of the Nibelung"
("RHINEGOLD," "VALKYRIE," "SIEGFRIED" and "TWILIGHT OF THE GODS")
By RANDLE FYNES. 2s. 6d.
"PARSIFAL," by RANDLE FYNES, and "TRISTAN," by LOUIS N. PARKER. 2s. 6d.
Of all Booksellers
JOHN MURRAY

"THE PRETTIEST SPOT IN TOWN"
CAFÉ MARGUERITE
171 Oxford St., W.1
Gerrard 1273
Licensed until Midnight

Imperial Restaurant for Dinner and Supper

Not to be excelled for TONE, TOUCH and DURABILITY
CHAPPELL PIANOS
50 New Bond St., London, W.1
Exclusively used at this Theatre

Boots
TOILET SPECIALISTS AND PERFUMERS
Chief London Branches:
182 Regent Street, W.1
112-118 Edgware Road, W.2
15 New Bond Street, W.1
Boots Pure Drug Co., Ltd.

BY APPOINTMENT
Apollinaris
The Fashionable Mineral Water for Private Entertaining

BY APPOINTMENT TO HIS MAJESTY THE KING
GILL & REIGATE LTD.
FURNITURE DECORATION
73-77 OXFORD ST. LONDON, W.1.

Fieden Brown & Co. Ltd., Craven Street, Strand

Cast and Season list pages from the programme for *The Twilight of the Gods,* 22 May 1922.

As with previous *Ring* operas, the performance was chiefly notable for the magnificent orchestral playing under Mr Albert Coates, whose conducting was the mainspring of the whole performance. The playing he obtained in the great symphonic interludes – the Journey to the Rhine and the Funeral March – was wonderful for brilliance and poetic expression, while throughout the evening the glorious orchestral fabric was given its full beauty. Some excellent work was done by the principals. Mr Frank Mullings was an heroic Siegfried, singing and acting dramatically, and Miss Beatrice Miranda was an equally good Brünnhilde. The role is, of course, one of the most exacting in all opera, but Miss Miranda stood the ordeal very well, singing with fine intensity, and giving real dramatic force to her great scenes with Siegfried. (*Daily Chronicle*)

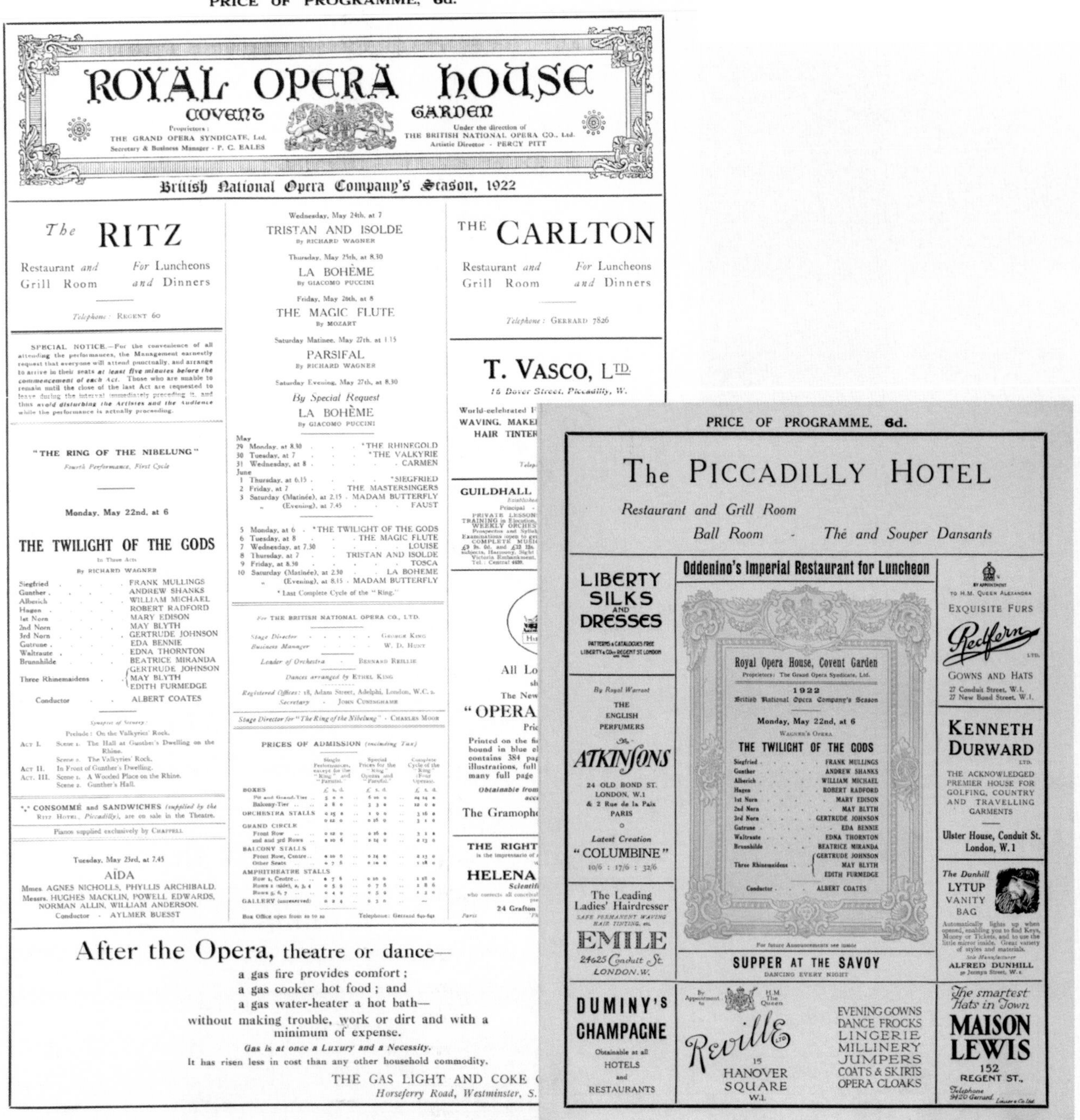

PRICE OF PROGRAMME, 6d.

ROYAL OPERA HOUSE
COVENT GARDEN

Proprietors: THE GRAND OPERA SYNDICATE, Ltd.
Secretary & Business Manager - P. C. EALES

Under the direction of THE BRITISH NATIONAL OPERA CO., Ltd.
Artistic Director - PERCY PITT

British National Opera Company's Season, 1922

The RITZ
Restaurant *and* Grill Room
For Luncheons *and* Dinners
Telephone: REGENT 60

SPECIAL NOTICE.—For the convenience of all attending the performances, the Management earnestly request that everyone will attend punctually, and arrange to arrive in their seats ***at least five minutes before the commencement of each Act.*** Those who are unable to remain until the close of the last Act are requested to leave during the interval immediately preceding it, and thus ***avoid disturbing the Artistes and the Audience*** while the performance is actually proceeding.

"THE RING OF THE NIBELUNG"
Fourth Performance, First Cycle

Monday, May 22nd, at 6

THE TWILIGHT OF THE GODS
In Three Acts
By RICHARD WAGNER

Siegfried . . . FRANK MULLINGS
Gunther . . . ANDREW SHANKS
Alberich . . . WILLIAM MICHAEL
Hagen . . . ROBERT RADFORD
1st Norn . . . MARY EDISON
2nd Norn . . . MAY BLYTH
3rd Norn . . . GERTRUDE JOHNSON
Gutrune . . . EDA BENNIE
Waltraute . . . EDNA THORNTON
Brunnhilde . . . BEATRICE MIRANDA
Three Rhinemaidens . . . GERTRUDE JOHNSON, MAY BLYTH, EDITH FURMEDGE
Conductor . . . ALBERT COATES

Synopsis of Scenery:
Prelude: On the Valkyries' Rock.
ACT I. Scene 1. The Hall at Gunther's Dwelling on the Rhine.
Scene 2. The Valkyries' Rock.
ACT II. In Front of Gunther's Dwelling.
ACT. III. Scene 1. A Wooded Place on the Rhine.
Scene 2. Gunther's Hall.

*** CONSOMMÉ and SANDWICHES *(supplied by the* RITZ HOTEL, *Piccadilly)*, are on sale in the Theatre.

Pianos supplied exclusively by CHAPPELL

Tuesday, May 23rd, at 7.45
AÏDA
Mmes. AGNES NICHOLLS, PHYLLIS ARCHIBALD.
Messrs. HUGHES MACKLIN, POWELL EDWARDS, NORMAN ALLIN, WILLIAM ANDERSON.
Conductor - AYLMER BUESST

Wednesday, May 24th, at 7
TRISTAN AND ISOLDE
By RICHARD WAGNER

Thursday, May 25th, at 8.30
LA BOHÈME
By GIACOMO PUCCINI

Friday, May 26th, at 8
THE MAGIC FLUTE
By MOZART

Saturday Matinee, May 27th, at 1.15
PARSIFAL
By RICHARD WAGNER

Saturday Evening, May 27th, at 8.30
By Special Request
LA BOHÈME
By GIACOMO PUCCINI

May
29 Monday, at 8.30 . . . *THE RHINEGOLD
30 Tuesday, at 7 . . . *THE VALKYRIE
31 Wednesday, at 8 . . . CARMEN
June
1 Thursday, at 6.15 . . . *SIEGFRIED
2 Friday, at 7 . . . THE MASTERSINGERS
3 Saturday (Matinée), at 2.15 . MADAM BUTTERFLY
" (Evening), at 7.45 . . . FAUST

5 Monday, at 6 . *THE TWILIGHT OF THE GODS
6 Tuesday, at 8 . . . THE MAGIC FLUTE
7 Wednesday, at 7.30 . . . LOUISE
8 Thursday, at 7 . . . TRISTAN AND ISOLDE
9 Friday, at 8.30 . . . TOSCA
10 Saturday (Matinée), at 2.30 . . . LA BOHEME
" (Evening), at 8.15 . MADAM BUTTERFLY

* Last Complete Cycle of the "Ring."

For THE BRITISH NATIONAL OPERA CO., LTD.
Stage Director . . . GEORGE KING
Business Manager . . . W. D. HUNT
Leader of Orchestra - BERNARD REILLIE
Dances arranged by ETHEL KING
Registered Offices: 18, Adam Street, Adelphi, London, W.C. 2.
Secretary - JOHN CUNINGHAME

Stage Director for "The Ring of the Nibelung" - CHARLES MOOR

PRICES OF ADMISSION *(including Tax)*

	Single Performances, except for the "Ring" and "Parsifal."	Special Prices for the "Ring" Operas and "Parsifal."	Complete Cycle of the "Ring" (Four Operas).
	£ s. d.	£ s. d.	£ s. d.
BOXES			
Pit and Grand-Tier	5 0 0	6 10 0	24 14 0
Balcony-Tier	2 8 0	3 3 0	12 0 0
ORCHESTRA STALLS	0 15 0	1 0 0	3 16 0
	0 12 0	0 16 0	3 1 0
GRAND CIRCLE			
Front Row	0 12 0	0 16 0	3 1 0
2nd and 3rd Rows	0 10 6	0 14 0	2 13 0
BALCONY STALLS			
Front Row, Centre	0 10 0	0 14 0	2 13 0
Other Seats	0 7 6	0 10 0	1 18 0
AMPHITHEATRE STALLS			
Row 1, Centre	0 7 6	0 10 0	1 18 0
Rows 1 (side), 2, 3, 4	0 5 9	0 7 6	1 8 6
Rows 5, 6, 7	0 4 9	0 5 9	1 3 0
GALLERY (unreserved)	0 2 4	0 3 6	—

Box Office open from 10 to 10 Telephone: Gerrard 840-843

THE CARLTON
Restaurant *and* Grill Room
For Luncheons *and* Dinners
Telephone: GERRARD 7826

T. VASCO, LTD.
16 Dover Street, Piccadilly, W.
World-celebrated
WAVING, MAKE
HAIR TINTER

GUILDHALL

All Lo
The New
"OPERA
Printed on the fi
bound in blue cl
contains 384 pa
illustrations, full
many full page
Obtainable from
The Gramophone

THE RIGHT
HELENA
24 Grafton

After the Opera, theatre or dance—
a gas fire provides comfort;
a gas cooker hot food; and
a gas water-heater a hot bath—
without making trouble, work or dirt and with a minimum of expense.
Gas is at once a Luxury and a Necessity.
It has risen less in cost than any other household commodity.
THE GAS LIGHT AND COKE
Horseferry Road, Westminster, S.

PRICE OF PROGRAMME, 6d.

The PICCADILLY HOTEL
Restaurant and Grill Room
Ball Room - Thé and Souper Dansants

LIBERTY SILKS AND DRESSES

By Royal Warrant
THE ENGLISH PERFUMERS
ATKINSONS
24 OLD BOND ST. LONDON, W.1
& 2 Rue de la Paix PARIS
Latest Creation
"COLUMBINE"
10/6 : 17/6 : 32/6

The Leading Ladies' Hairdresser
EMILE
24&25 Conduit St.
LONDON. W.

Oddenino's Imperial Restaurant for Luncheon

Royal Opera House, Covent Garden
Proprietors: The Grand Opera Syndicate, Ltd.
1922
British National Opera Company's Season
Monday, May 22nd, at 6
WAGNER'S OPERA
THE TWILIGHT OF THE GODS
Siegfried . . . FRANK MULLINGS
Gunther . . . ANDREW SHANKS
Alberich . . . WILLIAM MICHAEL
Hagen . . . ROBERT RADFORD
1st Norn . . . MARY EDISON
2nd Norn . . . MAY BLYTH
3rd Norn . . . GERTRUDE JOHNSON
Gutrune . . . EDA BENNIE
Waltraute . . . EDNA THORNTON
Brunnhilde . . . BEATRICE MIRANDA
Three Rhinemaidens . . . GERTRUDE JOHNSON, MAY BLYTH, EDITH FURMEDGE
Conductor . . . ALBERT COATES
For future Announcements see inside

SUPPER AT THE SAVOY
DANCING EVERY NIGHT

By Appointment to H.M. Queen Alexandra
EXQUISITE FURS
Redfern
GOWNS AND HATS
27 Conduit Street, W.1.
27 New Bond Street, W.1.

KENNETH DURWARD
THE ACKNOWLEDGED PREMIER HOUSE FOR GOLFING, COUNTRY AND TRAVELLING GARMENTS
Ulster House, Conduit St. London, W.1

The Dunhill
LYTUP
VANITY BAG
ALFRED DUNHILL

DUMINY'S CHAMPAGNE
Obtainable at all HOTELS and RESTAURANTS

By Appointment to H.M. The Queen
Reville Ltd
15 HANOVER SQUARE W.1.
EVENING GOWNS
DANCE FROCKS
LINGERIE
MILLINERY
JUMPERS
COATS & SKIRTS
OPERA CLOAKS

The smartest Hats in Town
MAISON LEWIS
152 REGENT ST.

Bruno Walter, whose first *Ring* performance at the Royal Opera House was with *Das Rheingold* on 5 May 1924, the first night of that year's Grand Opera Season, which marked a return to pre-war glamour and practices: the German language was restored to the *Ring* cycle and the cast included a good number of foreign – including some German – performers. In addition, after the 1922 and 1923 *Ring* opera performances principally under the batons of Albert Coates and Eugene Goossens, the employment of Walter as conductor made an eloquent statement on the return of operatic internationalism after World War I.

Walter 'is a small, pale man, with long black hair, and his methods with the baton were decidedly spectacular and interesting to watch. At moments when Wagner's terrific music needed special amplification he would throw down his baton, fling his arms high and endeavour "to mould" melody in the air with his long white fingers'. (*Daily Mirror*) He 'acquitted himself of his task with all the mastery for which he is justly famous. His grip over an orchestra whose acquaintance he has only just made is as firm as if he had controlled it for years. The authority of his reading and the plasticity with which he brings out every theme are beyond praise. With all his care for detail he never loses sight of the big patches of Wagner's music.' (*Manchester Guardian*)

Walter and the orchestra were particularly applauded before the third act of *Götterdämmerung*, with the *Daily News* reporter summarizing a widely held view of the conductor's interpretation of the score as 'the biggest and most heroic we have heard for years and years, and the most consistent'. The stage presentation had also been developed by Charles Moor, with more reliance on lighting effects and stage suggestion that allowed the music to dominate the way such set pieces as the Ride of the Valkyries and Brünnhilde's immolation/the burning of Valhalla were evoked.

As to the glamour, there was much amusement in the press at the sight of men in evening dress and women in ball gowns and copious jewellery, all

sitting round in Covent Garden market in the afternoon sun, waiting for a performances of *Die Walküre* and *Siegfried* that began at 5.00 and a *Götterdämmerung* that started at 4.30. It was also reported that some of the audience arrived in afternoon clothing, were chauffered off at the first interval, then returned in evening wear. Such observance of the formalities of dress was possible as it was also the year in which long supper intervals (40 minutes between the first and second acts) were reintroduced; the restaurants of hotels in the area provided 'dîner à l'opéra', a series of small courses, quickly served and bearing the names of singers or characters appropriate to that evening's performance. The combination of dining with doses of Wagner prompted some musing on the new gilded iron and mahogany handrail that had been installed up the middle of the staircase from the foyer to the salon in the Royal Opera House: was it there to help fed and flagging Wagnerites haul themselves up to their seats for the final act?

In a letter from Berlin to Lieut.-Col. Blois (managing director of Covent Garden), dated 2 February 1931, Walter recommended Fritz Wolff as the best casting for Loge, also suggesting Walter Kirchhoff ('because artistry, expression, variety, temperament, diction… are qualities that matter and far less the voice') and Richard Schubert as other possibilities. Wolff had already played the role in London in 1930 and, in fact, did so in five further Seasons: 1931, 1932, 1933 (when he also played Siegmund), 1937 and 1938. 1931, however, proved to be the last year that Walter conducted the *Ring* at Covent Garden.

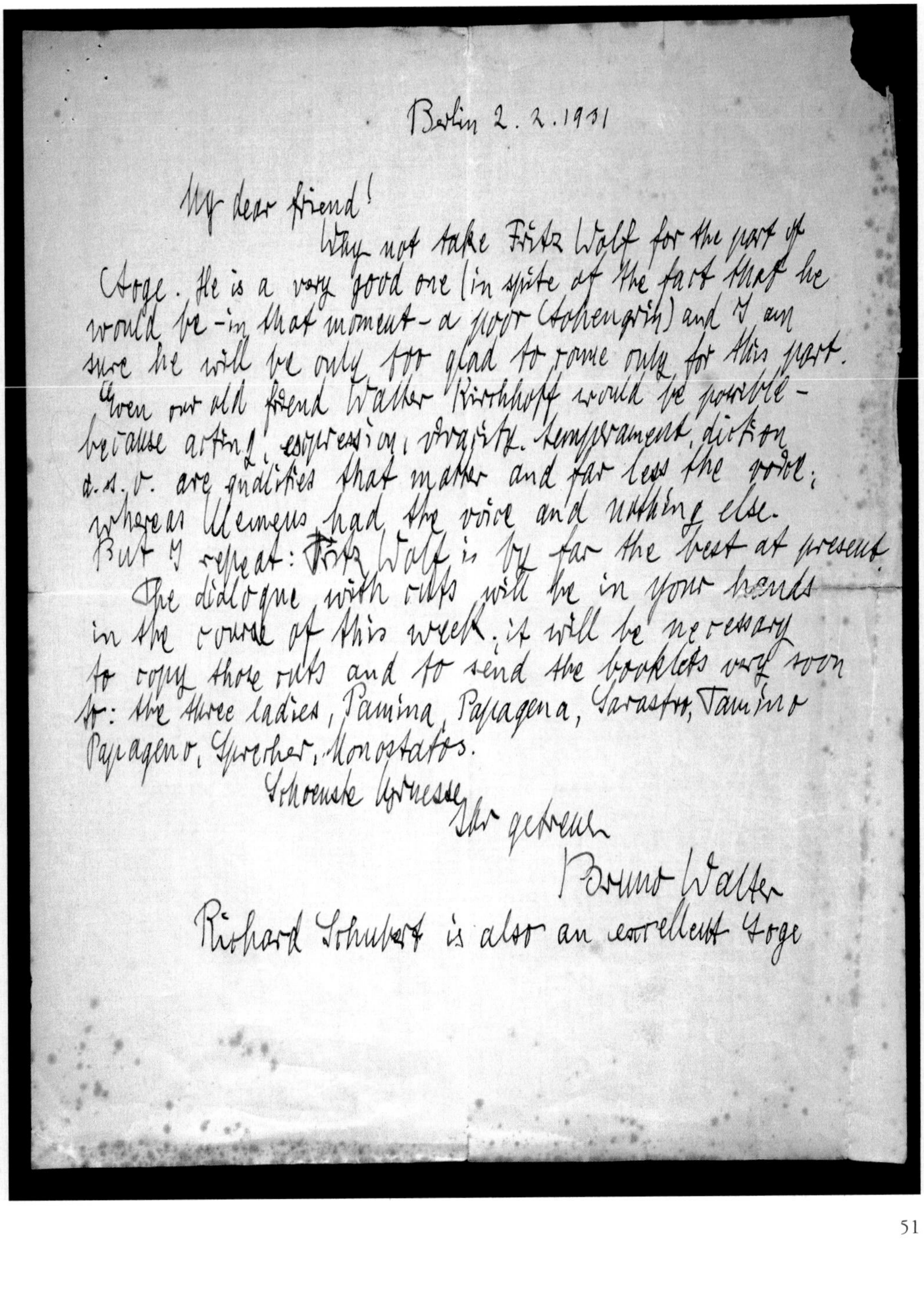

Berlin 2. 2. 1931

My dear friend!

Why not take Fritz Wolf for the part of Loge. He is a very good one (in spite of the fact that he would be – in that moment – a poor Lohengrin) and I am sure he will be only too glad to come only for this part. Even our old friend Walter Kirchhoff would be possible – because acting, expression, variety, temperament, diction u.s.w. are qualities that matter and far less the voice; whereas Clemens had the voice and nothing else. But I repeat: Fritz Wolf is by far the best at present.

The dialogue with cuts will be in your hands in the course of this week; it will be necessary to copy those cuts and to send the booklets very soon to: the three ladies, Pamina, Papagena, Sarastro, Tamino Papageno, Sprecher, Monostatos.

Schönste Grüsse

Ihr getreuer

Bruno Walter

Richard Schubert is also an excellent Loge

The programme for the first *Walküre* performance, 21 May 1925, signed by the conductor, Robert Heger. After the artistically successful *Ring* of 1924 (if not a financially successful Season), only *Die Walküre* was performed in 1925. The three performances (21 and 29 May and 3 June) were conducted by Robert Heger, making the first of many appearances in the pit with the *Ring* operas. Heger had been a conductor at Munich when Bruno Walter was Music Director, and it was to be these two in alternation who were at the helm of most *Ring* performances at the Royal Opera House until the early 1930s.

These performances also marked the return of Fritz Soot, this time as Siegmund and without the last-minute drama of his 1924 Siegfrieds; his Sieglinde, Delia Reinhardt, made her first and last appearances at the Royal Opera House in the role, although she returned in the *Ring* in 1926 for the first of several Gutrunes and in 1927 as Freia. For the second and third performances, Fricka was sung by Maria Olczewska, who had pretty much claimed the part as her own at Covent Garden from her first appearance in 1924 (when she also sang Waltraute, a role she also repeated many times); in 1926–8 she also sang Erda in *Siegfried.* The *Times* description for these 1925 performances of Fricka serves as well as any to indicate the praise she consistently garnered for both her singing and acting:

> We are so used to Frickas who strive and cry, but convince no one except Wotan, but Mme. Olczewska in every musical phrase and every gesture, but perhaps most of all in the way she maintained a pose either of command or entreaty, made Fricka appear neither the prude nor the *Hausfrau,* but the outraged goddess whose honour must be vindicated at all costs. She was, in fact, the Fricka of Wagner's intention.

PRICE OF PROGRAMME. 3d.

THE CARLTON
Restaurant *and* Grill Room
For Luncheons *and* Dinners
Soupers Dansants from 10.30 p.m.
Telephone: GERRARD 7826

The RITZ
Restaurant *and* Grill Room
For Luncheons *and* Dinners
DANCING IN THE RESTAURANT EVERY NIGHT AFTER DINNER
Telephone: REGENT 60

LIBERTY SILKS AND DRESSES
PATTERNS & CATALOGUES FREE
LIBERTY & CO LONDON & PARIS

BUELHOFF PIANOS
65 Wigmore Street, LONDON

ARCHIBALD RAMSDEN, Ltd
12 Park Row, LEEDS

Royal Opera Covent Garden
Proprietors: The Grand Opera Syndicate, Ltd.
LONDON OPERA SYNDICATE, Ltd. SEASON
THIS EVENING'S PERFORMANCE
Thursday, May 21, 1925, at 7
WAGNER'S OPERA
DIE WALKÜRE
(In German)

Siegmund	FRITZ SOOT
Wotan	FRIEDRICH SCHORR
Hunding	EMANUEL LIST
Brunnhilde	GERTRUD KAPPEL
Sieglinde	DELIA REINHARDT
Fricka	BELLA PAALEN
Gerhilde	EDA BENNIE
Ortlinde	MAY BUSBY
Waltraute	BELLA PAALEN
Schwertleite	MARION BEELEY
Helmwige	ROSEL LANDWEHR
Siegrune	MAY BLYTH
Grimgerde	EDITH FURMEDGE
Rossweisse	EVELYN ARDEN
Conductor	ROBERT HEGER

Originality, Distinction and keen Value in Gowns for all occasions.
Ninette
47, Cranbourn Street,
(Facing Daly's Theatre)
London, W.1
Phone: Gerrard 2244 & 8141

STEINWAY
The Instrument of the Immortals
Also the chosen Piano of the world's greatest living pianists: Paderewski Josef Hofmann Pachmann Rachmaninoff
STEINWAY & SONS
STEINWAY HALL 115-117, WIGMORE ST LONDON, W.1

"VALAZE"
BEAUTY PREPARATIONS
and exclusive treatments to remedy every beauty flaw.
Helena Rubinstein
NEW YORK
46, West 57th Street
PARIS
126, Faubourg St. Honoré
LONDON
24, GRAFTON STREET, W.1
(Off Bond St—Facing Hay Hill)

The Leading Ladies' Hairdresser
Permanent Waving, Hair Tinting, etc., etc.
EMILE
24 & 25 Conduit St.
LONDON, W.

SUPPER AT THE SAVOY
DANCING UNTIL 2 A.M.

ROTAX
ELECTRIC LIGHTING & STARTING EQUIPMENT
The only system to complete a 25,000 mile official R.A.A. test without a fault.
May we send you our latest Lists?
ROTAX (MOTOR ACCESSORIES) Ltd
Willesden Junction, London N.W.10

Not to be excelled for
TONE, TOUCH
and
DURABILITY
CHAPPELL PIANOS
50 New Bond St., London, W.1
Exclusively used at this Theatre

Reville
COURT DRESSMAKERS
Gowns-Wraps-Hats & Furs
HANOVER SQUARE, W.1.

ANTIQUES DECORATIONS REPRODUCTIONS
The HOUSE for FINE FURNITURE
GILL & REIGATE

The Swedish soprano Nanny Larsén-Todsen appeared as Brünnhilde in 1927 (second cycle) and in 1930 (*Siegfried* and *Götterdämmerung*), covering a similar period to her Bayreuth performances in the role.

Frida Leider as Brünnhilde and Rudolf Bockelmann as Wotan. They played these roles opposite each other on the Royal Opera House stage in the second cycle *Die Walküre* of 1930 and then in 1934–7.

Leider repeatedly gained the critics' praise through her combination of lyrical singing and convincing acting. For example, of *Die Walküre* (1927): 'Her motionless figure and the aloof and even tones of her voice in the scene of her summoning Siegmund to Walhalla and the electric change of tone in the first moment of her pity showed the same grasp of the implications of character which has made her Isolde a thing of exceptional power. The scene of her protection of Sieglinde, her last meeting with and her appeals to Wotan were no less impressive and true in feelings.' (*The Times*) And of *Götterdämmerung* a few night later: 'Madame Frida Leider added to her reputation here by a rendering of Brünnhilde well measured in every detail. She rose to the finest point in the second act, in which the scene of her recognition of Siegfried as her betrayer had some attribute of greatness. In the last

scene of all she gave great poignancy to the more tranquil moods in which the heroine (even more the heroine of *Götterdämmerung* than of *Die Walküre*) sees the approaching end of all things. But her voice thrilled when from the contemplation of her dead love she turned to swift action ending with the setting [of] the torch to the pyre which is to rise and engulf Walhalla.' (*Daily Telegraph*). On 25 May 1931, she seemed additionally suited to her famous role through an ability to follow Wagner's stage directions: 'Brünnhilde really did ride on Grane into the flames, and the sight of her flying figure (does Mme Leider add horsemanship to her other accomplishments?) added a dramatic touch which showed that Wagner's extravagant demands for realism may have some justification; it was as exciting as it was surprising.' (*The Times*)

Bockelmann, pictured here on an autographed card from 1937, essayed several of the main Wagnerian roles for his voice – Wotan/Wanderer, Gunther, Kurwenal, Hans Sachs and the Dutchman – regularly performing them at Bayreuth from the late 1920s on. He was noted in particular for the authority and grandeur he brought to his *Ring* performances.

Eduard Habich and Erich Zimmermann as Alberich and Mime. Habich was Covent Garden's leading Alberich from 1924 through to 1936, and a Bayreuth stalwart in the role from 1911. He appeared as Alberich with Zimmermann as Mime in the two cycles under Beecham in 1934; Zimmermann (who also appeared regularly in the role at Bayreuth) played Mime in the 1937 cycles and first 1938 cycle (both under Furtwängler).

Stage designs by Gabriel Volkoff for the 1934 *Ring* cycles:

Hunding's hut, *Die Walküre* Act I.
The destruction of Valhalla, *Götterdämmerung* Act III.

Stage designs by Gabriel Volkoff for *Siegfried* in the 1934 *Ring* cycles. The designs directly follow the atmospheric progression of the work:

Act I:
enclosed, underground and dark
Act II:
at ground level and in the forest
Act III:
beginning in the mountains and finally moving to the high open space of Brünnhilde's rock

Season booking form for the 1935 Imperial League of Opera Season and the programme for the second performance of *Siegfried*, on 2 October.

Royal Opera  Covent Garden

Managing Director - - GEOFFREY TOYE
Manager - - . C. A. BARRAND

LONDON & PROVINCIAL OPERA SOCIETY, LIMITED, SEASON
in conjunction with
THE IMPERIAL LEAGUE OF OPERA

GRAND OPERA FESTIVAL

under the Artistic Direction of

Sir THOMAS BEECHAM, Bart.

Monday, September 23rd, 1935

FOR TWO WEEKS ONLY

Repertoire :

In English		In Italian	
SIEGFRIED - -	*Wagner*	**UN BALLO IN MASCHERA**	*Verdi*
KOANGA - - - (First Performance)	*Delius*	**LA BOHÈME** - - -	*Puccini*
DER FREISCHÜTZ	*Weber*	**LA CENERENTOLA** - -	*Rossini*

Royal Opera  Covent Garden

GRAND OPERA FESTIVAL

Under the Artistic Direction of SIR THOMAS BEECHAM, Bart.

LONDON & PROVINCIAL OPERA SOCIETY, LIMITED, SEASON
in conjunction with
THE IMPERIAL LEAGUE OF OPERA

SEPTEMBER 23—OCTOBER 5, 1935

APPLICATION FORM

To the Box Office Manager, Royal Opera House, Covent Garden, London, W.C.2.

I wish to book the following seats :

Please state number of seats required — Please fill in Dates and Operas.

_____ Grand-Tier Box @ £5 for_____
_____ Balcony-Tier Box @ £3 for_____
_____ Orchestra Stalls @ £1 for_____
_____ ,, ,, @ 15/- for_____
_____ ,, ,, @ 12/6 for_____
_____ Stalls Circle @ 15/- for_____
_____ ,, ,, @ 12/6 for_____
_____ Dress Circle @ 15/- for_____
_____ ,, ,, @ 12/6 for_____
_____ Balcony Stalls @ 10/- for_____
_____ Amphitheatre Stalls @ 7/6 for_____
_____ ,, ,, @ 5/- for_____

for which I enclose remittance £_____

I am a member of The Imperial League of Opera, Reference Number_____, and claim the privileges quoted in your prospectus. (Please strike out if not applicable.)

I should like to become a member of The Imperial League of Opera and enclose an additional sum of_____ for_____ membership(s). (Please strike out if not applicable.)

*Name*_____

*Address*_____

*Date*_____ _____

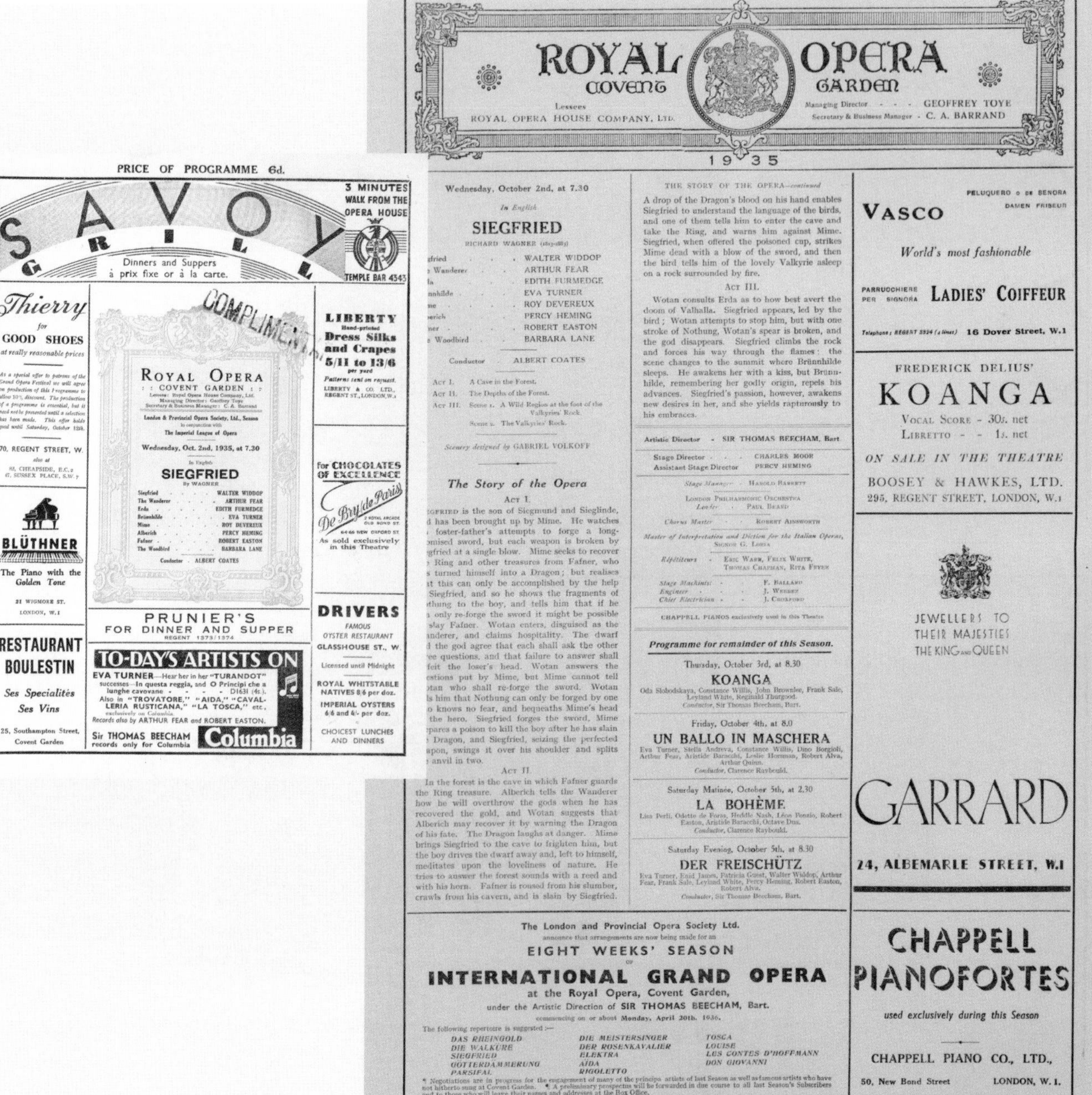

PRICE OF PROGRAMME 6d.

SAVOY GRILL
Dinners and Suppers
à prix fixe or à la carte.

3 MINUTES WALK FROM THE OPERA HOUSE
TEMPLE BAR 4343

Thierry
for
GOOD SHOES
at really reasonable prices

As a special offer to patrons of the Grand Opera Festival we will agree on production of this Programme to allow 10% discount. The production of a programme is essential, but it need not be presented until a selection has been made. This offer holds good until Saturday, October 12th.

70, REGENT STREET, W.
also at
83, CHEAPSIDE, E.C.2
67, SUSSEX PLACE, S.W.7

COMPLIMENTARY

ROYAL OPERA
: : COVENT GARDEN : :
Lessees: Royal Opera House Company, Ltd.
Managing Director: Geoffrey Toye
Secretary & Business Manager: C. A. Barrand

London & Provincial Opera Society, Ltd., Season
in conjunction with
The Imperial League of Opera

Wednesday, Oct. 2nd, 1935, at 7.30

In English
SIEGFRIED
By WAGNER

Siegfried	WALTER WIDDOP
The Wanderer	ARTHUR FEAR
Erda	EDITH FURMEDGE
Brünnhilde	EVA TURNER
Mime	ROY DEVEREUX
Alberich	PERCY HEMING
Fafner	ROBERT EASTON
The Woodbird	BARBARA LANE

Conductor . ALBERT COATES

LIBERTY
Hand-printed
Dress Silks and Crapes
5/11 to 13/6
per yard
Patterns sent on request.
LIBERTY & CO. LTD., REGENT ST., LONDON, W.1

for CHOCOLATES OF EXCELLENCE
De Bry (de Paris)
2 ROYAL ARCADE OLD BOND ST.
64-66 NEW OXFORD ST.
As sold exclusively in this Theatre

BLÜTHNER
The Piano with the *Golden Tone*
21 WIGMORE ST.
LONDON, W.1

PRUNIER'S
FOR DINNER AND SUPPER
REGENT 1373/1374

RESTAURANT BOULESTIN
Ses Specialités
Ses Vins
25, Southampton Street, Covent Garden

TO-DAY'S ARTISTS ON
EVA TURNER—Hear her in her "TURANDOT" successes—In questa reggia, and O Principi che a lunghe cavovane - - - - D1631 (4s.).
Also in "TROVATORE," "AIDA," "CAVALLERIA RUSTICANA," "LA TOSCA," etc., exclusively on Columbia.
Records also by ARTHUR FEAR *and* ROBERT EASTON.
Sir THOMAS BEECHAM records only for Columbia
Columbia

DRIVERS
FAMOUS
OYSTER RESTAURANT
GLASSHOUSE ST., W.
Licensed until Midnight
ROYAL WHITSTABLE NATIVES 8/6 per doz.
IMPERIAL OYSTERS 6/6 and 4/- per doz.
CHOICEST LUNCHES AND DINNERS

PRICE OF PROGRAMME 6d.

ROYAL OPERA
COVENT GARDEN

Lessees
ROYAL OPERA HOUSE COMPANY, LTD.

Managing Director - - - GEOFFREY TOYE
Secretary & Business Manager - C. A. BARRAND

1935

Wednesday, October 2nd, at 7.30

In English

SIEGFRIED
RICHARD WAGNER (1813-1883)

...gfried	WALTER WIDDOP
... Wanderer	ARTHUR FEAR
...la	EDITH FURMEDGE
...nnhilde	EVA TURNER
...me	ROY DEVEREUX
...erich	PERCY HEMING
...ner	ROBERT EASTON
... Woodbird	BARBARA LANE

Conductor . ALBERT COATES

ACT I. A Cave in the Forest.
ACT II. The Depths of the Forest.
ACT III. Scene 1. A Wild Region at the foot of the Valkyries' Rock.
Scene 2. The Valkyries' Rock.

Scenery designed by GABRIEL VOLKOFF

The Story of the Opera

ACT I.

...EGFRIED is the son of Siegmund and Sieglinde, ...d has been brought up by Mime. He watches ... foster-father's attempts to forge a long-...omised sword, but each weapon is broken by ...gfried at a single blow. Mime seeks to recover ... Ring and other treasures from Fafner, who ...s turned himself into a Dragon; but realises ...at this can only be accomplished by the help ... Siegfried, and so he shows the fragments of ...thung to the boy, and tells him that if he ... only re-forge the sword it might be possible ... slay Fafner. Wotan enters, disguised as the ...anderer, and claims hospitality. The dwarf ...d the god agree that each shall ask the other ...ee questions, and that failure to answer shall ...feit the loser's head. Wotan answers the ...estions put by Mime, but Mime cannot tell ...otan who shall re-forge the sword. Wotan ...ls him that Nothung can only be forged by one ...o knows no fear, and bequeaths Mime's head ... the hero. Siegfried forges the sword. Mime ...pares a poison to kill the boy after he has slain ... Dragon, and Siegfried, seizing the perfected ...apon, swings it over his shoulder and splits ... anvil in two.

ACT II.

In the forest is the cave in which Fafner guards the Ring treasure. Alberich tells the Wanderer how he will overthrow the gods when he has recovered the gold, and Wotan suggests that Alberich may recover it by warning the Dragon of his fate. The Dragon laughs at danger. Mime brings Siegfried to the cave to frighten him, but the boy drives the dwarf away and, left to himself, meditates upon the loveliness of nature. He tries to answer the forest sounds with a reed and with his horn. Fafner is roused from his slumber, crawls from his cavern, and is slain by Siegfried.

THE STORY OF THE OPERA—*continued*

A drop of the Dragon's blood on his hand enables Siegfried to understand the language of the birds, and one of them tells him to enter the cave and take the Ring, and warns him against Mime. Siegfried, when offered the poisoned cup, strikes Mime dead with a blow of the sword, and then the bird tells him of the lovely Valkyrie asleep on a rock surrounded by fire.

ACT III.

Wotan consults Erda as to how best avert the doom of Valhalla. Siegfried appears, led by the bird; Wotan attempts to stop him, but with one stroke of Nothung, Wotan's spear is broken, and the god disappears. Siegfried climbs the rock and forces his way through the flames: the scene changes to the summit where Brünnhilde sleeps. He awakens her with a kiss, but Brünnhilde, remembering her godly origin, repels his advances. Siegfried's passion, however, awakens new desires in her, and she yields rapturously to his embraces.

Artistic Director - SIR THOMAS BEECHAM, Bart.

Stage Director - - - CHARLES MOOR
Assistant Stage Director PERCY HEMING

Stage Manager - HAROLD BARRETT

LONDON PHILHARMONIC ORCHESTRA
Leader . PAUL BEARD

Chorus Master - - ROBERT AINSWORTH

Master of Interpretation and Diction for the Italian Operas,
SIGNOR G. LANZA

Répétiteurs - ERIC WARR, FELIX WHITE, THOMAS CHAPMAN, RITA FRYER

Stage Machinist - - F. BALLARD
Engineer - - - J. WEBBER
Chief Electrician - - J. CRAWFORD

CHAPPELL PIANOS exclusively used in this Theatre

Programme for remainder of this Season.

Thursday, October 3rd, at 8.30
KOANGA
Oda Slobodskaya, Constance Willis, John Brownlee, Frank Sale, Leyland White, Reginald Thurgood.
Conductor, Sir Thomas Beecham, Bart.

Friday, October 4th, at 8.0
UN BALLO IN MASCHERA
Eva Turner, Stella Andreva, Constance Willis, Dino Borgioli, Arthur Fear, Aristide Baracchi, Leslie Horsman, Robert Alva, Arthur Quinn.
Conductor, Clarence Raybould.

Saturday Matinée, October 5th, at 2.30
LA BOHÈME
Lisa Perli, Odette de Foras, Heddle Nash, Léon Ponzio, Robert Easton, Aristide Baracchi, Octave Dua.
Conductor, Clarence Raybould.

Saturday Evening, October 5th, at 8.30
DER FREISCHÜTZ
Eva Turner, Enid James, Patricia Guest, Walter Widdop, Arthur Fear, Frank Sale, Leyland White, Percy Heming, Robert Easton, Robert Alva.
Conductor, Sir Thomas Beecham, Bart.

VASCO
PELUQUERO de SEÑORA
DAMEN FRISEUR
World's most fashionable
PARRUCCHIERE PER SIGNORA
LADIES' COIFFEUR
Telephone: REGENT 5524 (4 lines) 16 Dover Street, W.1

FREDERICK DELIUS'
KOANGA
VOCAL SCORE - 30*s.* net
LIBRETTO - - 1*s.* net
ON SALE IN THE THEATRE
BOOSEY & HAWKES, LTD.
295, REGENT STREET, LONDON, W.1

JEWELLERS TO THEIR MAJESTIES THE KING AND QUEEN
GARRARD
24, ALBEMARLE STREET, W.1

The London and Provincial Opera Society Ltd.
announce that arrangements are now being made for an
EIGHT WEEKS' SEASON
OF
INTERNATIONAL GRAND OPERA
at the Royal Opera, Covent Garden,
under the Artistic Direction of SIR THOMAS BEECHAM, Bart.
commencing on or about **Monday, April 20th, 1936.**

The following repertoire is suggested:—

DAS RHEINGOLD	*DIE MEISTERSINGER*	*TOSCA*
DIE WALKÜRE	*DER ROSENKAVALIER*	*LOUISE*
SIEGFRIED	*ELEKTRA*	*LES CONTES D'HOFFMANN*
GÖTTERDÄMMERUNG	*AÏDA*	*DON GIOVANNI*
PARSIFAL	*RIGOLETTO*	

¶ Negotiations are in progress for the engagement of many of the principal artists of last Season as well as famous artists who have not hitherto sung at Covent Garden. ¶ A preliminary prospectus will be forwarded in due course to all last Season's Subscribers and to those who will leave their names and addresses at the Box Office.

CHAPPELL PIANOFORTES
used exclusively during this Season
CHAPPELL PIANO CO., LTD.,
50, New Bond Street LONDON, W.1

From the cast of *Siegfried,* 2 October 1935, Arthur Fear in Act I as the Wanderer and Walter Widdop as the young hero.

The performances of *Siegfried* given in this Imperial League of Opera Season were two of the few of the Wagner *Ring* operas in English in the 1930s (there had been three English *Valkyries* under Boult in 1931). Although the *Ring* in English had proved successful as far back as 1908–9, and the use of the national language for opera was increasingly popular immediately post-World War I, the return of international performers in the mid-20s inevitably brought with it a return to original-language performance. Arthur Fear had appeared as Donner and Gunther, singing in German, in the 1930 *Ring* cycles; this later appearance was his only Covent Garden Wanderer in either language (Robert Parker had sung the role at the first of the two *Siegfrieds*, on 4 September).

Walter Widdop was a regular leading tenor with the British National Opera Company, and his first and only previous appearance at Covent Garden as the eponymous hero of *Siegfried* had been with that company in the two English language performances given at the start of 1924. They had been conducted by Eugene Goossens, with Joseph Farrington as the Wanderer and Florence Austral as Brünnhilde. At both performances in 1935, the maid of the mountain that Widdop awakened was Eva Turner, last heard as Brünnhilde as far before as 1921, when the language was also English. Widdop had also played Siegmund in 1929 (in German; a performance conducted by Albert Coates, separate from the cycles of that year under Walter and Heger) and 1932 (in the second cycle and again in German; Melchior had sung in the first).

The programme for the performance of *Götterdämmerung,* 1 June 1937. This was the final performance of the two cycles given that year, which for the first time at the Royal Opera House were under the baton of Wilhelm Furtwängler. He had a first-rate cast for both cycles: the first had Frida Leider and Max Lorenz as Brünnhilde and Siegfried, with Margarete Klose as the *Götterdämmerung* Waltraute; the second, as shown here, had Kirsten Flagstad, Lauritz Melchior and Kerstin Thorborg in those roles.

Opposite: wardrobe copy of the costume design by Gabriel Volkoff for Mary Jarred as Erda in the 1933 performances of *Das Rheingold* and *Siegfried.*

ROYAL OPERA
COVENT GARDEN
Artistic Director: Sir THOMAS BEECHAM, Bart.
Secretary & Manager: CHARLES A. BARRAND

GÖTTERDÄMMERUNG

The Story of the Opera

In the darkness of the first scene the three Norns, or Fates, are dimly seen on the Valkyries' Rock. Attaching their golden rope to a tree, they tell in turn of the early coming of Wotan, who had fashioned his spear from the World ash-tree, of how Siegfried had broken the spear, and how Wotan and the gods have made firewood of the World ash as a pyre for Valhalla when the end should come. But the golden rope breaks before they can foretell what will happen, and they vanish. Day dawns, and Siegfried and Brünnhilde appear from their cavern. Brünnhilde has given Siegfried her armour, which makes him invulnerable except in the back, and also her horse Grâne. Siegfried gives Brünnhilde the Ring as a pledge of fidelity, and rides forth in search of adventure.

Act I.

The crafty Hagen, son of Alberich and half-brother of Gunther, laments that neither Gunther nor Gutrune are married. He speaks of the fire-girt Brünnhilde and suggests that Siegfried the fearless might win her for Gunther. Hagen has brewed a magic philtre whereby Siegfried will love Gutrune and forget all other women. Siegfried's horse is heard, and the hero arrives, drinks the potion, forgets Brünnhilde, and desires to wed Gutrune. Meanwhile Brünnhilde is visited by Waltraute, who tells her of the gloom in Valhalla, where the gods await the end. The curse upon the gods will be removed if Brünnhilde will return the Ring to the Rhine Maidens; but she refuses to give up Siegfried's love pledge. Siegfried enters,

Royal Opera Covent Garden
LONDON & PROVINCIAL OPERA SOCIETY SEASON
Artistic Director: Sir Thomas Beecham, Bart.
Secretary & Manager: Charles A. Barrand

Der Ring des Nibelungen
RICHARD WAGNER

Tuesday, June 1st, 1937, at 5
In German

GÖTTERDÄMMERUNG

Siegfried	LAURITZ MELCHIOR
Gunther	HERBERT JANSSEN
Hagen	LUDWIG WEBER
Alberich	EUGEN FUCHS
Brünnhilde	KIRSTEN FLAGSTAD
Gutrune	MARIA NEZADAL
Waltraute	KERSTIN THORBORG
Die drei Nornen	MARY JARRED CONSTANCE WILLIS MAE CRAVEN
Woglinde	STELLA ANDREVA
Wellgunde	JOSE MALONE
Flosshilde	LINDA SEYMOUR
Conductor	Dr. WILHELM FURTWÄNGLER

Synopsis of Scenery:
Prelude. The Valkyries' Rock.
Act I. Scene 1. The Hall of Gunther's Dwelling on the Rhine.
Scene 2. The Valkyries' Rock.
Act II. Outside Gunther's Dwelling.
Act III. Scene 1. A Wooded Place on the Rhine.
Scene 2. Gunther's Hall.

Assistant Artistic Director - PERCY HEMING
Stage Director - CHARLES MOOR
Stage Managers: Harold Barrett, Emil Brotze, K. O. Koch, Sydney Russell
LONDON PHILHARMONIC ORCHESTRA
Leader - David McCallum
Chorus Master - Robert Ainsworth
Assistant Chorus Master - Robert Alva
Musical Staff: Hermann Weigert, Norman Feasey, George Coop, Edorado Pedrazzoli
Accountant & Treasurer - G. C. Reynolds
Press Representatives: Alan Bland and Andrew Reid
CHAPPELL PIANOS exclusively used in this Theatre
Wigs by CLARKSON

The Story of the Opera—continued

changed by the Tarnhelm to the likeness of Gunther, and deprives the horrified Brünnhilde of the Ring.

Act II.

Hagen and his father Alberich, who appears in a vision, plan to steal the Ring and gain world power. Siegfried appears, followed by Gunther and Brünnhilde, and claims Gutrune as his bride; and the furious Brünnhilde, seeing the Ring on his finger, claims Siegfried as her husband. He, under the influence of the philtre, denies the claim and swears his innocence. Brünnhilde swears to his treachery, but the hero cannot understand, and goes away in high spirits with Gunther and the vassals. Brünnhilde, Hagen and Gunther plan the hero's death while he is hunting.

Act III.

The first scene is in a forest near the Rhine, Siegfried, wandering from his companions, encounters the Rhine Maidens, who plead for the return of the Ring. He refuses, and is threatened with impending death. The hunting party appears, and Siegfried entertains the men with the story of his life. Hagen puts a herb in his wine, which restores his memory. As he is telling of his first meeting with Brünnhilde Hagen stabs him in the back. The scene changes back to the Hall of the Gibichungs. Gutrune awaits Siegfried, hears from Hagen that he is dead, and swoons when Siegfried's body is brought in. Hagen claims the Ring, but is opposed by Gunther, whom he then kills. When Hagen attempts to remove the Ring from Siegfried's finger, the dead hand is raised in menace at the moment Brünnhilde enters. All is clear to her now; she longs to join her beloved Siegfried in death. Commanding a funeral pyre to be built, she takes the fateful Ring from the hero's finger and puts a brand to the pyre, upon which Siegfried's body has been placed; Brünnhilde soon throws herself into the flames. A great conflagration envelops the scene; the waters of the Rhine rise in flood and the Rhine maidens recover the Ring. Hagen is drowned in an attempt to snatch it from them, and finally the glow of the burning Valhalla is seen in the heavens.

Wed., June 2, at 8 PELLÉAS ET MÉLISANDE

Erda

OPERA
ROYAL HOUSE
DIEU ET MON DROIT
COVENT GARDEN
THE ROYAL OPERA HOUSE, COVENT GARDEN, LTD.
(IN ASSOCIATION WITH THE ARTS COUNCIL OF GREAT BRITAIN)
presents
THE
COVENT GARDEN
OPERA
in
DER RING DES NIBELUNGEN
Words and Music by RICHARD WAGNER
Scenery and Costumes by LESLIE HURRY
Producer: RUDOLF HARTMANN
Conductor: RUDOLF KEMPE
FIRST CYCLE
MAY 10 DAS RHEINGOLD at 7 p.m.
MAY 14 DIE WALKÜRE at 6 p.m.
MAY 19 SIEGFRIED at 6 p.m.
MAY 27 GÖTTERDAMMERÜNG at 6 p.m.
SECOND CYCLE
JUNE 8 DAS RHEINGOLD at 7 p.m.
JUNE 10 DIE WALKÜRE at 6 p.m.
JUNE 14 SIEGFRIED at 6 p.m.
JUNE 17 GÖTTERDAMMERÜNG at 6 p.m.
THE COVENT GARDEN ORCHESTRA
(Leader: CHARLES TAYLOR)
BOX OFFICE 10-7.30
Telephone: COVent Garden 1066
Claridge, Lewis & Jordan Ltd., 68/70 Wardour Street, London, W.1

Poster for the 1955 *Ring* cycles at The Royal Opera House. Conducted by Rudolf Kempe, the cast included Hans Hotter (Wotan), Margaret Harshaw (Brünnhilde), Otakar Kraus (Alberich), Peter Klein (Mime), Maria von Ilosvay (Fricka), Erich Witte (Loge), Ramón Vinay (Siegmund), Leonie Rysanek (Sieglinde), Frederick Dalberg (Hunding) and Set Svanholm (Siegfried).

CHAPTER THREE

BREAKING WITH TRADITIONS

1948–1971

In 1948, the first Season of the new National Opera Company put Wagner back on the Covent Garden stage with three revivals: *Mastersingers* (in English), *Tristan und Isolde* (in German) and, as the sole representative of the *Ring, The Valkyrie* (in English). Friedrich Schramm, a director from Basle, came over to stage a production that kept to what Harold Rosenthal – writing at only a decade's distance – would recall as 'the usual static Wagnerian manner'; the scenery was pre-war with some new additions by Reece Pemberton. There were six performances scheduled, beginning on 3 March, all of them conducted by Karl Rankl, who had been appointed Musical Director of the new Company in 1946. He had the benefit of strong casting on stage, with Hans Hotter and Kirsten Flagstad as Wotan and Brünnhilde, and Doris Doree and Arthur Carron as Sieglinde and Siegmund. These portrayals prompted Scott Goddard to write in his review for the *News Chronicle*: 'One had the impression in a degree that seldom obtains in this opera, of two God-like characters and two mortals contrasted with true dramatic force.' Edith Coates was also well-received as Fricka, stressing the part of the justifiably angry woman, rather than the imperious goddess.

The performance was in English, and the significance of this was not lost on the audience; *The Times* described Flagstad's uneasy foray into English-language performance as 'a valuable service... to the company and the cause of English national opera'. Hotter was also uncomfortable with the language, although the rest of the predominantly home-grown cast were not similarly troubled. The performance attracted some attention in the press for two other reasons, one on- and one off-stage. Present in the audience were The Queen and her youngest daughter, Princess Margaret; the former in a white dress with a sable cloak, the latter in a pink dress with an ermine coat. They drank coffee from vacuum flasks in the first interval, then retired to an ante-room during the longer second interval for a supper brought from Buckingham Palace. What they thought of the on-stage incident was not reported, for near the close of the opera Hotter lost his footing on some scenic 'rocks' and fell nearly two metres onto the back of the stage; fortunately, he recovered rapidly and completed the act. This was not, however, what the *Daily Telegraph* had in mind when describing 'a performance that will be remembered for years', but rather it was Hotter as 'superbly authoritative and powerful, a full-scale lord of Valhalla'.

In November 1948 – but the following opera Season – both *Die Walküre* and *Siegfried* were given in their original language and with pre-war designs; by 1949 a complete cycle was mounted in May–June. Some writers at the time tried to build up the event by describing it as the first European full cycle of *The Ring* since the end of the war, and thus a source of national pride. Harold Rosenthal corrected this view in a letter to *The Times* that cited performances in Stockholm, Bordeaux, Lyon, Marseilles, Toulouse and Lisbon. But in the mood of the time – theatrically uncertain of national confidence in the West End, whether straight play, musical or opera – such bolstering publicity is understandable, and in the case of opera was to find its reward in rising performance standards and status through the 1950s. Hotter was unfortunate again, his annual hay fever setting in a little earlier than anticipated, so necessitating Kenneth Schon as a last-minute transatlantic replacement before Paul Schoeffler could take over Gunther as scheduled for the last performance of the cycle. Overall, the performances met with a mixed reception, the orchestra promising but lacking finesse; the staging included some minor alterations, with at least one critic convinced that the serpent into which Alberich transformed himself in *Das Rheingold* was a familiar friend from *Die Zauberflöte*. But the event itself was what really mattered: the *Ring* was back at Covent Garden. Not only did this allow older audience members to revisit a favourite work for the first time in a decade, but it gave younger operagoers their first chance to experience the tetralogy on stage. Further complete cycles that followed in June 1950 and May 1951 consolidated this return to the main repertory.

However, the pattern of the previous decades of Wagner staging now took a turn that proved to be literally vital for the *Ring,* not just at Covent Garden but world-wide. Winifred Wagner, the English-born widow of Wagner's son Siegfried, had kept the annual Bayreuth Festival running through the war, with the support of Hitler (until 1940 a regular visitor), as late as 1944. It was only in 1951 that the Festival was allowed to restart, but under the charge of Winifred's sons (and Wagner's grandsons) Wieland and Wolfgang. With the first production of the reinstated Festival, *Parsifal*, and then with his first Bayreuth *Ring*, Wieland instigated a new style of Wagner staging. In part, this arose from the need to provide some distance from the recent political associations of Winifred and hence the festival with Hitler, but it was also an opportunity to respond to more general reappraisals of theatre presentation and function whose origins are principally associated with Adolphe Appia and Edward Gordon Craig. Gone were the big sets, the painted naturalism, the stage props, the ornate and often heavy costumes; instead, it was the stage pared down to its basics, animated with lighting and projections, and the inhabitants of this new symbolist world accordingly dressed in more simple, less literal costumes. This became known as the 'new Bayreuth style' and provided that crucial break with what had established itself as Wagner tradition, and so made possible the multiplicity of ways of staging Wagner that we experience now.

What happened at Bayreuth in 1951 was bound to be influential precisely because it took place at the Wagnerian spiritual home (control of the Festival had continued in a direct line of descent from the composer to his widow, Cosima, to his son Siegfried and, in turn, to Siegfried's widow, Winifred). As a consequence, the old look and old style of *Die Walküre* and *Siegfried* by the Covent Garden Opera Company at the Royal Opera House in October 1953 appeared badly dated to the critics and Wagner aficionados who had experienced the Bayreuth revolution. In fact, action had already been taken at the Royal Opera House in arranging a new cycle for May–June 1954, although it was in the event to seem in part an evolution from the previous production rather than a building-up entirely on new foundations. The tetralogy was to be under the direction of Rudolf Hartmann, a German director principally based in Munich and particularly associated with Strauss opera (he had recently directed *Elektra* for Covent Garden, in 1953). His *Meistersinger* for Bayreuth in 1951 had shown him to be at odds with Wieland Wagner's approach, with the result that he directed nothing else there, but something of the Bayreuth lesson was taken for his new London *Ring*. The production cleared the stage space and adopted more suggestion in action and image than explicit statement; Hartmann's 'straightforward and dignified' approach meant that the dramatic turning points of character and the sustained confrontations worked well, if such grander moments as the entry to Valhalla consequently lost out.

For the new designs, by Leslie Hurry, there was a similar pared-down naturalism and a simplification of effect rather than a completely new angle. Hurry had visited Germany to see the changes in technique underway there, and combined traditional and more symbolic approaches. There were built sets, although not of the pre-war scale and detail, and now the stage was raked. The naturalism of skies, water, fire and so on was to be achieved both through images (static and moving) projected onto the rear cyclorama and a mostly fixed front gauze and through the extensive use of lighting to create mood, albeit in the event often set too dim. One significant advantage of this method was that the main curtains did not need to be lowered and raised for most of the scene changes, a marked improvement on previous practice for the dramatic continuity of *Das Rheingold* in particular. Front gauzes are often criticized for creating a feeling of emotional distance between performers and audience, but here, for *The Stage* at least, the gauze 'does much to drop a poetic mist between our down-to-earth seats and singers, posturing among stage rocks, who might sink to prosaic levels without such protection'. It was noticeable to several commentators that the scenes in the most open settings of the drama (Brünnhilde's rock and the banks of the Rhine, for example) worked better than the more enclosed ones (Hunding's hut was 'shrouded in gloom murkier than a London smog'). *Siegfried*, with the front gauze lifted for the most part, allowed for some welcome, brighter colours and lighting; and if the bear had been a casualty of the simplifications of staging, at least there was 'a dragon to delight the child in every Wagnerite, a huge and fantastical beast, like an overgrown cactus, that emerges modestly exhaling a smoke ring or two, only later to show the force of his exhaust' (*The Times*); the stage hands nicknamed the beast 'Big 'Arry'.

In its first outing, the Hartmann-Hurry interpretation was assessed as promising more than it managed to realize, and the staging was improved under revival director Peter Potter through incremental changes from Season to Season until the final cycles in 1960. These performances were more significant, however, for their outstanding roster of singers, mostly under the baton of Rudolf Kempe (although Fritz Stiedry had introduced the production), than for the production itself: The years 1954–60 saw casts that included Hotter as Wotan, Ramón Vinay as Siegmund, Set Svanholm as Siegfried, Wolfgang Windgassen as both Siegmund and Siegfried, Otakar Kraus as Alberich, Erich Witte as Loge and Peter Klein as Mime. As Brünnhilde, Margaret Harshaw dominated through 22 appearances (seven cycles and an extra *Walküre*), with Birgit Nilsson next at ten (two cycles and two *Götterdämmerungs* in 1957 and a *Siegfried* and *Götterdämmerung* in 1960), Astrid Varnay next at nine appearances (two cycles in 1958, one in 1959), Martha Mödl three (the second 1959 cycle) and finally Sylvia Fisher a single *Walküre* on 19 September 1958 (she had previously played the role on tour with the Company to Liverpool and Birmingham in 1956). At the time, this Royal Opera House *Ring* was felt to be a significant achievement, such that Harold Rosenthal could describe it in 1958 as 'what has generally been considered the finest *Ring* in the world'. Yet it appears now to have been a transitional interpretation that mixed – uneasily at times – familiar Wagner staging with the newer approach that seemed copied and added rather than integrated. And so a replacement cycle was begun at the start of the 1961/2 Season, again with *Die Walküre,* with the expectation of further breaks with Wagnerian convention.

When *Die Walküre* opened on 29 September 1961 it did indeed show major changes from the previous year's performances; in every important way it was new. First, the production was by Hans Hotter, bringing an intimate and experienced performer's eye on the *Ring* to the directorial role and also playing Wotan, 'a feat which brought a welcome solution to the problem of production', as the Annual Report of the Royal Opera House for 1961–2 put it. What seems particularly to have been appreciated was that Hotter did not over-direct the performers, but allowed them to command the stage undistracted for significant periods. He described his approach thus: 'We have to ban the over-traditional or we cannot keep this baby alive. The style of acting of Wagner has changed just as the style in the speaking theatre has changed. One underplays rather than overplays – and, the more you leave out, the more personality you have to put in.' The *Times* correspondent thought Hotter's direction 'tactful, lucid and very effective', adding that

> it makes the drama and the characters live, and is particularly successful in the calculations of stage movement during Wagner's symphonic meditations. An example is the long and poignant orchestral passage after the harum-scarum departure of the Valkyries from their rock. Wagner says that the positions of Wotan and Brünnhilde should not change; Mr Hotter allows himself as Wotan just enough movement to convey that he is discovering the cause of Brünnhilde's disobedience in his own, restrained wishes – and that his conscience is further troubled.

The same review then leads into the second of the big changes for 1961:

> It is a measure of the production's success that the contributions of Mr Hotter and his scenic designer Mr Herbert Kern, can hardly be considered independently. The extremely striking set for the second act maintains its excitement through the producer's use of it; and likewise, when Mr Kern omits to provide a door for Hunding's hut, Mr Hotter backs him to the hilt, building up tension to the sudden appearance of moonlight through the distant treetrunks. If it is not quite what the drama demands, it is both practical and beautiful.

With his new design, Kern had kept an eye on the Bayreuth shift of a decade before; but despite what *The Times* suggests, the reception that his sparse, bold sets received was not generally so positive. This was made clear – more marked through its brevity – in the Annual Report quoted above, which simply stated that 'There was some criticism of the décor of the new *Walküre*', then footnoted that 'the entire new *Ring* is now to be designed by Mr Schneider-Siemssen, whose décor for Schönberg's *Erwartung*... won high praise'.

Third, where Kempe had been the dominant conductor since 1955, now it was the turn of Georg Solti, who had only recently taken up the position of Music Director with the Company. He was very widely praised for the standard of playing he drew from the orchestra and the well-shaped emotional drive of the score; Donald Mitchell's comments for the *Daily Telegraph* were typical: 'From the very start of the opera with the thrilling storm prelude which opens Act I, it was obvious that Mr Solti can convey the intense degree of physical excitement which is so much part of Wagner's genius.'

And so to the fourth area of change: the singers. There were three prominent newcomers: Michael Langdon a 'successfully sinister' Hunding, Claire Watson a 'warm, impulsive' Sieglinde and Anita Välkki a 'credible, indeed endearing' Brünnhilde. Langdon was (almost) the sole Hunding through to 1968; Watson sang Sieglinde for three Seasons, Välkki for two (if not consecutive ones, and in 1964 it was to replace Amy Shuard who had to withdraw through illness). But despite the glowing reception Jon Vickers had received for his debut as Siegmund at Covent Garden in 1958, his return this time to the part with The Royal Opera was also to be his last.

The Hotter-Kern production did not last beyond three revival performances in December 1962 of *Die Walküre,* and even before these, on 7 September, a new production of *Siegfried* had marked the start of a new cycle, still with Hotter as director, but now with Schneider-Siemssen's designs. The central feature of this new look was a giant ring, 14 metres in diameter with the performing platform of its circumference 2 metres wide. This metal-framed structure was assembled in sections and supported on hydraulic jacks 5.5 metres below the stage which enabled it to be tilted in any direction; it was almost large enough to fill the width of the stage and strong enough to support an assembled chorus of 80 in *Götterdämmerung*. The centre space of the ring platform could either be left empty – to become the watery home of the Rhinemaidens, for example – or it could be used for trees, pillars, rocky outcrops and so on, with the platform circumscribing the world round them. On the opening night of *Siegfried* the audience's first view of the construction was of a ring tilted backwards, its upper lip forming the cave entrance; tree trunks filled in the background in a return to solid scenery after back projections. For the second act, the ring platform tilted forwards, its centre opening as Fafner's cave, with smoke and the dragon rising up from within. In Act III, a bare ring with a sloping central rock provided for Brünnhilde's mountain top. The changing positions of the platform were done manually, which required the use of curtains between acts or scenes to conceal the changeovers. Desmond Shawe-Taylor (in the *Sunday Times*) did not think this added to the atmosphere in *Siegfried* Act III: 'Instead of Wagner's billowing transformation scene we soon found ourselves staring morosely at the royal monograms on the house curtains. And when the curtains parted again to reveal a re-tilted ring under a grey-black sky, there was no hint of the radiant morning light demanded by the composer and unmistakably painted in his music.' He was also reminded of 'an ill-wiped windscreen' by the constant presence of a streaked gauze at the front of the stage, and as irritated by it as were several others.

But Schneider-Siemssen's designs were on the whole considered to be very effective, as at the start of *Siegfried* Act III, when the metal ring was tilted at 45 degrees 'so that the colloquy between the Wanderer and Erda appeared to be taking place on the outer rim of Earth', and Erda was able to rise up from within the ring 'instead of, as in recent years, stepping out from behind a rock', as one observer dryly compared. There were restrictions with a doughnut-shaped performing area, but Hotter often used the space to bring out the dynamics between the characters. For example, in *Die Walküre* Act II, the Valkyries were ranged round one side of the curved platform, Brünnhilde stood opposite, and between them at the front Sieglinde lay on the ground; later, Wotan appeared high at the back, standing on a rock and outlined by a blazing sun behind him, commanding his world. The huge ring structure could also be raised right up above the heads of the cast. In *Die Walküre* Act I, it acted as the roof of Hunding's hut, with the World Ash Tree rising through the centre and splitting high above into hard, spreading branches; for the Gibichung Hall in *Götterdämmerung*, it encircled the pillars of the building (for the final destruction, scenically impressive, the metal ring slipped and the towers tumbled). But this also brought with it problems for the sightlines of anyone in the Balcony upwards, resulting in some disembodiment of those onstage – legs but no body or vice versa depending on the angle of view. (The upper part of the auditorium was altered in the summer of 1964, so that when the third and fourth instalments of the new production were shown in a complete cycle that September, the formerly separate gallery and amphitheatre had become one large amphitheatre with 600 tip-up seats instead of the previous benches. In fact, first to use the newly arranged space, at a dress rehearsal for *Die Walküre,* were

The Friends of Covent Garden, whose five-hour queue caused traffic chaos in the area.)

The period 1964–70 was a musically notable one for the *Ring* at the Royal Opera House. Under Solti's direction there was consistently fine singing and playing, and the reviews for him and the results he brought forth were regularly packed with superlatives. In 1964, when he first conducted right through the cycle, there was a consensus of praise for him for individual nights and the whole event. To take just two of many examples:

> There was all the precision-turned instrumental detail and the keen, taut vigour that one expects when Solti is conducting – the opening storm, for instance, lashed and howled with extraordinary pictorial vividness – but the details were all blended and the rhythm was never pulled too taut. Solti, in fact, conducted with an expressive warmth and a sense of broad epic paragraph such as he has rarely, if ever, achieved before in this theatre.
> (Edmund Tracey on *Die Walküre* for *The Observer*)

> Chief splendour is the orchestra: during his three years as musical director, Georg Solti has achieved both a fine balance for the acoustic of the theatre, plus a tremendous increase in the standard of playing among the various sections. Opera goers are not the only ones to benefit from this, of course; it means that the taxing ballets of Stravinsky and Ravel are that much more rewarding. Mr Solti's interpretation of the Ring is intense and powerful, but never just that; it is carefully related to the events of the drama, so though the passages relating to natural phenomena – storm, water, fire – are hair-raising, those that accompany human activity have greater impact. This is made explicit in the magnificent third act of *Die Walküre* where a natural storm becomes a storm of human emotion; the cracking of a human heart is more devastating that the cracking of a thundercloud, a fact known to Wagner and projected by Mr Solti.
> (J. Roger Baker for *The Tatler*)

The Times put this into an interpretational context:

> This is not (as Mr Solti's heterogeneous, romantically drawn out cadences contradictorily confirmed) a stately, euphoniously generalized view of the old school, as we know it from descriptions and recordings and from live performances by such relics of the romantic tradition as Furtwängler and Konwitschny (Beecham's lightweight majesty was revealing but typically eccentric – Wagner for the unconvinced Wagnerite); nor is it the lucid, almost classical edifice that Mr Kempe has erected in past seasons at Covent Garden and Bayreuth, or the neo-romantic treatment of Mr Karajan. Mr Solti seeks a synthesis of the modern interpretations contrasted in those of the two last-named conductors, with a highly but not extravagantly spiced flavour of his own.
> (on *Götterdämmerung*)

One characteristic of Solti's orchestra was that it could be given its head to resounding effect, but there was some reaction to this: after singing the *Götterdämmerung* Brünnhilde at Covent Garden in 1963, Birgit Nilsson did not sing in the 1964 cycles, making no comment as to why. Thomas Stewart, her fellow performer at Bayreuth and also a Covent Garden Gunther in 1963–4, was, however, direct: 'Let's face it. Solti's orchestra is too damn loud. The singers on the stage hardly stand a chance. Solti is a very exciting conductor, but he has got to decide if he just wants a visual effect plus orchestra or allow the singers to be really heard.'

Hans Hotter is an important figure in any review of Covent Garden *Rings*. There was his towering interpretation of Wotan over nearly twenty years – his first complete cycle at the Royal Opera House was in 1948, his last in 1965 (illness prevented him completing all but the first opera in 1967). However, the new productions of the *Ring* in the 1960s were unveiled with Hotter as director and David Ward as Wotan, and it was Ward who was to be the dominant Wotan through to the early 1970s. The national card was played for his first appearance, in the 1962 *Siegfried,* with the *Evening News* proclaiming the headline 'British Wotan Triumphs', and continuing that: 'Mr Ward, the first British artist to sing the great role of Wotan since before the war, sang throughout with the utmost assurance, pouring forth a stream of rich bass tone that was wonderfully free from "wobble" even under pressure. It was an immensely important stage in the career of this distinguished artist, and he rose to it in style, taking full advantage of the guidance of producer Hans Hotter, himself the leading Wotan of to-day.'

In a continuation of what has been an undercurrent of national appropriation for Wagnerian performance, other singers of British origin and training were acclaimed in the 1960s' Covent Garden *Rings*. Amy Shuard made her debut as Brünnhilde at Covent Garden on 7 December 1962, the evening upon which Kirsten Flagstad died, as several critics noted (here Noël Goodwin for *Music and Musicians*): 'The great Norwegian Valkyrie would, I think, have been proud of the latest recruit to leadership of the immortal corps. Shuard has the role well within her grasp. If her performance showed the possibilities for future development, it is not to deny her very real achievement already. She revealed a keen sense of vocal character, radiant in her delight at Wotan's affection for his favourite daughter, troubled by his predicament, and noble in her submission to his punishment.' The Annual Report of the Royal Opera House for 1962–3 took particular pleasure in commenting on this debut: 'Especially gratifying for the Opera House in the German section was the success of Amy Shuard in her first *Walküre* Brünnhilde, which the Musical Director had encouraged and helped her to undertake. Miss Shuard's vocal accomplishment was sure and the interpretation sympathetic, so that her progress now to the even more taxing role in *Götterdämmerung* and as Isolde seems only a matter of time. A British soprano of star quality for these is an exciting prospect, and evidence again, if evidence is needed, that the resident company has become a starting place for world fame.' She went on to alternate as Brünnhilde in the whole cycle with Ludmila Dvoraková from 1964 through to 1971.

Shuard had previously appeared as Gutrune in 1959–60, and in 1965 (to continue the roster of British performers) Heather Harper made her first Covent Garden appearance in the role – the same performances that saw Gwyneth Jones and Rita Hunter sharing Third Norn! Harper returned in the role in 1967–9 (she made her impressive Bayreuth debut as Elsa in 1967), but found herself with an unexpected conjunction of performances on 5 October 1967. She had been booked for *Götterdämmerung* on 7 October, but Hotter, who was scheduled to sing in *Siegfried* on 5 October was unable to perform; his replacement, Herbert Fliether, could not manage that evening, so the last two operas of the cycle were switched: *Götterdämmerung* in place of *Siegfried* and *Siegfried* in place of *Götterdämmerung*. Unfortunately, Harper had already rehearsed to sing the Brahms *Requiem* under Jascha Horenstein at the Festival Hall on 5 October. Somewhat cheekily, she made the suggestion that – provided someone else sang Act II – she could perform Act I at Covent Garden, cross the river to sing the *Requiem* and still return in time for Act III. To her surprise, this offer was taken up, and so Sylvia Fisher sang Act II while Harper changed costumes and venues, in the process performing on the same night the work of two composers sometimes presented as antithetical.

The list of those British born or trained continues through to 1970, and includes: Josephine Veasey as a much admired Fricka, Michael Langdon as the resident Hunding, and John Dobson first as Froh, then Loge. Gwyneth Jones made a particularly favourable debut as Sieglinde in 1966 (she returned in the same role in 1968): 'her singing is the genuine article' (*The Times*), her voice 'combined radiance and strength' (*The Standard*) and it was 'a debut not just of promise but of present achievement' (*Daily Express*). There are many other British performers in these cast listings, especially through the Rhinedaughters (with a strong Welsh contingent in their casting – including Jones who is from Monmouthshire), Valkyries and Norns. This is a significant reflection of the way the resident Company had built up its own identity and individuality from its post-war beginnings. But beyond this, through its home on the historic Covent Garden site, the Company's reputation was inevitably perceived more generally as a major indicator of the fortunes of British opera. In addition, the *Ring* – as a pivotal repertory work – was bound to be considered a principal indicator of such national and international operatic health. The Company's standing was felt to be in its ascendancy, its *Ring* cycles one of the major manifestations of such talent. Indeed, this confidence was sufficiently evident in 1963 to provoke Wilfrid Mellers to declare: 'Let British trumpets sound as far as Bayreuth.'

ROYAL OPERA HOUSE

COVENT GARDEN

OPERA SEASON

1949

The programme for *Das Rheingold* on 12 May 1949, the opening of the first cycle to be presented at Covent Garden since 1939.

Thursday, 12th May, 1949

DAS RHEINGOLD

Opera in one act and four scenes

(being the first part of "Der Ring des Nibelungen")

Words and music by Richard Wagner

Conductor - KARL RANKL

Producer - FRIEDRICH SCHRAMM

THE COVENT GARDEN ORCHESTRA

Leader - JOSEPH SHADWICK

RICHARD WAGNER, 1813–1883

This opera was first produced at the Court Opera, Munich, on 22nd September, 1869. It was first produced in England on 5th May, 1882, at Her Majesty's Theatre in German. It was first performed in English on 27th January, 1908, at Covent Garden.

CHARACTERS IN ORDER OF APPEARANCE

Woglinde	MURIEL RAE
Wellgunde	ROSINA RAISBECK
Flosshilde	JEAN WATSON
Alberich	GRAHAME CLIFFORD
Fricka	EDITH COATES
Wotan	HANS HOTTER
Freia	BLANCHE TURNER
Fasolt	MARIAN NOWAKOWSKI
Fafner	DAVID FRANKLIN
Froh	EDGAR EVANS
Donner	RHYDDERCH DAVIES
Loge	SET SVANHOLM
Mime	PETER KLEIN
Erda	EDITH FURMEDGE

Hans Hotter was not only the Covent Garden Wotan for the majority of performances from the late 1940s through to 1966, but was also through most of this period the leading interpreter of the role at Bayreuth and world-wide.

> As for Hotter, he dominated the drama. The voice, though liable to spread under extreme pressure, is still a mighty instrument, and the singer's subtlety of vocal inflexion can never have been more marvellously displayed than in the opening bars of Wotan's monologue. But it is as an actor of godlike power and suffering that Hotter is carved most grandly on the memory. For one thinks, no one else can handle a seven-foot spear with such casual magnificence, so that it becomes an adjunct and symbol of authority, not the source of slightly ludicrous embarrassment that it is to most Wagnerian singers who trail the puissant pike. (Adam Bell in 1957 for *The Observer*)

Not only a favourite performer at Covent Garden, he also directed most effectively the new *Ring* productions 1961–4: his 1961 staging of *Die Walküre* was, for Andrew Porter, 'self-effacing, conventional in the best way, quite simply *right* at almost every point'; his *Götterdämmerung* in 1963 was 'splendidly clear, direct and unmannered' to Desmond Shawe-Taylor and conveyed 'a sense of the drama's monumental descent' to John Warrack.

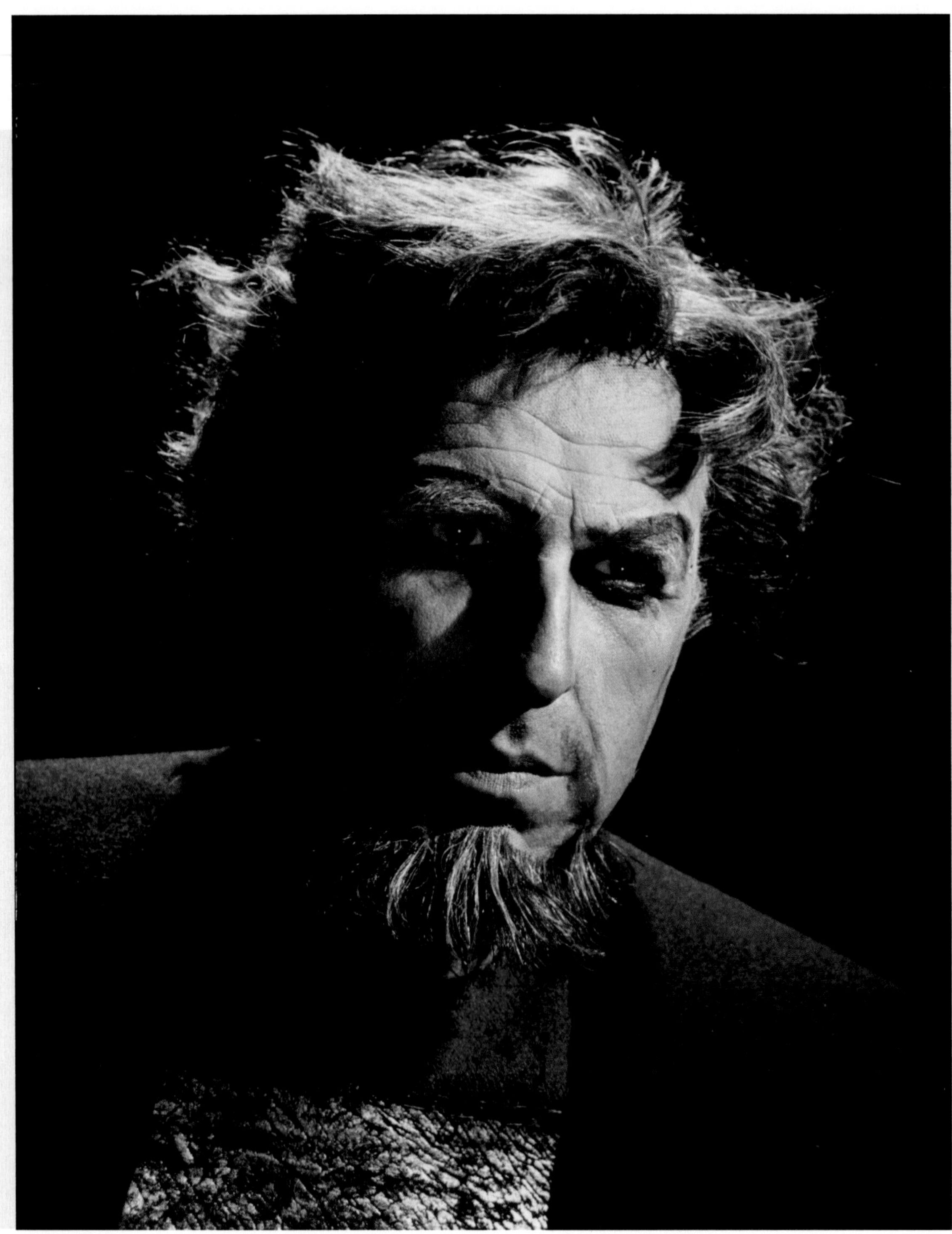

Kirsten Flagstad and the dress she wore post-war as Brünnhilde in *Götterdämmerung* at the Royal Opera House, with two performances each year 1949–51 (she had first appeared in the role pre-war in 1936).

Autographed photograph of Margaret Harshaw as Brünnhilde. She sang the role at The Royal Opera House in the October 1953 performances of the old productions of *Die Walküre* and *Siegfried* with pre-war sets and in the first three Seasons (1954–6) of the new production of the cycle by Rudolf Hartmann.

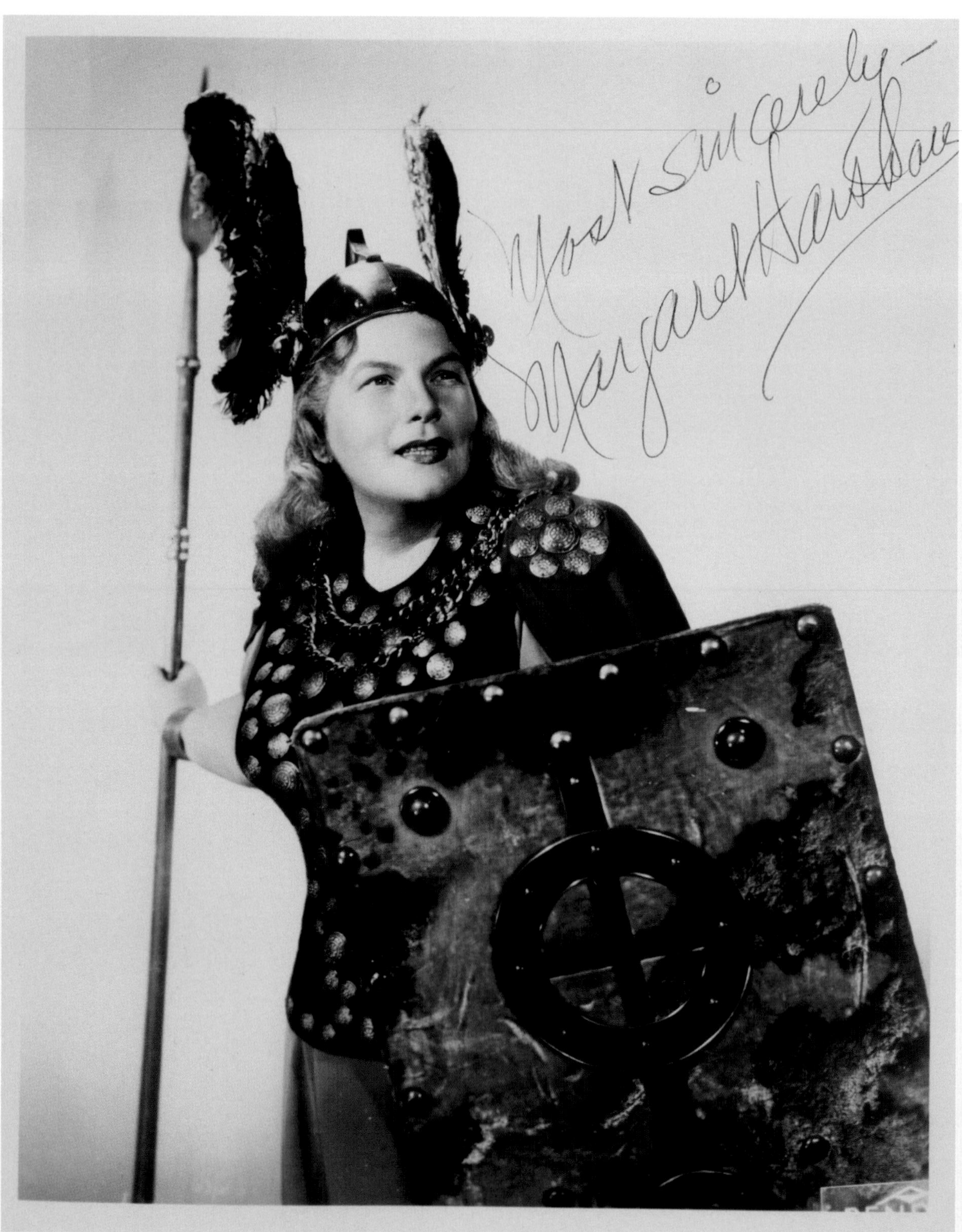

Constance Shacklock as Erda in 1954. She was an important core member of the emerging Covent Garden opera companies after the war, and between 1948 and 1954 regularly sang Grimgerde, First Norn and the *Götterdämmerung* Flosshilde; she appeared as Fricka in 1950 in alternation with Edith Coates. Shacklock also sang Erda for the first productions of the new Hartmann staging (and was also Grimgerde and Second Norn), but the role was not best suited to her voice, and in subsequent revivals of the production the part was taken in turn by Jean Madeira (1955/6), Maria von Ilosvay (1957), Rut Siewert (1958) and Marga Höffgen (1959/60). Shacklock continued to appear in the cycle as Grimgerde (to 1956) and Second Norn (to 1960), accumulating an impressive number of appearances over all six roles.

Otakar Kraus played Alberich for the first time at Covent Garden in 1951, and then appeared in the role throughout all of the Hartmann production and the first runs of the new Hotter production. His final appearances as Alberich were in 1968.

Projection designs by Leslie Hurry for the new production of the *Ring* in 1954. Hurry based his concept on the use of 150 hand-painted slides, blown up to 70 times their original size by projectors on stage and in a specially built box in the balcony stalls (which necessitated the removal of some twenty seats). He took a year of trial and error to perfect his technique and for the sheer quantity of detailed work said 'I never expect to have such a difficult job again'. There were projectors for both static and animated film, which were seen on a gauze that filled the proscenium arch, between stage and auditorium, and on the vast rear cyclorama, 21 metres high and 42 metres long. The projections could produce the effects of mist, storms, clouds, flowing or rippling water and fire – from Mime's glowing forge to a scorching rock for Brünnhilde (several critics wondered if she could possibly arise unscathed from it in *Siegfried*). The rainbow effect was achieved with light directed onto the stage through a prism.

Set Svanholm was the first post-war Siegfried. He appeared first in the opera of the same name in 1948, then played the role in all but one performance through to 1955; he performed all the *Götterdämmerung* Siegfrieds from 1949 to 1955. With his Siegfried for the opening of the new production in 1954, *The Times* summed him up as 'a graduate in forgework to music, an athletic figure whose characterization, vocal and histrionic, well conveys the naïve, hearty, natural bully in Siegfried, a virile voice that softens, in his forest meditations, to most sympathetic effect – all these inform his most advantageous assumption'. Wolfgang Windgassen next took over as the House Siegfried through to the mid-1960s. But Svanholm also made one further, if unexpected, appearance in a Covent Garden *Ring*. In 1957 Ramón Vinay was scheduled to make his London debut as the *Götterdämmerung* Siegfried in the performances of 14 and 17 October (Windgassen played the *Siegfried* title role); but throat problems were evident with his Siegmund on 27 September: 'Ramón Vinay is a virile Siegmund in those parts of the role which lie in the baritone *tessitura*; above the stave it is a case of what a critic called *can belto*; but alas, for much of the time he cannot.' (*The Observer*). Walter Geisler was lined up to fly in and take over Siegmund on 8 October, but his plane was delayed; Vinay began the performance, and Geisler was rushed from the airport just in time to take the stage for Act II. Replacements were found for *Götterdämmerung,* with Svanholm (by then Director of Stockholm Opera) flown in for 14 October and Bernd Aldenhoff for 17 October. This gave the chance for witty comparison on the part of Philip Hope-Wallace in the *Manchester Guardian:*

> Owing to Mr Vinay's disposition, we have heard three different Siegfrieds in less than a week. Mr Windgassen is the most mellifluous singer; Mr Svanholm the most energetic, and Mr Aldenhoff the most good-natured looking of the heroes, the latter quite a decent Helden tenor type. Wagnerian acting is not the crude arm-wagging it is sometimes taken for. Each of these Siegfrieds has a different manner of dying. For instance, Mr Windgassen collapses slowly like a chloroformed dog and one is never quite sure if he is dead yet. Mr Svanholm, however, goes over on his back with such a bang that one is rather alarmed lest he might indeed be so. Mr Aldenhoff takes it with resignation.

Poster for the two cycles in September–October 1958. A cast of distinction included Hans Hotter as Gunther while still holding on to Wotan's spear for the first three operas (he had done this once before at the Royal Opera, in 1949). Especially noted at the time was Jon Vickers's Covent Garden debut as Siegmund (he had just sung the role at Bayreuth). In the *Daily Telegraph,* Clive Barnes considered Vickers had 'in one bound… arrived in the ranks of international heroic tenors. He looked right and sounded right. His lustrous ringing top notes were as impressive as the warmth of his soft singing. All in all, it was among the best Wagnerian tenor singing heard at Covent Garden since the war'. The poster does not give the full casting story, however, for Windgassen was sufficiently unwell as to have Karl Liebl flown in from Wiesbaden to be on standby in the wings for the *Siegfried* of the second cycle (9 October); Windgassen completed Act I, but left Liebl to finish the performance.

Rudolf Kempe, shown here both in a portrait and in rehearsal for *Tannhäuser* at the Royal Opera House in November 1955, conducted the *Ring* cycle with what had become his characteristic awareness of the grand sweep that drives through the cycle, and the whole musical effect provoked Neville Cardus to claim it 'the best *Ring* to be heard anywhere at the present time'.

Set designs by Herbert Kern for *Die Walküre,* first presented on 29 September 1961: above, Act I; centre, Act II; below, Act III. The reception that Kern's designs received was mixed, but tended mostly towards disappointment. Philip Hope-Wallace found them 'utterly conventional' and 'very much what we had before and quite unimaginative visually'. David Cairns's summary for *The Spectator* was that they were '[Leslie] Hurry without the emotion' – in other words, no great advance on what was there before. Yet Paul Bowen (*News Daily*) wrote 'a word of praise' to Herbert Kern, whose sets 'were truly magnificent… imposing, combining starkness of the modern conception of Wagner presentation with the essentials of realism. Thus, Hunding's hut had walls and was built around the tree, yet the doors were not flung open to allow the lovers to escape, but there was instead a sudden lighting up of the pale blue curtain at the back of the stage'. Kern was not used for the designs of the other *Ring* operas, but replaced by the Austrian theatre designer Günther Schneider-Siemssen.

Costume designs (two with fabric swatches) by Herbert Kern for Alberich, Mime and Erda. Of Kern's approach in *Die Walküre,* Paul Bowen (*News Daily*) wrote: 'In costumes there was the identification of colour with class of character. Thus, Wotan and Fricka, the Gods were in strong blue and red, respectively, the Valkyries were in darker blue, Siegmund and Sieglinde, the two half-god mortals, in yellow, and Hunding, the one true mortal, in sombre brown.' The designs shown here remained unrealized after Kern was replaced for the rest of the new cycle.

Günther Schneider-Siemssen's design for the back gauze of scene 4 of *Das Rheingold.* In 1962 he had completed his first design for Covent Garden, with Peter Ustinov's production of *Erwartung;* well received, it was this that led on to his first *Ring* design for Covent Garden – replacing Herbert Kern – with *Siegfried,* in September 1962, then *Götterdämmerung* in September 1963 and finally *Das Rheingold* and *Die Walküre* in September 1964. The photograph showing the backdrop on stage was taken at a rehearsal for *Das Rheingold* in 1970, and has Donald McIntyre as Wotan and Helen Watts as Erda.

Costume designs by Günther Schneider-Siemssen for Hans Hotter's 1964 production: Wotan, Brünnhilde and Siegfried.

Amy Shuard as Brünnhilde. She performed her first Brünnhilde in *Die Walküre* on 7 December 1962, and continued in the role at the Royal Opera House through to 1971. She appeared as Brünnhilde in the other two operas at Covent Garden for the first time in 1964 on 12 September (*Siegfried*) and 19 September (*Götterdämmerung*). She is also seen here as Brünnhilde at the dress rehearsal of *Siegfried* in 1965 (with Wolfgang Windgassen) and with Georg Solti.

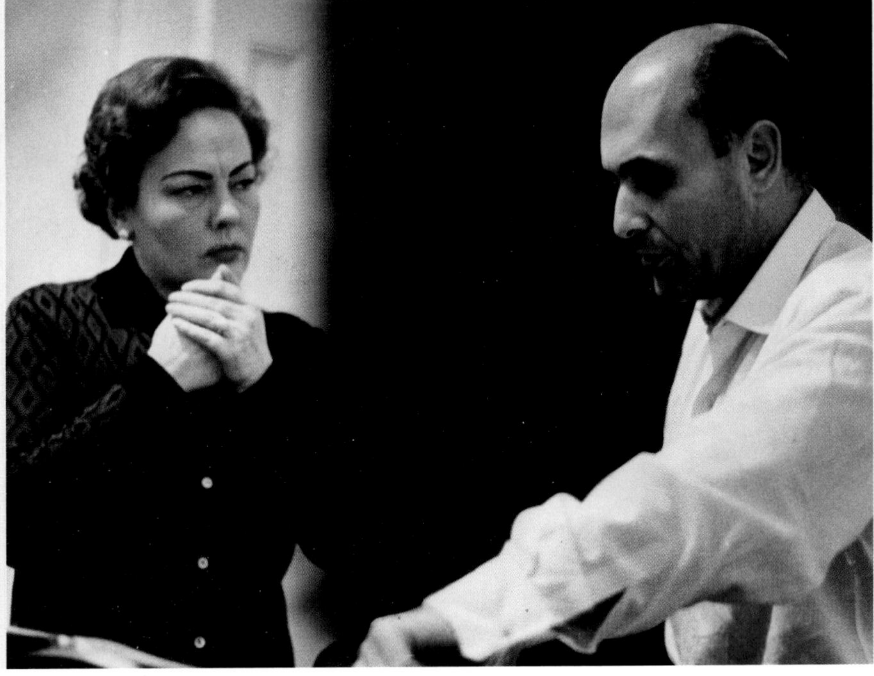

David Ward as the Traveller *(Siegfried)* in September 1962, the first performances of the new production by Hans Hotter; the translated role title was used throughout the life of this production, rather than the original, and more usual, Wanderer. Wotans have been relatively long-lived at Covent Garden, a pattern set by those early performance records of Anton van Rooy and Clarence Whitehill, and, notably, Hotter himself. Ward appeared regularly in the role in Royal Opera *Rings* through the1960s and early 70s. He first sang Fasolt and Hunding (1960), then took on the Traveller (1962; 'in exceptionally fine voice' for his debut, according to *News Daily*). *The Times* thought his first Wotan in *Das Rheingold* (1964) was 'rough, short tempered, craggy… with rusty windswept hair and flashing eye', while his *Walküre* Wotan a few days later was played 'more robustly, with less spirituality and nobility, so that the picture of Mad Wotan is moved several notches towards realism, and the relationship between Warfather and his warrior daughter is interestingly altered'. With regular appearances in these roles for the next decade, he made his final Covent Garden appearances in the 1975 *Ring* as the *Rheingold* Wotan (8 October) and the Traveller (11 October).

Scenes from the Hans Hotter production with designs by Günther Schneider-Siemssen:

Das Rheingold (1970): Scene 1, Alberich (Zoltán Kélémen) and the Rhinemaidens (Elizabeth Bainbridge, Anne Howells and Elizabeth Robson). Scene 2, Loge (John Dobson, centre) advising Wotan (David Ward, right) on how to pay Fafner and Fasolt (Michael Langdon and Martti Talvela, centre back) for Valhalla; Fricka (Josephine Veasey, centre left) disapproves, while Freia, Donner and Froh (Eva June, John Shaw and Ermanno Mauro, left) look on.

Die Walküre (1970): Act II, the slain Siegmund (James King).

Die Walküre (1970): Act III, the Valkyrie rock.

Siegfried (1965): Act II, Siegfried (Wolfgang Windgassen).

Götterdämmerung (1970): Prologue, Brünnhilde (Ludmila Dvoraková) and Siegfried (Karl-Josef Hering).

ROYAL
OPERA
HOUSE
COVENT GARDEN
IN
ASSOCIATION WITH
COMMERCIAL
UNION
ASSURANCE
PRESENTS
RICHARD WAGNER'S
DER
RING DES
NIBELUNGEN
ON THE OCCASION OF THE CENTENARY OF THE FIRST
PERFORMANCE OF THE RING CYCLE AT BAYREUTH IN 1876

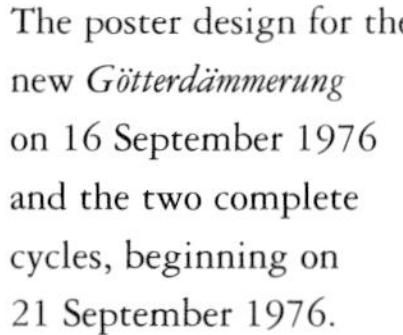

The poster design for the new *Götterdämmerung* on 16 September 1976 and the two complete cycles, beginning on 21 September 1976.

CHAPTER FOUR

A RING FOR THE 70s

1974–1982

It begins with a flickering red smudge erupting out of the blackness, like a malignant volcano, the feeble whirr of the projector that sends us this image, contrasting sharply with the sonority of the score.

The red splash enlarges menacingly, turns to blue, then green, and the whole stage slowly rises upward, propelled by a mighty piston, a black pillar, crowned with a rock of gold.

So – spellbindingly – begins Covent Garden's long-awaited new Ring. (David Gillard: *Daily Mail,* 1 October 1974)

The impetus for a new Royal Opera *Ring* in the mid-1970s came from two main directions. First, a significant historical anniversary, and second, the desire of the Royal Opera Music Director to tackle this central part of the repertory. The anniversary was the centenary of the very first cycle at Bayreuth, in August 1876. To mark this, a new *Ring* would be built up by The Royal Opera in instalments, to complete the first full cycle at the start of the 1976–7 Season: *DasRheingold,* 30 September 1974; *Die Walküre,* 1 October 1974; *Siegfried,* 17 September 1975; and *Götterdämmerung,* 16 September 1976. Two completed cycles were given in 1976: the first on 21, 25 and 29 September and 1 October; the second on 4, 5, 7 and 9 October.

John Tooley, then General Administrator of the Royal Opera House, suggested to Colin Davis that a possible director for the new production would be Götz Friedrich, a German director who was then principal director at the Hamburg Staatsoper. Davis met Friedrich in Berlin and discovered that they got on very well. A fortnight at Covent Garden spent going through the work 'word by word, note by note... some of the most marvellous days of my life', as Davis recalled, cemented the relationship, leading one commentator at the time to talk of 'something of an artistic love affair' between director and conductor.

Their chosen designer was Josef Svoboda, a Czech widely acknowledged as one of the greatest theatrical designers in Europe. His central idea provided for a new versatility and visual impact of the performing area, as the *Daily Mail* critic David Gillard described the opening sequence of *Das Rheingold* on 30 September 1974. The stage itself became mobile, with a square platform supported on a central hydraulic support that enabled it to twist, tilt, turn and lift, so presenting the heights of the gods above and the depths of the earth beneath. 'If this production has a symbol', Friedrich explained, 'it is this central piston which is the source of energy and movement.' The potential of this kinetic acting space was further demonstrated in *Das Rheingold* when the stage tilted up to reveal a mirrored surface underneath that reflected to the audience the Rhinemaidens, dancing and cavorting from below the stage floor level. (In the early runs of the opera the use of dancers as stage doubles combined with the mirrors to suggest nine Rhinedaughters; the staging was refined for the first complete cycles in 1976 to present the requisite three!) Next, the raised platform provided for the open rocky space of the assembled gods, before allowing Loge and Wotan to descend on ropes to ground level, while the mirrored underneath reflected the bright lights of Nibelung miners' helmets in the depths below. For the conclusion of the opera, the level platform transformed into a broad, steeply raked stairway for the gods to ascend to Valhalla.

A similar flexibility extended through the following operas: *Die Walküre* began with the rearing and turning platform as the setting for a chase of Siegmund while the stormy prelude played. Diagonally opposing planes on the raised platform made for a sparse and spectacular Act III setting for Wotan to confront the Valkyries and Brünnhilde. *Siegfried* saw it tilted at an angle towards the front of the stage presenting the forest above and Mime's cave below, yet the platform could rear up dramatically with Wotan at its height looking down to Erda entangled in the roots of the World Ash Tree beneath him. Fires in the pit under the stage allowed the audience to see the reflection of Siegfried walking through them before the revelation of Brünnhilde's rocky mountain top as a bare tilted platform with a single raised plane jutting above for the Valkyrie's sleep. What added to the drama, was that the stage moments were part of the dynamic imagery of the production, not simple scene changes; the use of the three-dimensional performing space – height, depth and distance all played a vital part – was an inversion of the expected, in which the stage floor was fixed, and the people and sets moved on and round it.

But hydraulics on their own do not make for a production. Here the lighting, by William Bundy, played a large part in evoking the mood. The moving platform did its stuff against a background cyclorama onto which were projected atmospheric effects often in primary colours whose reds, greens and blues contrasted with sets that were predominantly black, grey and white. Sometimes the projections were suggestive of clouds and storms; streams of moving light on the tilted platform evoked the Rhine in *Götterdämmerung*, giving way to a cold and hard light for the Gibichung Hall. At the end of the whole cycle, an image of the gods burning in Valhalla was presented high up at the back. Elsewhere shadows were dramatically used: the assembled Valkyries were thrown into relief by harsh shadow; Hagen's appearance was made more menacing by his shadow literally looming large over the scene. The image of the murdered Siegfried lying still and alone on a dark stage in a bright shaft of light through the Funeral March was particularly memorable.

In his programme essay on the full cycle, Friedrich established at the outset what he saw as the main concern his new staging had to address: 'Every artistic realization, often described by the too narrow term "interpretation", must establish its "today" and "here" in order the better to understand the time span which Wagner projects from a mythical past through his own epoch and on into the distant future. And each artistic realization must take into account the risks and limitations of its own reality which will be measured in relation to the Utopian.' Part of Friedrich's solution was to combine in the imagery elements from the time of the work's original setting, the time of its creation and the time of the performance itself, in the process creating 'synthetic time'. This synthesis then drew on another time period, that of the ideas of human aspiration itself in a continuum from the past stretching forward into our future. 'The world: the theatre. The stage: a world' is how Friedrich summarized his approach. The production was not supposed to create some sort of alternative discreet world, but rather the production should draw into it a variety of elements to which the audience could relate – and from whatever sources – provided that they brought out the intellectual content of the operas. Fundamentally, the form of the stage fitted this inclusive, illustrative view: instead of a closed ring-shaped platform – as had been used in the previous Covent Garden staging as a visual embodiment of Alberich's ring – the square platform represented a world open on four sides, and so mirrored the contrasting but complementary sections of the operatic tetralogy.

The costumes were designed by Ingrid Rosell to create a strong visual identity for each individual character, in tune with Friedrich's idea to make each clearly stand out, yet not represent a particular time or place. The timelessness of the production came through in such contrasts as what seemed to be space suits for the giants, who carried giant drills as though offensive weapons, set alongside an ermine robe for the formal propriety of Fricka; Wotan's features were framed by what was something between a vast ruff and a caricature of a winged collar. This was echoed in the Valkyrie costumes, made in black and silver, with Brünnhilde not made immediately distinguishable from her sisters. Siegfried went from the dirty working clothes of a young blacksmith to a patterned jacket that matched Gunther's when later drawn into the Gibichung world.

Underlying all this was Friedrich's Marxist interpretation, demonstrating where the power lay. His *Rheingold* had the political and social building blocks of founding revolutionaries, heads of government and the proletariat. His *Walküre* moved to a domestic, middle-class 19th-century world that was ultimately, for Friedrich, the beginning of the end. *Siegfried* became one vision – and a suspect one – of the Utopian ideal that society was striving for, with nature as both refuge and a source of trauma. *Götterdämmerung* showed 'the glittering glamour of the last civilization, a distorted image of the once heroic struggle to stave off downfall' and ultimately was a 'future society without a future'. The intellectual predominated in this interpretation, and the calculating, strategic element came through in Friedrich's description of the end of the cycle: 'The great conflict is over. The game is ended.' What needed some work as the cycle went through its early revisions was the introduction of some warmth that the distancing effects and a certain intellectual rigour had tended to subdue. The final scene of *Siegfried* was one such case, where the awkward and adolescent hero did not seem to interact with his newly encountered love sufficiently strongly in the first performances; the scene was emotionally warmed up when the cycle was performed in its entirety.

With the first run of *Das Rheingold* Colin Davis attracted a mostly unenthusiastic reception. Two aspects of his interpretation were welcome: an attention to instrumental detail and a control of orchestral volume and phrasing to make the singers rightfully prominent. But a third was not: the performance was very slow, one critic suggesting that Reginald Goodall (famously 'spacious' in his Wagner tempos) was the equivalent of a racing driver by comparison. To be more precise, it was not so much the slow speeds as a sense that there was not a sufficiently strong underlying momentum to propel the work inexorably from one detail, one climax, to the next. Davis had identified the dots but failed to join them up, so that the architecture of the score seemed to be missing. Similar observations would come up in later decades as conductors tackled the score for the first time, and thus the response to Davis should be no surprise.

Der Ring des Nibelungen is a work of theatre, and so it requires the experience of live performance to hone its effect; it is just as important for a conductor to gain this sense of how it all fits together as for the director, the performers and the audience. Time and again, the first outing of the first part of a new *Ring* receives a less subtle performance and provokes a less sympathetic response than when it is later incorporated into full cycles, by which time it is more settled in style and has an integrity from all its elements placed in context. Davis gradually came to architectural grips with the score as the cycle progressed, with admittedly some faster speeds, but more importantly no sense of hurry.

By the first complete cycle, Andrew Porter (*Financial Times*) thought Davis 'conducted with so apt a blend of naturalness and passion; with power and eloquence in the orchestral playing but not training of spotlights, as it were, on individual instrumental marvels of the conductor's artfulness; with buoyant, "breathing" support for the singers, alert, not dictatorial'.

Through all the performances of this particular production, certain performers remained pretty much constant. Donald McIntyre was Wotan at the opening of this new production, and for most of the revivals of the cycle. In a gradual passing on of the baton – or, more precisely, the spear – McIntyre had shared the part of Wotan/Wanderer with David Ward in the final couple of revivals of the previous production; Ward now slowly bowed out through appearances as the Wanderer in the fourth performance of the opening run of *Siegfried* and for one performance of the first revival of *Das Rheingold*. Norman Bailey also played Wotan, twice for *Das Rheingold* and *Siegfried,* three times for *Die Walküre.* There was one casualty of the set that provoked a near-Wotan convention for the 1975 revival of *Das Rheingold.* Gwynne Howell fell foul of the stage with a fall from the platform and had to withdraw through injury from the role of Fasolt. Raymond Herincx, who had played Wotan the previous year for ENO, was already cast as Donner, and so appeared alongside Ward, who stepped into the role of Fasolt (for the performances when he was not singing Wotan) and McIntyre as Wotan. William Mann noted: 'The arguments between Fasolt and Wotan at this performance were unusually virulent and sparkling in their give-and-take, each contestant determined to out-sing and out-point the other. A fair judge may well have awarded Freia to the giants and thereby altered the world's course completely.' But McIntyre remained the commanding head god of this cycle, growing in technique and interpretation, again to quote Mann (on the 1975 *Siegfried*), who considered McIntyre had 'learnt to declaim and sing arioso with gripping intensity and incisiveness as well as ease and beauty of tone; he inspires fear but is tragically anxious himself, aware that in the crucial conflict his impotence will be more obvious than his gruesome half-mask or vaunted control of ravens and mountain-top'.

For the first of the two principal women in this Wotan's life, Fricka was played by the same person all through the 1970s performances of this production: 'In *Rheingold* Josephine Veasey is unmistakably a spoiled wheedling wife... In *Walküre* she rounds on Wotan with a show of venom that leaves him like a whipped dog.' (*Financial Times*) Yvonne Minton took over for the final two revivals of 1980 and 1982 ('A strong, urgent Fricka', according to Stanley Sadie in *Musical Times* on the latter revival). The principal Brünnhilde throughout the establishment of the new production and its first revivals was Berit Lindholm (Katalina Kasza also sang some performances). Lindholm brought a vocal strength and clarity to the part that rode over the orchestral sound; several reviewers thought the performance too cool at the conclusion of *Siegfried,* but overall she gave a reliable and firm performance through several Seasons, and her interaction with McIntyre in particular was always effective. This made for a contrast with the production's later alternate Brünnhilde, Gwyneth Jones, who made her Royal Opera debuts in the part in this production for two of the cycles at the start of the 1978–9 Season. Jones was uneven in her performances: on the one hand there could be an erratic and prominent vibrato, a lack of precision, broken phrasing; on the other, there was huge vocal stamina, intense commitment and a powerful build-up to a heroic, dignified and compelling conclusion that Max Loppert summarized as 'blazing nobility'.

There was more of a rolling change than a sharing of performances with the Siegmunds and Siegfrieds. To Richard Cassilly's widely praised Siegmund were added those of René Kollo, then Peter Hofmann, who was also much appreciated, with 'a haunted animal-like wildness and despair with a voice of exceptional beauty and sensuality to match the urgency of his acting' (*The Spectator*). In the title role, Helge Brilioth opened the first *Siegfried* on 17 September 1975, his only performance for this *Ring* production. He was not well received, and something of the unheroic interpretation of Friedrich seemed to have rubbed off technically in the form of poor pitching and under-par presentation, the kinder critics noting that the effects of a summer illness may still have been making their mark. Brilioth was immediately succeeded by a more agile Jean Cox, and latterly by Alberto Remedios.

Loge and Alberich had a particular place in Friedrich's scheme, as they were characters who could well be used at the edges of the platform or even come right off it to the sides or the front of the stage, in effect to pose questions to the audience through their role in the drama. George Shirley's Loge was understood and appreciated in this way from the outset. To Peter Heyworth (for *The Observer*), Shirley played Loge 'brilliantly... as a sinister magician, a cynical, sardonic conjuror out of a short story by Thomas Mann, who plays with the weaknesses of others with Mephistophelian virtuosity'. Furthermore, Shirley was an African-American performer whose colour particularly made a point that his fellow gods were, in the words of Conrad Wilson in *The Scotsman,* 'a bunch of white cheats and thugs'. Zoltán Kélémen's Alberich was equally impressive, 'formidable', 'resonant with evil'.

In a pattern that was to be repeated for future Royal Opera *Rings,* what at first appeared to be diverse and even contradictory elements in the interpretation by Friedrich, Davis, Svoboda, Rosell and Bundy gained for many of the audience a clear coherence by the time of the cycle's completion such that William Mann for *The Times* described how its 'manifestations, previously jostling for attention, [were] now subsumed by Wagner's music into a single experience, rich, moving, inspiring'. Others were equally convinced. 'Such was the power and conviction of both the musical and the dramatic performance', wrote David Cairns (*Sunday Times*) of the effect from one opera to the next, 'that... the great machine continued to hum and the work to live on in the intervening days, dominating our imaginations. ... There is no *Ring* that I will be able to relive more easily in my mind's eye above all for the overwhelming sight of men and women in their griefs and exaltations.' Tom Sutcliffe for *The Guardian* noted that the production 'becomes more secure in detail and masterly in interpretation with each repetition. ... The truth about this *Ring* production is that its extraordinary complexity takes time to settle down on stage, time to gel for the audience.'

Not everyone agreed. In *The Times,* while Bernard Levin went into panegyrics on the merits of the production, Andrew Porter thought it 'a disaster, scenically, dramatically and therefore – since the elements cannot be separated – musically' (although this did not prevent him praising Davis, as quoted above). Porter was one of the observers who considered that the departures by Friedrich from the spirit and often the letter of Wagner's original weakened the interpretation considerably, and found the images often mistimed with the score: 'the visual equivalent of a singer's entry several bars too early.' Like Porter, Stanley Sadie (also for *The Times*) did not like the dramatization of the various opera and act preludes, and the consequent 'superimposition of meanings that its creator could not have envisaged, seems close to the borderline of legitimacy'. Sadie gave a specific example: 'the *Walküre* prelude: dark, agitated music, hinting perhaps at Wotan's inner turmoil, at the strife surrounding Wälse and his brood, at physical storms, at Siegmund's battles, or at each of these, and more, all mutually symbolic. Staging it merely as a pursuit makes it specific: the music now scarcely more significant than that accompanying a chase in a television thriller.'

But a directorial genie, that had long threatened to escape, was now well and truly out of the bottle. Coinciding with this Royal Opera *Ring* was the new centenary cycle at Bayreuth, directed by Patrice Chéreau. His interpretation was also part-Marxist critique like Friedrich's (the Covent Garden programme quoted extracts from Shaw's well-known left-wing interpretation), yet more extreme, as with its *Rheingold* hydro-electric dam that became a rusty dried-up industrial plant by *Götterdämmerung,* or through Siegfried clothed in a dinner jacket. This did colour some of the critical responses to the Friedrich *Ring,* for the Bayreuth production had been unveiled in its entirety only some six weeks or so before the first complete Covent Garden cycle; if anything, Chéreau's approach made Friedrich's seem less extreme, even conventional. But what both directors did share fundamentally was important: neither the naturalism that marked the first half-century and more of the *Ring*'s staging history, nor the pared down spaciousness that followed in the 1950s were to be the first choice of either director or their designers. Very much in the air were concepts and imagery clearly beyond Wagner's own knowledge and experience – that hydro-electric dam again – and such an attitude to overt directorial illumination (if you like it) or imposition (if you hate it) grew in increments to compile a veritable interpretational language for *Ring* staging worldwide. The staged *Ring* really did cease to be solely Wagner's image, but was conceived as a presentation *inter alia:* Patrice Chéreau's *Ring,* Harry Kupfer's *Ring*, Götz Friedrich's *Ring*… and so it would continue. The presentation of gods, giants, dwarfs and dragons went beyond the literal to the symbolic, so that Brünnhilde's rock could be as much on a mountain top as on the roof of a skyscraper, or – as when Friedrich returned for a second production at Covent Garden in the late 1980s – in an underground bomb shelter.

Poster for *Götterdämmerung,* 1 October 1976, the last opera of the first complete presentation of the cycle in the production by Götz Friedrich, conducted by Colin Davis. The poster features a costume design by Ingrid Rosell for Brünnhilde.

Costume design by Ingrid Rosell for Brünnhilde and Waltraute in *Götterdämmerung*. Opposite, the realization of the design in September 1976, with Berit Lindholm (Brünnhilde) and Yvonne Minton (Waltraute).

Donald McIntyre as Wotan in the Hotter production designed by Schneider-Siemssen and Norman Bailey as the Wanderer in the Friedrich production with designs by Rosell. The different design approaches are evident here, with McIntyre in the former (1970) and Bailey in the latter (1980). When the Rosell design was first seen (1975) William Mann wrote: 'Wanderer-Wotan has a literally two-faced appearance, black-and-white, death's head on the left, swarthy and bearded on the right for amiability.'

Zoltán Kélémen as Alberich in the Hotter and Friedrich productions (1970 and 1974) provides an equally strong contrast as the Wotan designs.

Friedrich's two principal Brünnhildes: Berit Lindholm (below) and Gwyneth Jones (opposite). For the new cycle's *Walküre,* Wotan's favourite daughter was sung by Lindholm, who sang it at Bayreuth in 1973; Jones also sang the part in the centenary production at Bayreuth (she had first appeared as Sieglinde there ten years before).

Although Katalin Kasza alternated with Lindholm in 1974–6, for all subsequent revivals it was Gwyneth Jones who shared the role and was to provide the major link of casting with the following production of the cycle by The Royal Opera in 1989–91.

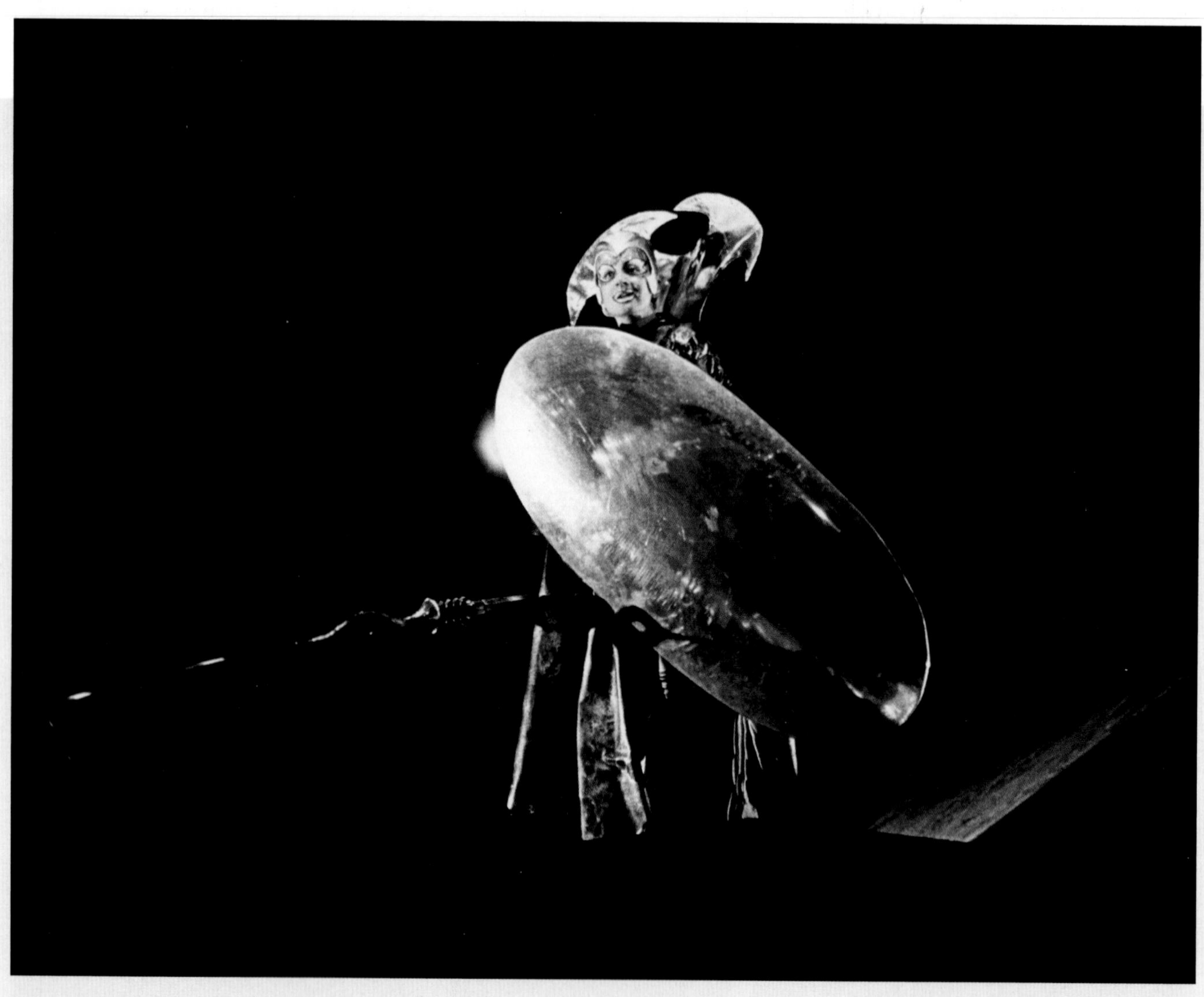

Colin Davis (left) and Götz Friedrich (director) during rehearsals for *Siegfried* in September 1975.

The Rhinedaughters and the gold in the opening scene of *Das Rheingold.*

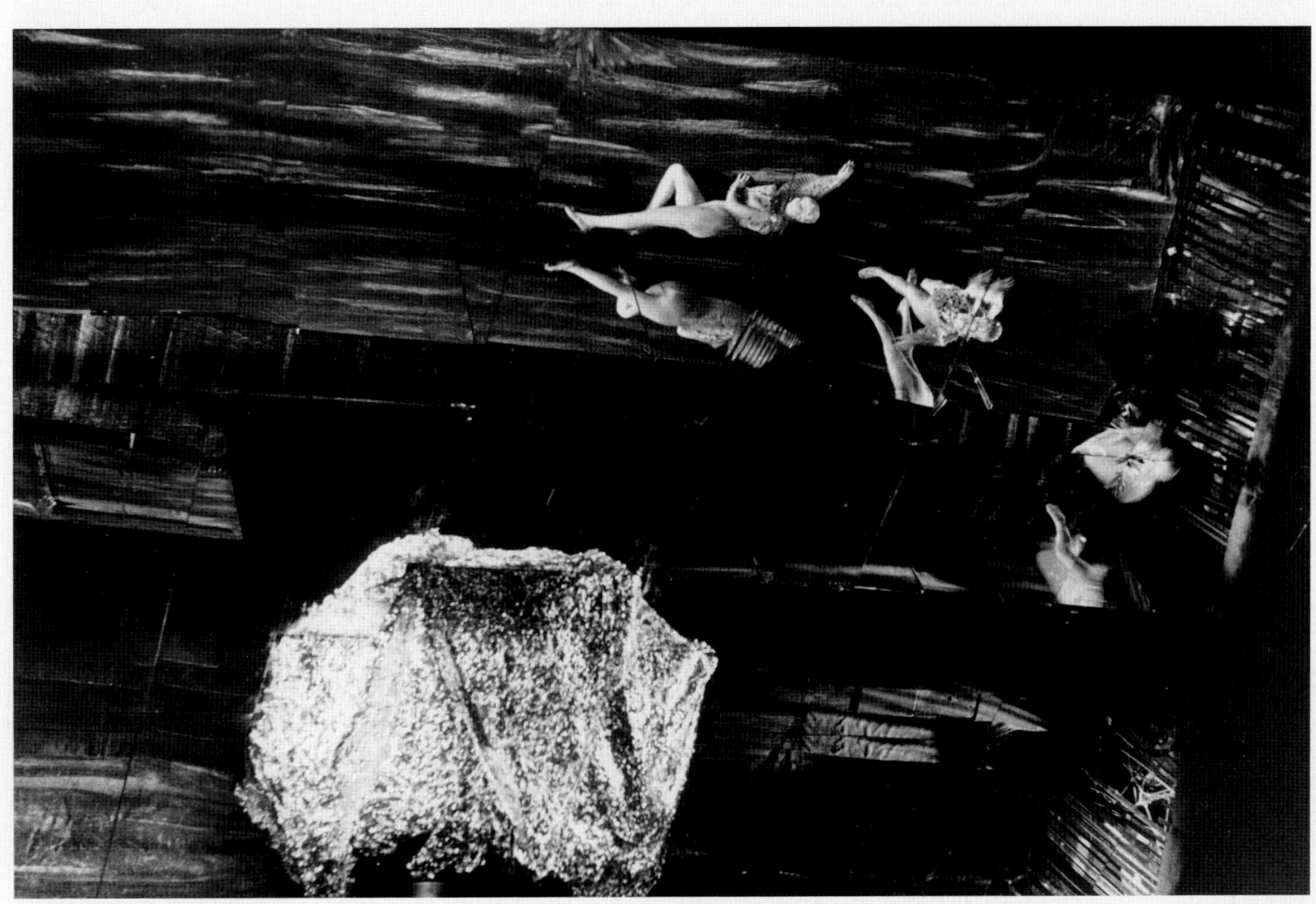

Nibelheim. A view of the tilted platform, from the auditorium, shows how the acting area below stage level (here for Nibelheim) could be seen through its reflection in the platform's mirrored underside. A second view, from the wings, with George Shirley as Loge, shows the open pit from which the hydraulic stage platform was supported. In front is Alberich's hi-tech control tower, 'a strange crystal contraption that became his pulpit of evil doctrine' (*Sunday Times*). Shirley was a 'complete success both visually and musically', as *The Times* described it; 'sulky, malicious, scornful and witty in flame-red tattered kaftan and slippers, he made us see the whole action (as the producer doubtless intended) through his cynical left-wing eyes.' *The Scotsman* commented further on this casting: 'Friedrich... treats Shirley's colour as an asset, thereby creating the world's first black Loge, suitably cool, hip and sardonic, up to date in his dress sense, and rightly recognising the rest of the gods as a bunch of white cheats and thugs.'

While Wotan, Donner and Froh (Donald McIntyre, Norman Bailey and Robert Tear) look on, Friea is finally obliterated from view by the pile of gold for the giants. Fafner and Fasolt (Donald Shanks and Matti Salminen) were 'space-fiction astronauts with ray-guns, supermen without superbrains' (*The Times*).

For *Das Rheingold*'s conclusion the flat platform was turned into a large flight of steps for the gods' ascent to Valhalla through the raising of seven wood stairways fitted into the surface of the stage platform. This floor was replaced with a reddish-brown wood surface for *Die Walküre* and metal (covered by various carpets) for *Siegfried* and *Götterdämmerung*; Brünnhilde's rock was set into these surfaces as required.

Costumes designed by Rosell for Fricka: silver lurex, silver plastic with silver lamé, and silver-shot dress with full-length fake-ermine cloak. Josephine Veasey played Fricka in the first four Seasons of this production (1974–6 and 1978); in the 1980 and 1982 revivals the part – and costumes – were taken over by Yvonne Minton.

Die Walküre Act I, with Marita Napier (Sieglinde), Aage Haugland (Hunding) and René Kollo (Siegmund), 1976.

The Valkyrie rock, *Die Walküre*; inset, Valkyrie armour bodice and skirt designed by Rosell.

Act I of *Siegfried,* showing the creation of Mime's cave in the dark area underneath the tilted central platform; 1975, with Ragnar Ulfung (Mime) and Helge Brilioth (Siegfried).

Act II of *Siegfried* (1975), behind whose hanging strips of forest vegetation lurks the dragon Fafner (Matti Salminen). Without a shadow of doubt, it was the dragon that grabbed many of the headlines for this *Siegfried*. Svoboda created a vast metallic creature that required four men to control the head section and a further 18 to move all the giant claws; in fact, it required the choreographic skill of Eleanor Fazan to animate it effectively. At the end, the spectacle of the dying Fafner emerging from the insides – in the process, diminished in both status and physical scale – was especially poignant. But where some saw a *coup de théâtre,* thrilling and terrifying, others were happy to count the cost as a means of attacking the structure and purpose of opera itself. It was widely reported that the dragon cost £3400 and its operating staff of 22 included ten on a weekly wage for a mere eight minutes on stage. What extravagance, what waste, what wilful indulgence, complained the *Sunday Times* reporter; this produced a strong and irate clarification to the paper from the men obliged to operate the great beast:

> Our 'full weekly wage' is in fact only £28 per week. The agreement with our employers is effectively 'play as cast' and covers all the *Ring* cycle operas in production. The ten for whom Mr Fay says it is 'nice in particular' are involved in doubling for Wotan, Siegfried, Siegmund, Loge and Alberich, and in playing heroes, hunters and a beast as well as the dragon Fafner.
>
> Besides scheduled performances (Wagner operas can be five hours long), we have a total six-day week commitment to the Opera House and must be available for 33 hours per week rehearsal, morning, afternoon and evening as called. (Overtime rate 35p per hour). A situation some workers might consider a sale of soul as well as body in other professions, and one which, I think you'll agree, demonstrates Mr Tooley's careful House-keeping rather than any 19th-century excess!

[As the original typescript letter shows, the newspaper edited out John Tooley's name when it printed the response.]

Elizabeth Bainbridge as Erda (*Siegfried,* 1975). She sang Erda in both *Das Rheingold* and *Siegfried,* thoughout the life of the production, sharing the role principally with Patricia Payne, but also latterly with Marta Szirmay.

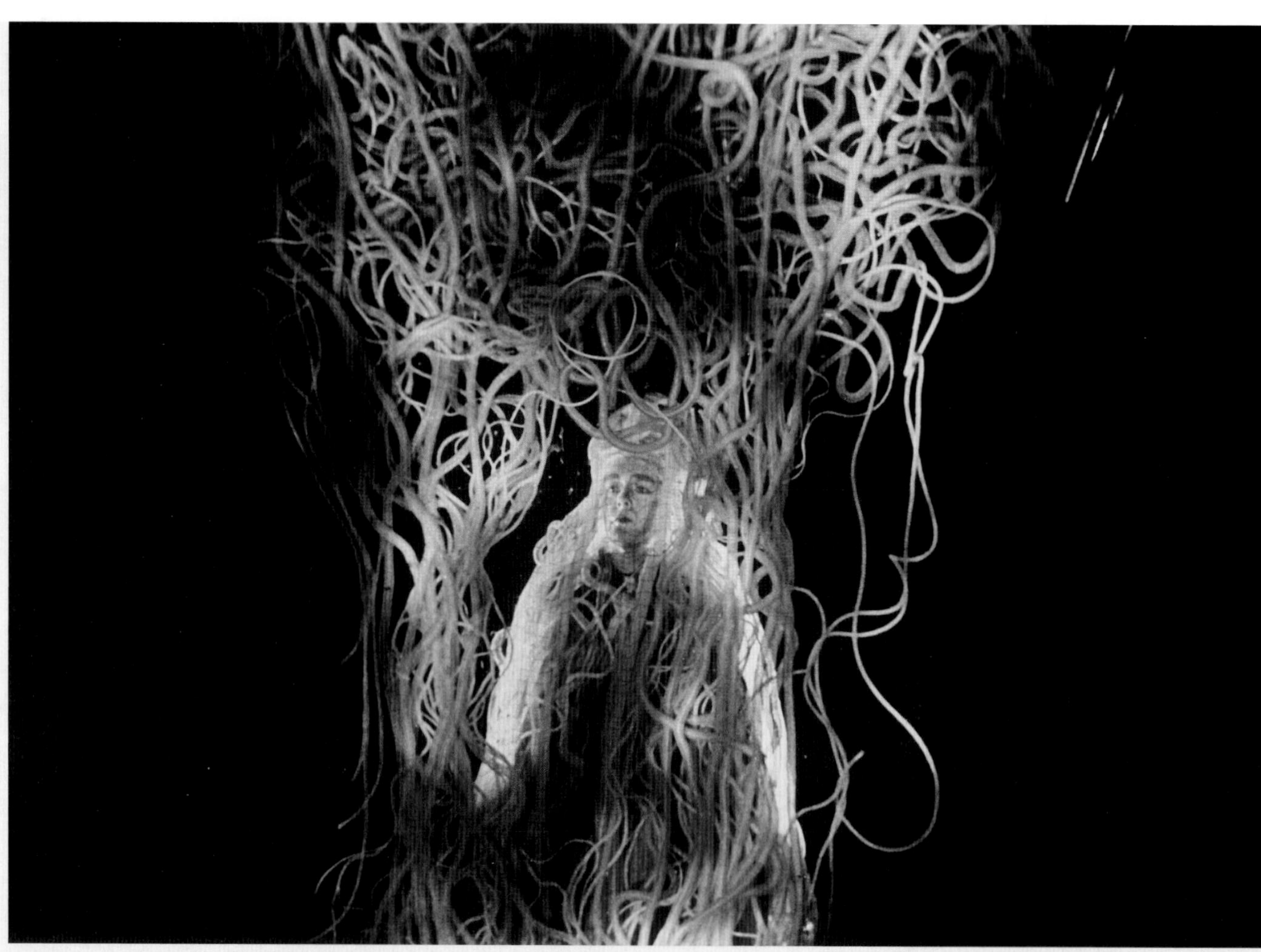

Elizabeth Bainbridge as Erda and Donald McIntyre as the Wanderer (*Siegfried,* 1975). Right, the costume for Erda made to Rosell's design.

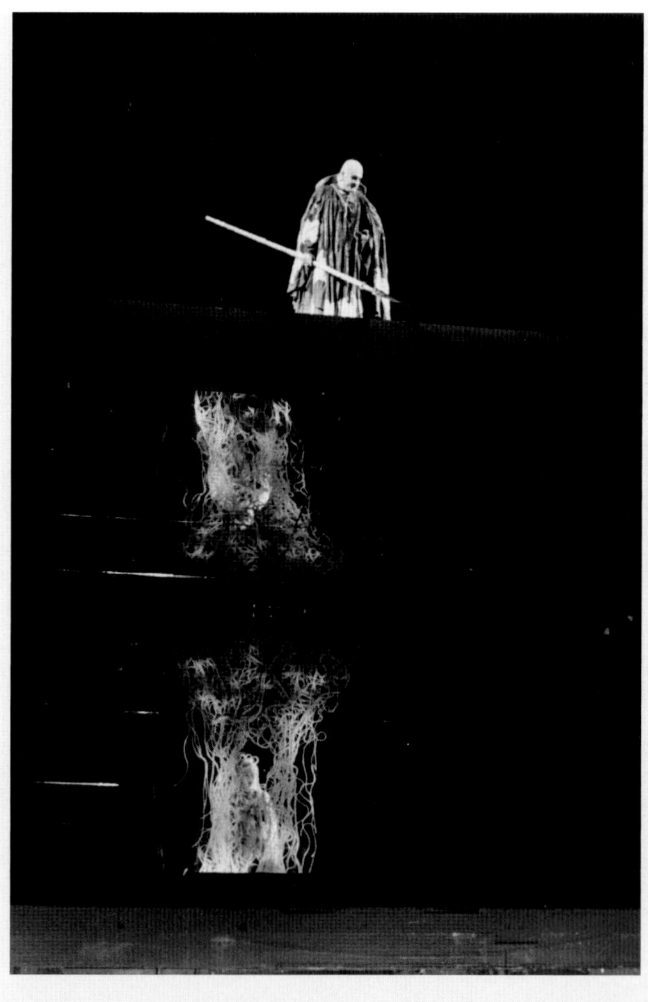

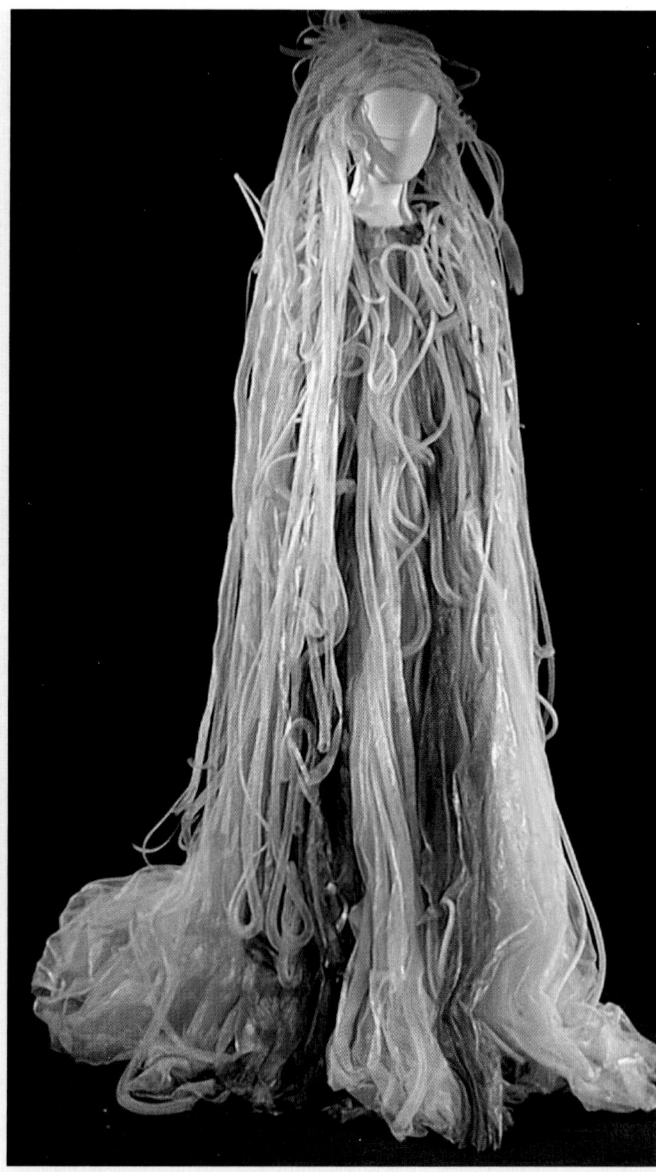

The concluding scene of *Siegfried*, with Helge Brilioth (Siegfried) and Berit Lindholm (Brünnhilde) in 1975. The setting is effectively but simply conveyed through the tilted central platform to which has been added a raised section for Brünnhilde's sleep, its stark line emphasized and extended by William Bundy's atmospheric lighting.

The huge Fresnel lenses used in *Götterdämmerung* (opposite) were a source of some contention in the production, along much the same lines as those of the dragon. It was a memorable image to see Hagen looming large over the action he manipulates, his face magnified and distorted. This was a stage mechanism that focussed on the internal dark motives of a dark mind, like a cinema close-up. Yet at £1000 for each lens plus the cost of transport from Japan, it was expensive staging; and for those sitting in seats at an angle to the magnifying lenses, sideways or from above, the effect was limited or non-existent. Stanley Sadie in *The Times* saw the device as a wry metaphor for the production itself: 'some aspects are hugely inflated, others scarcely to be seen.' Shown here, from 1976, are Hagen (Bengt Rundgren) watching over Gutrune (Hanna Lisowska), in turn, with Gunther (Siegmund Nimsgern) and Siegfried (Jean Cox).

Act III of *Götterdämmerung,* 1976.
Opposite: Siegfried (Jean Cox) encounters the Rhinedaughters Flosshilde, Wellgunde and Woglinde (Gillian Knight, Eiddwen Harrhy and Valerie Masterson).

Below opposite: the hall of the Gibichungs, 1976, with Bengt Rundgren (Hagen), Berit Lindholm (Brünnhilde), Hanna Lisowska (Gutrune), Siegmund Nimsgern (Gunther) and Jean Cox (Siegfried).

Opposite (inset): costume designed for Gutrune by Ingrid Rosell, worn by Hanna Lisowska in the opening run of performances of this production, September– October 1976. The role was played in later Seasons by Helena Döse, Linda Esther Gray and Anne Evans.

Below: the conclusion of the cycle, showing the destruction of Valhalla and the gods. The image was filmed on the stairs by the Crush Bar of the Royal Opera House with actors in costume against a backing cloth; flame imagery was superimposed over the photography of the figures and the result projected on to the stage. Additional cloud and flame on stage was achieved with hand-painted discs rotating in front of a projection light.

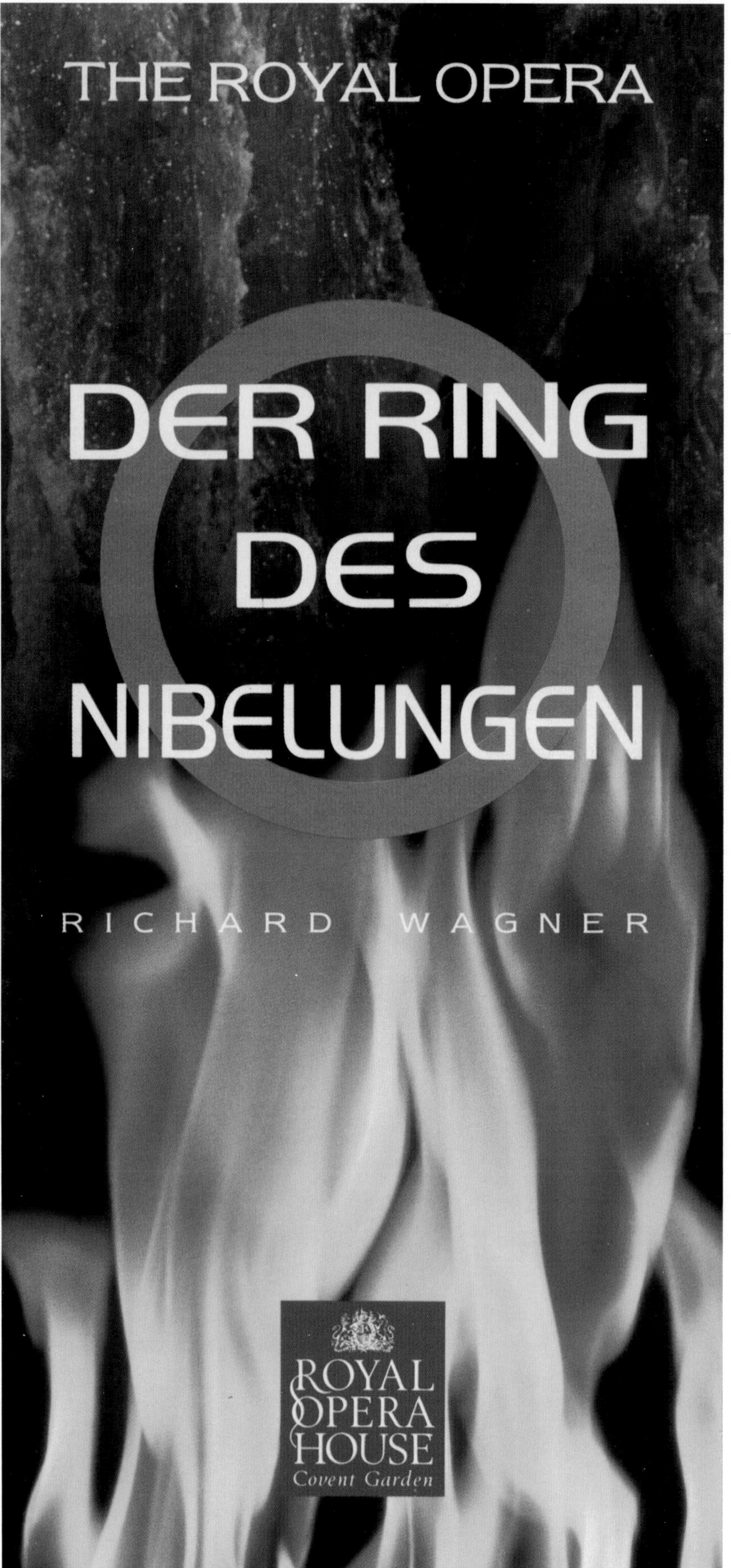

Cover of the booking form flyer for the production by Götz Friedrich, first seen at the Berlin Deutsche Oper and presented in a revised staging as a cycle by The Royal Opera in 1991.

CHAPTER FIVE

CHANGING DIRECTION

1988–1991

When Bernard Haitink took over as Music Director of The Royal Opera in 1987, he was keen to conduct the *Ring*. Leaving aside the desire of Music Directors to stamp their own individuality on the cycle through the creation of a completely new production, taking over the previous Friedrich-Svoboda-Rosell celebrated staging was not a realistic option for several reasons. In particular, the revolving, twisting hydraulic platform at the centre of the set had become noisy, while its domination of the stage space caused logistical problems: no other work could be shown in repertory while it was in place, and this led to the loss of around eighteen nights of performance for other repertory works, and consequently to a considerable loss of income.

There were two further issues. First, a proposal to close the Royal Opera House for much-needed refurbishment, scheduled initially to begin in 1993, was likely to last several years. Second, budget constraints were especially tight – there simply wasn't the money to finance a production on a grand scale. The parameters of a new staging of the *Ring* were now in place. It was to be a contrast to what had gone before, with Haitink keen on a simpler staging to complement his own intentions; as he told one interviewer, 'There has been far too much messing around on stage, and that doesn't help the music. I want to restore some balance.' The restriction of technical demands would also allow the work to be performed in repertory and at other theatres – Royal Albert Hall performances were in mind, for example – during the redevelopment closure.

The director was to be Yuri Lyubimov, a great figure of the Russian stage through his work as founder-director of the avant-garde Taganka Theatre; criticisms of the Soviet regime led to his exile in 1983, and by the time of the new *Ring* in 1988 he was settled in Israel. Two years before he had directed what turned out to be a successful *Jenůfa* at Covent Garden – first critical disapproval, then popular success – with Haitink as conductor. So the new Wagner project seemed to be building on that beginning, even if Lyubimov expressed some surprise at this second offer to collaborate with Haitink, saying of his experience with Haitink and *Jenůfa* that 'It was a complicated production and our relationship was not simple. It was hard for him to appreciate my theatrical vision. I expected he would be scared off.' Lyubimov intended to bring out in the production what he viewed as Wagner's view of the world: 'alarm, angst, warning and tragical anguish'. But there was also a desire to keep it all tied to the modern and recognizable, not – so the designer Paul Hernon explained – in a fairytale world of dwarfs and giants.

Hernon spent some two years in preparing ideas that took into account all the prescribed limitations. What he developed was a simple circular stage with a large central disc that could act as a performing surface or open as an entrance or exit for various characters: it was through its centre in *Das Rheingold* that Wotan and Fricka arose in an embrace and Erda appeared more portentously, while its tipping and tilting wrong-footed Alberich in his slippery chase of the Rhinedaughters. Back projections on a screen that could be changed from a central aperture to a wide screen allowed for descriptive and complementary imagery, while fire for Loge and water (both real and projected) were the beginnings of the representation of the elements through the cycle that would have continued with earth in *Die Walküre*.

There were six performances of *Das Rheingold* in autumn 1988, the first on 29 September 1988; but the last, on 13 October, was to prove the final one of not only this production but indeed the whole cycle. There had been signs of difficulty early on when Lyubimov publicly expressed his worry at a rehearsal period of just four weeks, a very tight schedule for a director used to the slow development of ideas through workshop methods right up to the last possible moment, rather than firm decisions in advance as opera staging frequently demands on technical grounds. On top of this, Lyubimov spoke no English or German and had what was kindly described as an 'extraordinary temperament', causing tensions in rehearsals, especially with Haitink. Citing 'intellectual differences in artistic interpretation', Jeremy Isaacs (the Opera House's General Director at the time) announced that the cycle would not be completed with the team of Haitink-Lyubimov-Hernon.

Inevitably, the cancellation of the project and what happened next – the need to find a replacement production, and quick! – has tended to colour assessment of this production of *Das Rheingold*. In fact, while the backstage situation may already have been indicating a stormy opening for *Walküre* preparations in more ways than the obvious one, in the auditorium the audience response to *Das Rheingold* was warm when it opened. Critical detractors were easily balanced by those who enthused, 'lacking in motivation' for one but 'an impressive start' for another. And if the common consent seemed to be that the design was overfussy on occasion, and if the introduction of extra characters by Lyubimov was felt unnecessary – a silent figure of Justice, an extra bevy of Rhinedaughters – nonetheless there was also a shared feeling that a promising start had been made on the cycle. There was praise for Haitink, to whom the *Ring* at this stage was a new undertaking in the theatre (indeed, he had only just begun his recording of it for EMI), and the strong cast (many with role or Company debuts) was appreciated: James Morris as Wotan, Helga Dernesch as Fricka, Ekkehard Wlaschiha as a particularly commanding Alberich and Kenneth Riegel as a show-stealing Loge.

So what to do next? The casts were booked, the schedules made and The Royal Opera wanted to keep the *Ring* in its repertory as planned. Other up-and-running *Rings* were considered, but the chosen solution also brought the return of Götz Friedrich, who agreed to rework his cycle made in 1984–5 for West Berlin's Deutsche Oper (Friedrich was the General Manager and Principal Director there), and which was at that time touring to Japan and Washington. There was an extra advantage in that some of the booked cast was familiar with what had become known as the 'Time Tunnel' *Ring*. True, the Royal Opera version did have some new designs, it had a different conductor and some of the casting would be new to the Friedrich concept; but inevitably there was debate over just how new this reworking for London of an existing production would be.

The tunnel concept had first suggested itself to Friedrich in Salzburg (as he recalled for the *Sunday Times* in 1988), where an underground car park with huge metal security doors provoked the idea of a space that was at the same time protective yet also completely confining. This served as a metaphor for Friedrich's interpretation: 'It's as though we have lost sight of heaven, or of the sky. In the 19th century, sky still existed. People depicted it on backdrops or projections in the theatre. If we look around now, civilization happens in an underground labyrinth. We fill the sky, instead, with satellites, bombs, smog.' For the transference from idea to stage reality Peter Sykora, the designer, drew on the distinctive coffered vaulting of the Washington Metro by creating a long receding tunnel in which, with openings and inserts for the different scenes, everything would take place, and whose industrial imagery amplified Friedrich's apocalyptic vision. Such a vision was further influenced by Henry Moore's *Tube Shelter Perspective* (1941), one of a series of images from Blitz-torn London, described when first shown as 'a terrifying vista of recumbent shapes, pale as all underground life tends to be pale; regimented, as only fear can regiment; helpless yet tense, safe yet listening, uncouth, uprooted, waiting in the tunnel for the dawn to release them'.

In a programme note, Friedrich wrote: 'Our stage is to be understood as a "Time Tunnel". Every character, every situation is both present and past. What is above is turned upside down and becomes the below. Hope has been turned into fear which once again imagines what freedom is. The beginning is the end and the end is a new beginning.' One piece of staging made clear this approach, as though mankind were trapped in a cycle from creation to destruction that kept repeating to infinity. The close of *Götterdämmerung* mirrored the opening of *Das Rheingold*: the stage covered as if by a shroud, with stooped and cowled mystical figures in attendance waiting for the next, inevitable descent from rebirth to catastrophe. But for a pragmatic reason this effect could not make its mark until *Das Rheingold* was presented for the first time in September 1991. Friedrich's first opera had to be *Die Walküre,* not *Das Rheingold,* as the timetable necessarily continued from where Lyubimov had left off.

Act I of the first *Die Walküre,* on 27 September 1989, revealed Hunding's hut defined by large metal panels, whose louvres let through the headlights of Hunding's approaching car. These panels drew back as Sieglinde and Siegmund's incestuous love became clear to reveal a tunnel that seemed to stretch beyond the horizon. Act II saw Wotan brooding over the models of destroyed cities in what seemed his war bunker, and one *coup de théâtre* came as he stripped himself of the costumes that symbolized his power – white coat, white jacket, breastplate – and stepped forward for the words 'Das Ende' into a bright white light, his perspective shifting from god to vulnerable man. The leather-clad and metal-studded Valkyries inevitably attracted comment, with Friedrich describing them as 'a crazy horrifying gang of good-looking girls'. One newspaper cartoon depicted a nervous Front-of-House Manager facing an approaching gang of Hell's Angels, while the man selling papers outside reminds him, 'I told you it would attract the wrong kind of audience.' The black leather of Brünnhilde was tolerated, her high-winged helmet was generally not. However, her descent into sleep provided a particularly effective moment for the close of the opera as she was encircled by erupting pools of real flame.

In contrast to the close of *Die Walküre,* the first act of the first night of *Siegfried,* on 4 October 1990, presented a riot of colour, with a child-like rainbow vision of a forest dropped into the tunnel. Its symbolism was strengthened with a romper suit for the young hero and toys around the place: Mime was keeping Siegfried in an infantile state for his own ends. The forest and Fafner's lair were conveyed through netting draped in the tunnel, and the dragon himself continued the technological theme with Willard White inside what was variously described in reviews as 'an angry combine harvester with a face like a Halloween mask' and 'a combination of armoured tank and cinema organ and fairground dodge car'. The Woodbird was in part depicted as a small moving light, and incarnated in the first runs of the opera by Judith Howarth, lowered from the flies on a trapeze. But instead of Siegfried's journey to brilliant sunlight, he found his Brünnhilde asleep in the gloom of the tunnel, protected by large bolted doors. This dark enclosure of the final scene of Act III was subject to a good deal of criticism for its taking exactly the opposite approach to what seemed to be required: confined, colourless and lacking any visual impact to match the power of the finally triumphant mood.

Götterdämmerung opened on 4 February 1991 for the first of five performances on its own (not taking its place in the cycle until 8 October of the same year). The tunnel proved in this case very suitable for the Hall of the Gibichungs, into which were added the large magnifying lenses that had been part of the design in Friedrich's previous *Ring* to Svoboda's design, used as though for eavesdropping on key characters at key moments. The seated ranks of Gibichung warriors listened as Siegfried's memory returned to him, before covering their heads to create a pre-echo of the final minutes of the whole cycle in which the becloaked gods appeared to be burning, after which the audience was left with a final picture of shrouded Norn figures in the now shrouded tunnel.

It was these same figures who appeared for the Prelude to *Das Rheingold* (16 September 1991; the first of two separate performances before two full cycles). Next, the Rhinedaughters were placed behind a shimmering drape to represent the Rhine, while the gold behind them glowed as though the nucleus of what resembled an atomic model. The second scene showed a projection of Valhalla high up at the back of the stage – a statement of what immediately precipitated the crisis for the gods. In addition, the restrictive setting of the tunnel imagery was now fully in place. It allowed for such moments as the appearance of the workers in Nibelheim as just points of light moving over the ground, revealed to be the lamps on the miners' helmets in an underground world that had Alberich at the centre of control, monitoring everything through television screens as piles of gold roll through on conveyor belts. Erda appeared from among voluminous silk that turned into her own dress, covering the entire floor as if to mirror on the ground that sense of total enclosure of the tunnel above.

Through both the change from Lyubimov to Friedrich and then through the gradual revealing of the Friedrich cycle, consistencies in what was thought a very fine cast helped maintain a sense of continuity. At the centre were James Morris's Wotan/Wanderer and Gwyneth Jones's Brünnhilde. The former made a great impression ('the Wotan of our time' for the *Independent on Sunday*) with a sustained sense of dignity matched by a vocally rich tone, while the latter impressed in so many of the key moments – a riveting Immolation in particular – but took time to warm up and was thus sometimes considered a bit wayward. Kenneth Riegel and Helga Dernesch were the Loge and Fricka for both Lyubimov and Friedrich. John Tomlinson (himself a world-beating Wotan) was Friedrich's Hunding and a very effective Hagen. Alternating as Mime through the operas were John Dobson and Alexander Oliver, and as Siegfried René Kollo and Reiner Goldberg (with an additional single appearance by Spas Wenkoff). Ekkehard Wlaschiha was an impressive Alberich, and although Roderick Earle played the part in the first *Götterdämmerungs,* it was Wlaschiha who returned later in 1991 to play the whole cycle. A consistent grouping of Elizabeth Bainbridge, Phyllis Cannan and Christine Teare portrayed the eternal trio of Norns, while the roles of the Rhinedaughters were mainly taken by Jane Turner, Gillian Webster, Monica Groop and Judith Howarth (Anne Mason and Martha Sharp also appeared).

There were opposing views of the production, many of them inevitably centred on the 'Time Tunnel' concept and its impact on the design. To take just two of the many contrasting summaries:

> One no longer insists on the rocks and trees of a naturalistic production, but the time-tunnel remains for me an unconvincing theatrical space; neither specific enough to serve as, say, a brutalistic industrialized landscape, nor sufficiently abstract to resonate with powerful primeval or diachronic images. What vindicated the production, then, was not any new insight in the social or political dynamic of the *Ring,* but the intensity with which it was projected as a musico-dramatic experience.
> (Barry Millington, *Sunday Times*)

> The basic set is one of this *Ring*'s assets. Peter Sykora's much-maligned 'Time Tunnel' creates both an enclosed, stultifying world and a space of great depth as well as width – timeless, really, as it could be an ancient cave-temple or a giant sewer, or most characteristically, a vaulted 19th-century warehouse, later converted to an up-market apartment with skyscape for the Gibichungs.
> (Robert Maycock, *The Independent*)

Friedrich was also in the unusual position of inevitably inviting comparison between his two consecutive stagings for The Royal Opera. There seemed – maybe inevitably – not enough of a development from that previous highly successful production; its grander and more animated staging – necessarily impractical in this later production, designed to be more portable in its staging – was felt by many to be missing. To take one of the comparisons noted (by Edward Greenfield for *The Guardian*), from the very start of *Die Walküre*: in 1976, using the central revolving and tilting platform, 'Siegmund was tossed around on it, until one heaved a sigh of relief when he found refuge in Hunding's hut. This time... a matronly Sieglinde sits calmly on a tube-framed chair through the storm. She moves not a muscle, when in through a heavy metal hatch a wild figure lurches. Siegmund dressed in an overcoat of rough skins with khaki fatigues underneath...'. The story was well enough told for most, but the extra emotional dimensions, especially the heroic, were not sufficiently strong in a physically and atmospherically dark production with a bleak ending (and its implied 'Groundhog Day' rebeginning).

Importantly, the cycle was a great musical success, and a personal one for Haitink. Finally, after various stops and starts, he had his first complete *Ring* with The Royal Opera, albeit not the one intended and not an entirely new one. Throughout the cycle his conducting was praised, although as it represented his first cycle it inevitably grew in effect as the individual operas moved towards full completion. Many commentators lavished praise on his interpretation and on the fine orchestral playing it drew. For example, for Michael Kennedy (in the *Sunday Telegraph*) Haitink's *Siegfried* had

> the lucidity and lightness of texture appropriate to the scherzo-like mood of the music of Act I, and poetic delicacy and finely chiseled detail in the nature-painting of Act II, with superlative woodwind playing and a distinguished solo performance of Siegfried's horn-calls. ... The stormy prelude to Act III, the Wanderer's world-weary music and the final rapturous love-scene after the awakening of Brünnhilde were impassioned and ideally paced, and found the orchestra in its most accurate and responsive mood. It made me wonder if Wagner wrote a more entrancing and virtuoso score.

Typical also was Robert Henderson's summary of Haitink's conducting of the opening night of *Götterdämmerung* (*Daily Telegraph*) as having 'a magisterial nobility and incandescence, combining throughout seamless breadth with graphic richness and clarity of detail'.

The 1990 performances of *Siegfried* had been dedicated to that great Wagnerian, Sir Reginald Goodall, who had recently died. For some, it was fitting that the musical standard of these early 90s *Rings* was compared with the performance heights of Hotter's time; before Solti as conductor in the 1960s, Hotter had appeared under Goodall in the later 1950s. Yet for others, it threw into relief both the different conducting approaches of Goodall and Haitink (especially in the level of communication between pit and stage) and the conducting opportunities each was offered through the *Ring* at Covent Garden. Although Goodall's association with The Royal Opera was long, given his reputation with Wagner it is surprising to realize that, apart from a single *Rheingold* in 1975, he only ever conducted two performances of *Die Walküre* at Covent Garden, one in 1959, the other in 1975; he also conducted *Walküre* performances with the Company on tour in 1954 and 1956. But never a complete cycle at Covent Garden. In such a context, this made the dedication seem to some pointed rather than poignant.

Nonetheless, the breadth of musical interpretation and such consistently fine casts – everyone achieved praise from some quarter, and most from a convincing majority – made the completed cycle in 1991 a musical feat that many treasured as part of a near-century-long association of a great work with a world-class opera house. Haitink's first *Ring* finished shortly before his 62nd birthday, but it was not to be his last with The Royal Opera. Before the House closed for redevelopment there was to be a further – and notably controversial – production for him to conduct.

The poster for *Das Rheingold,* the first – and, in the event, only – instalment of the Russian director Yuri Lyubimov's *Ring* cycle for The Royal Opera. The production opened on 29 September 1988 and was seen in five further performances in October.

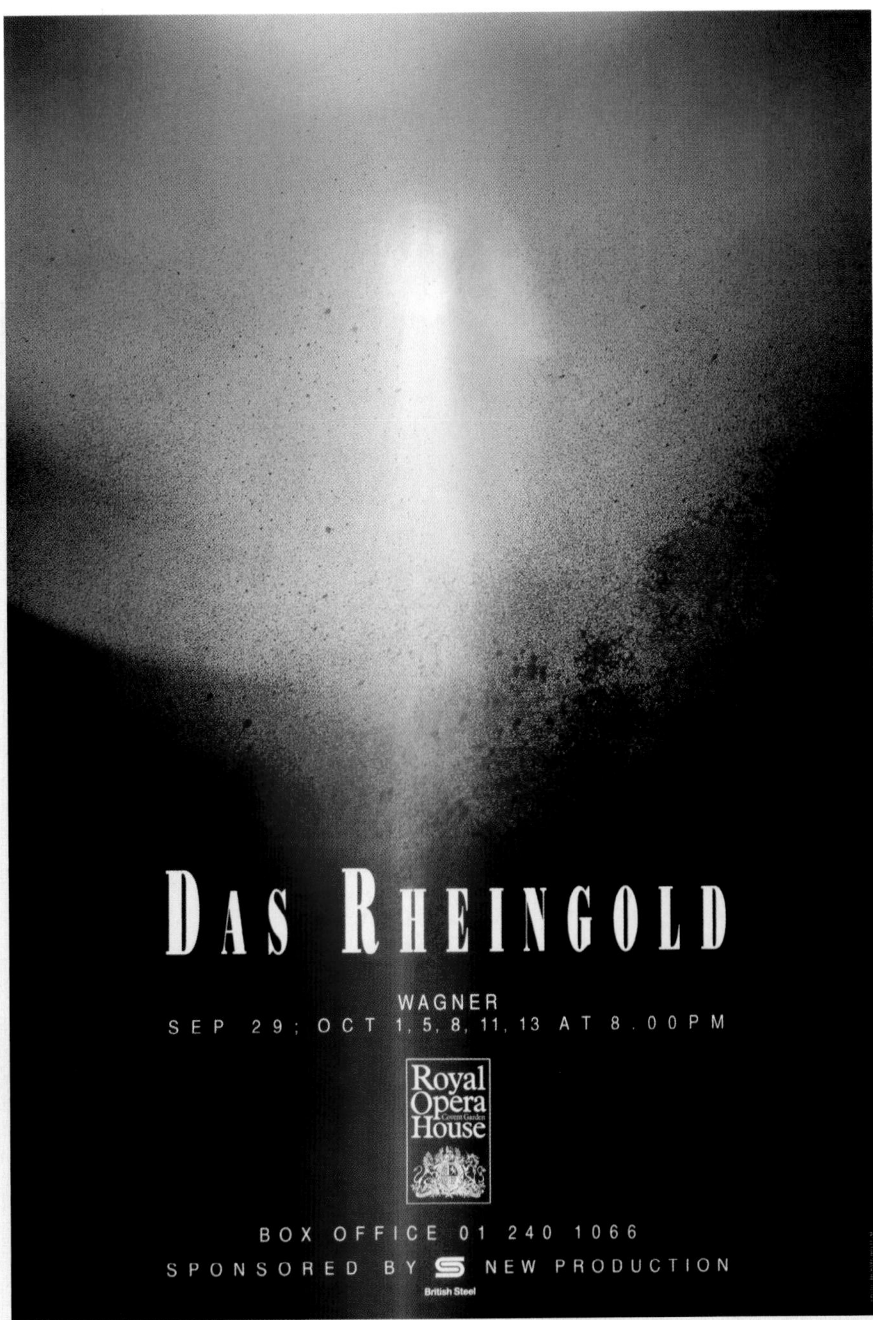

Costume designs by Paul Hernon for *Das Rheingold* (1988): Erda, Alberich and the Rhinedaughters.

Photographs of the model for Paul Hernon's set for *Das Rheingold.* The brief for the design included the need for it to be easily adapted to suit other venues during the anticipated closure of the Royal Opera House for redevelopment. A central floor with an adaptable circular opening was animated through lighting effects and projections.

The costume design by Paul Hernon for Loge (Kenneth Riegel) and the costume as also made for Loge's fire-eating stage double. Paul Griffiths (for *The Times*) reported Riegel's interpretation as that of 'a magician who is amused and surprised if his own tricks work. There is something appealingly sad and vulnerable in the way he sings his chicanery'.

The Observer (Nicholas Kenyon) wrote that 'The show is stolen… by the fire-god Loge of Kenneth Riegel. His brittle, edgy voice is perhaps conventionally moulded but is perfectly suited to the part, and his characterization as a schizophrenic red-and-black conjuror producing fire from the stage is one of the evening's solid successes.'

Das Rheingold, 1988. James Morris (Wotan), Helga Dernesch (Fricka) and Nancy Gustafson (Freia) with, at the back, Willard White and Roderick Kennedy (Fafner and Fasolt).

James Morris (Wotan) with Kenneth Riegel (Loge).

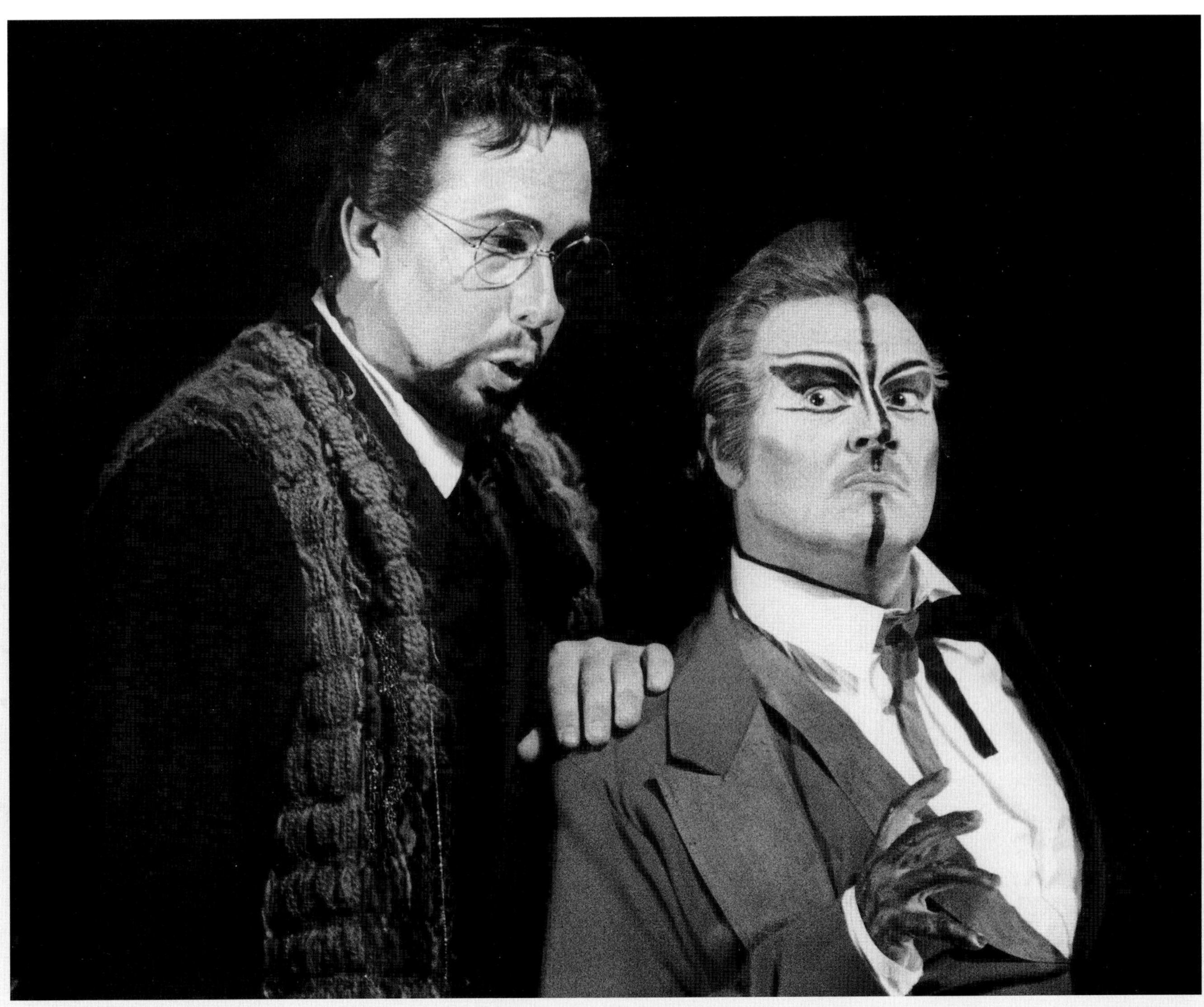

The backcloth design by Peter Sykora for the Royal Opera staging of Götz Friedrich's 'Time Tunnel' *Ring*. The first version of the production, for Deutsche Oper Berlin, took advantage of a very deep stage, permitting a tunnel of almost forty metres that really did appear to stretch into infinity. With the significantly more restricted stage at Covent Garden – less than half the depth originally required – this new backcloth had to suggest through painted perspective the seemingly endless tunnel.

The choice of such a circumscribed space for the entire cycle was seen by some as too restricting, by others as versatile and apt. In *Die Walküre* and *Siegfried* there is a geographical progression in which the restrictive and claustrophobic atmospheres of Hunding's hut and Mime's cave both give way to the height and openness of Brünnhilde's mountain top. Both involve images of nature, whether through high rock ridges and storms or forests and birds. While the tunnel could deal well with the man-made enclosed spaces (exactly what the tunnel represented), the open and natural context was harder to achieve – even inappropriate – in this interpretation. Although the design occasionally gave glimpses of a world whose horizons potentially stretched beyond the tunnel (as with *Die Walküre* Act I), it could not move to them and there was inevitably an ongoing tension between Wagner's work, Friedrich's concept and Sykora's design in this respect. Consequently it worked best in such scenes as those in Nibelheim, *Die Walküre* Act II or the Hall of the Gibichungs in *Götterdämmerung,* where the sense of constricted space could intensify a mood of concentration or confrontation.

Posters for the new productions of
Götterdämmerung (1991)
Die Walküre (1989)
and *Siegfried* (1990).

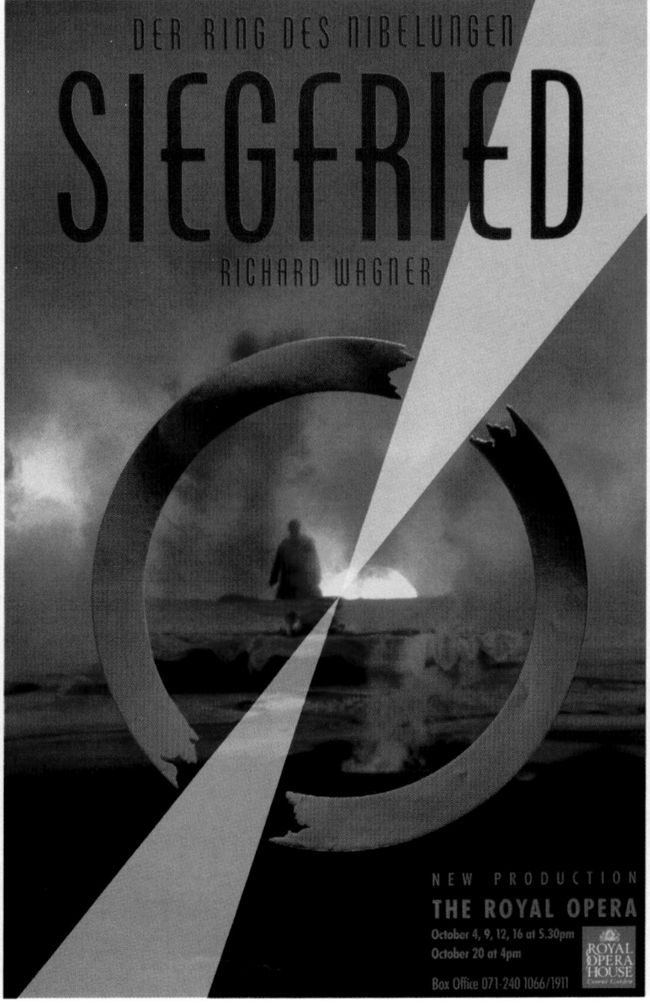

'To scale' designs by Peter Sykora for the Rainbow Forest of *Siegfried*.

Conductor and director: Bernard Haitink and Götz Friedrich during rehearsals for *Siegfried* (1990).

Das Rhinegold (1991).
The 'Time Tunnel' opening. Rhinedaughters and their Rhinegold: from left to right, Jane Turner (Flosshilde), Monica Groop (Wellgunde), Gillian Webster (Woglinde) and Ekkehard Wlaschiha (Alberich).

In Nibelheim. Kenneth Riegel (Loge; left) with Alexander Oliver (Mime).

Payment for Valhalla: from left to right, Franz-Josef Selig (Fafner), Deborah Riedel (Freia), Gwynne Howell (Fasolt), James Morris (Wotan), Kenneth Riegel (Loge), Helga Dernesch (Fricka), Kim Begley (Froh) and Donald Maxwell (Donner).

Inset, costumes designed by Peter Sykora. Froh: silver and white lurex with fake python skin, worn by Kim Begley. Donner: padded leather, white towelling and white sharkskin.

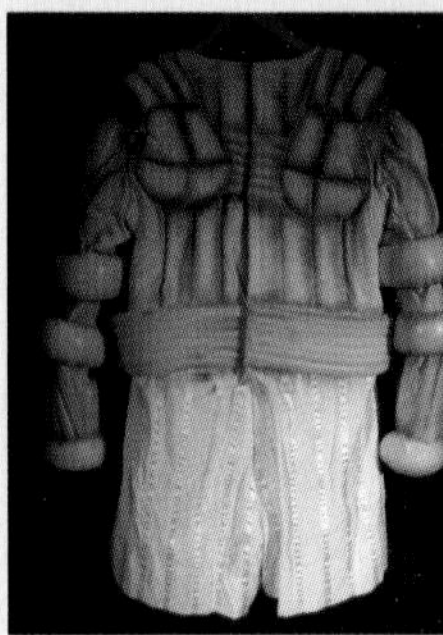

Die Walküre (1989).
Act I: top, John Tomlinson (left) and René Kollo as Hunding and Siegmund; middle, Gabriele Schnaut (Sieglinde) and René Kollo.

Act II: Fricka (Helga Dernesch) confronts Wotan (James Morris) while Brünnhilde (Gwyneth Jones) looks on.

Act III: Wotan (James Morris) summons Loge to protect the sleeping Brünnhilde (Gwyneth Jones).

Siegfried.
René Kollo (Siegfried) and Alexander Oliver (Mime) in Act I (1990) and with James Morris (Wanderer) in Peter Sykora's 'Rainbow Forest' setting.

Act II: Willard White as Fafner (1990); René Kollo and Franz-Josef Selig as Siegfried and Fafner (1991).

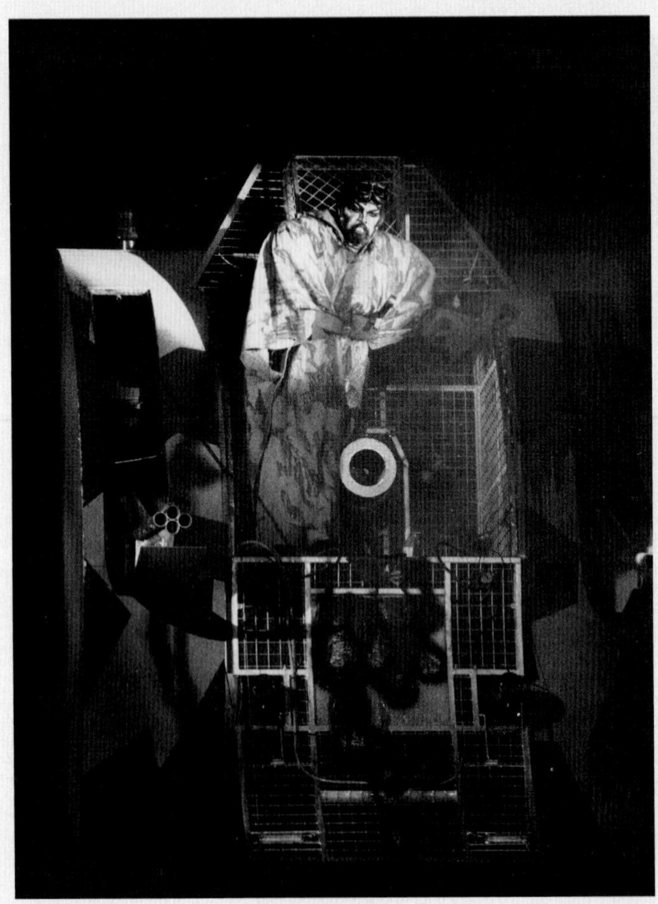

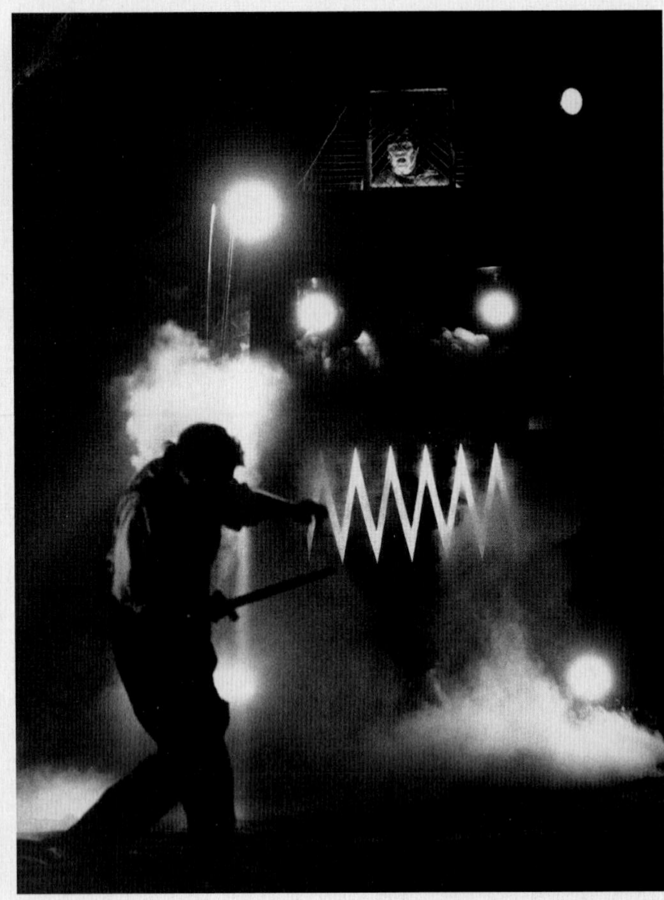

Götterdämmerung.
The opening of Act I: the three Norns, (left to right) Elizabeth Bainbridge, Phyllis Cannan and Christine Teare. Act II, with (left to right) Donald Maxwell as Gunther, Kathryn Harries as Gutrune, John Tomlinson as Hagen, Gwyneth Jones as Brünnhilde and René Kollo as Siegfried. The closing image of the opera, a return to the shrouded Norn figures in the seemingly endless tunnel with which *Das Rheingold* began the cycle.

Cover of the booking form flyer for the three cycles of the production by Richard Jones for The Royal Opera, autumn 1996.

CHAPTER SIX

ACCLAMATION AND THE ABSURD

1994–1996

During rehearsals people in the Opera House have said to me, 'What do you mean by that?'. I say, 'Well, what do you feel about that? What does it represent to you?'. From that point of view, I'd rather say our production was a vision of *The Ring* rather than an explanation. The images have to flow from one into another, and we've tried to make it very rich and resonant. I'd say, 'Reveal it in a mythic sense; don't explain it in a psychoanalytic or a Marxist sense. Ask more questions; don't give answers.' (Richard Jones speaking to Andrew Clements: *The Guardian,* 23 September 1996)

What connects a road traffic sign, a paper bag, a bearded lady and a 1950s Chevrolet? The Covent Garden *Ring* directed by Richard Jones and designed by Nigel Lowery immediately gives you the answer. The controversy began with the first night of *Das Rheingold,* on 13 October 1994, when the mixture of boos and cheers for the production first showed it as the 'love it or hate it' event it was to become. There was universal admiration for the musical interpretation both on stage and in the pit, under the direction of Bernard Haitink, The Royal Opera's Music Director. As to the staging, the sets were described by one critic as 'almost wantonly ugly and demonstrably wrong', but the whole event by another as 'not a production for people who want to leave their heads and hearts behind in the cloakroom'. The production was built up over a year, with *Die Walküre* the next night, *Siegfried* on 27 March 1995 and *Götterdämmerung* on 14 October 1995; three complete cycles followed near the start of the 1996/7 Season.

What was unexpectedly innovative was to realize that this was the first Covent Garden *Ring* to be in the hands of a British production team – and this just over a century after the first cycle was first seen at Covent Garden. True, there had been previous British influence in the early stage management and in later directorial assistance – Leslie Hurry had been well aware of his status as the first British designer of a complete cycle. Similarly within the ranks of performers, by the 1990s some of the greatest Wagnerian exponents in the world were of British origin, a far cry from the German dominated castings of a century before. Yet looking back through the names of directors and designers – Comelli, Hartmann, Hotter, Friedrich, Schneider-Siemssen, Lyubimov – is to see how the cycle had still tended to have key non-native elements in the production teams at the Royal Opera House for a century.

Richard Jones came to the project with a reputation for presenting works in unexpected ways, certainly without a sense of reverence for past interpretations and even a relish at confounding convention. Expectation was heightened by a *Ring* at Scottish Opera started under his direction and with designs by Nigel Lowery, but cancelled after its first two instalments for company rather than production reasons. Talking to Peter Conrad in *The Observer* about his ideas as rehearsals got under way at the Royal Opera House, Richard Jones described what had drawn him to Wagner's cycle: 'The *Ring* asks you to pick a planet – any planet – and then tells you a story about it. At the end of the story, the planet dies. Wagner was a great theatrical imaginist, that is, when he wasn't being a stupid git and philosophising. It's the sorcery in the *Ring* that fascinates me.' The visceral compulsion of the irrational in the human psyche was to underlie the production, and found its outlet in what appeared a freewheeling set of associations and juxtapositions: hence the traffic sign, the bag, the beard and the car. Jones's concept, with designs by Lowery, was developed from the Theatre of the Absurd, 'a meaningless universe in which people can consistently reinvent themselves for the purposes of their plans'. After those early naturalistic Bayreuth-styled sets and costumes of the first 50 years of the cycle's life at Covent Garden, a century had seen the work evolve on stage into what was now 'a vision of the *Ring* rather than an explanation'.

Das Rheingold presented the first-night audience with three cavorting Rhinemaidens in grossly padded naked latex suits, reminiscent of Beryl Cook's buxom characters rather than any lithe and seductive sirens; dancers in blue jumpsuits provided a physical manifestation of the flow of the Rhine. Alberich – a wonderfully manic Ekkehard Wlaschiha – arrived to woo them wearing frogman's flippers and a trilby hat, and discovered – as his reward for renouncing love – Rhinegold in the form of a Cinderella-like golden slipper. John Tomlinson as Wotan found that his spear had transformed into a one-way traffic sign, while Gwynne Howell and Carsten Stabell as the giants were presented literally as one – joined together, only to rip bloodily apart from each other when they disagreed over Freia and the gold. As Freia, Rita Cullis was neurotically in a world of her own, constantly clutching a doll, and it was this, rather than her, that was covered in golden shoes when payment for the giants' work was required, while a big red chimney represented Valhalla (with an aeroplane flying overhead) and the gods were led off at the end chasing it now metamorphosed into a bright star, tantalizingly just out of reach. Robert Tear as Loge in a plain dark suit was effective as a sober and poised contrast to the colourful parade (in appearance and interpretation) of other characters. This was a world formed from the collision of fairytale and uncomfortable dream; it was a bold concatenation of resonant images that jumped from reference point to reference point at differing times in fun, grossness and poignancy. The vivid colour and disparate nature of costumes and sets from Lowery helped strengthen this dislocation from previous *Rings* – with an eye on a Mediterranean Arcadia rather than a northern seriousness – to present something fresh and provocative that, in Andrew Clements's words (for *The Guardian*) was 'a staging with such a loose weave, which seems to bowl blithely along by free-association and sheer intuitive stage-craft'. Christopher Wintle (for the *Times Literary Supplement*) considered that Jones had 'stripped the cycle of Götz Friedrich's sententiousness, and replaced it with wit, wonder and humanity'.

But the first-night reception also showed that an opposing view was equally – even virulently – held. For some, this was a fiasco of a production, a cluttered assortment of facile ideas thrown together without any regard to the work's grandeur and scale. Some reporters found their glee in quoting the disgust of overheard audience members ('I'd have walked out if we weren't so far from the aisle') and predictably for the time it became a cause for complaint about public subsidy being put to no good use, notably from Alexander Waugh (for the *Evening Standard*) who declared: 'There is no justification for receiving any public funding for a show that is unanimously booed by all those who pay so heavily to go and see it. Nor can anyone pretend that the audience's reaction to this production was in any way unexpected.'

It is at this point, however, that the story takes a different turn from the expected one. This time there could be no change of direction as there had been after Lyubimov's *Rheingold,* for the new *Die Walküre* had its premiere the following night. The second dose in such quick succession confirmed for a few their dislike of the approach, for some confirmed their initial appreciation, but also for a good number turned a tide of initial hostility into rewarding enjoyment. And it is to the credit of several critics that they were not only open to persuasion as the cycle progressed but prepared to voice their changing views. Waugh reported this time that 'the director who only 24 hours before had an enraged audience baying for his blood has deftly earned his stay of execution here'. By the time of the third opera, he opined that '*Siegfried* now changes everything. I wonder who now, having seen this brilliant new production, will still want to throw rotten eggs at *Rheingold.*' Edward Seckerson (for *The Independent*) expanded on the idea by describing how Mime begins to explain 'the truth' to Siegfried in Act I: 'he blows the dust off a mysterious box. Inside is another, and another, and another. All of them empty. I imagine that a large percentage of Monday's Covent Garden audience will have seized upon this moment as a metaphor for the entire production. But the reverse is surely proving to be true. As each new box is opened, as each new instalment of the Jones *Ring* is placed in context, its quirkiness becomes more logical, its symbols more accessible, its surprises more intense.'

The staging of *Götterdämmerung* in particular created images of intense seriousness, beginning with the Norns, desperate to avoid what they could see would happen, and frantically trying to stop the frontcloth from being raised, thus – by implication – staving off the inevitable by stopping the theatre work itself. One moment was widely singled out as of particular power. In Act II, Hagen roused his vassals (still in their pyjamas) to witness the arrival of Brünnhilde. She was paraded down the table before them, a paper bag over her head (placed there when Siegfried as Gunther captures her) and her humiliation complete. As a direct portrayal of degradation it not only gave the clearest of indications of her change from warrior maid to human chattel, but provided the strongest of motivations for her incitement of the final cataclysm, to bring the world down on all their heads, to right Wotan's wrongs in the world and the wrongs towards her.

Single scenes apart, the sum of the imagery of the whole cycle remained for some a comic ragbag that trivialized the depth of the drama. There were the naïve stickman drawings of Nigel Lowery, a fly crawling up the side of a chimney, Mime as a type of pantomime dame, wardrobes with Narnia-like pretensions, a dragon with a pumpkin head, tricks with a light bulb that illuminated with no apparent power source. To Hugh Canning, as the final opera was unveiled, Jones and Lowery did for the *Ring* 'what the Marx Brothers did for Verdi's *Il Trovatore* in *A Night at the Opera*'. Here, the sheer diversity of cultural references made it more of a quiz show: those who felt they got the answers right could be self-congratulatory in their approval, those who didn't were inevitably bemused, irritated or excluded. In sum, the main text of the drama was taken for granted, and the subtext had become the overt element to be played out. Whether radical reinterpretation or literal staging, it was the choice of an extreme stance to putting the *Ring* on stage that generated the risk of alienating a significant proportion of the audience. But maybe Wagner's *Ring* has in effect become a no-win work for directors: a balance between literal and symbolic can seem an indecisive compromise from either side of the spectrum, while a succession of provocative visions of the cycle has accustomed audiences to expect – even if not consciously so – some shock value or scandal so that the high drama of the work is seen reflected in the biography of the production as well as on stage.

What does not change is the expectation of the musical interpretation, in which respect this last of the completed Covent Garden *Rings* was also one of the most distinguished. Haitink was universally praised for a spacious and mature approach to the score, impressive for detail and narrative pacing. There was evident audience acclaim for him at the end of each performance, and in 1995 he, with the Orchestra of the Royal Opera House, was awarded a Laurence Olivier Award for *Siegfried* and *Götterdämmerung*. Of the singers, John Tomlinson (Wotan), Deborah Polaski (Brünnhilde), Graham Clark (Mime), Siegfried Jerusalem (as his namesake hero), Jane Henschel (Fricka) and Philip Langridge (Loge) were mentioned with particular appreciation. Yet this is really to single out the 'first among equals', for strong casting in all roles invited a plethora of complimentary adjectives across the board.

For an unusual string of distinguishing elements beyond the expected, the performance of *Die Walküre* on 25 October 1996 did better than most. Planned features of the evening had the orchestra stalls seats removed for what was a Midland Bank Promenade performance, while the evening was recorded by BBC Radio 3. Unplanned were the illness of Anne Evans (she sang Brünnhilde only for Act II), her replacement by Penelope Chalmers (for Act III), in turn her replacement as Gerhilde by Patricia Cameron and the sign falling off Wotan's lollipop-spear during the last act. Unfortunately Evans's illness continued, so Carla Pohl sang Brünnhilde for *Siegfried* three days later. A month or so after, Plácido Domingo celebrated his 25th anniversary of performing with The Royal Opera by making his British stage debut in a Wagnerian role, as Siegmund in a single special *Walküre* on 6 December. He sang opposite Karen Huffstodt as Sieglinde (a replacement again for Evans). Just over a century of *Der Ring des Nibelungen* was marked with the end of the Haitink-Jones-Lowery *Ring* at Covent Garden. The House closed in July 1997 for redevelopment and did not open again for two and a half years.

There is a short coda to this production's history, at least musically, with Haitink conducting The Royal Opera in cycles given in September – October 1998 – one each semi-staged at the Royal Albert Hall and at Symphony Hall, Birmingham. An important interpretational continuity was provided with most of the singers associated with the cycle from either its first singly staged operas (including Graham Clark, Rita Cullis, Anne Evans, Matthias Hölle, Siegfried Jerusalem, Robin Leggate, Ekkehard Wlaschiha, John Tomlinson and Vivian Tierney) or the 1996 complete cycles. As consequence, home-grown performances from the Royal Opera House of the whole cycle spanned a century: from 1898 to 1998. So much for that London critic's impression in 1892, quoted at the start of Chapter 1, that the *Ring* 'will ever become popular here is unlikely'. The *Ring* has indeed become popular here. But more than that; it has become a core work of Western culture, a knowledge of which is as much a prerequisite of the operatic canon as are Shakespeare in literature or Turner in art.

The understanding of any new production of such a cultural masterpiece takes time to establish itself – without the luxury of a few decades! It takes time to settle in, most especially when it has been constructed to display a strong and personal interpretational slant on the part of the director, such that some suspension of judgement is required until a sense of the whole can be grasped. The pattern of a disliked new production, an appreciated complete cycle and a warmly welcomed revival is evident right through this production story. And probably this is exactly right. Each new *Ring* has to be thought out in the context of the people who present it and the people who watch it – while the appeal of Wagner's operas is ongoing, a production is essentially of its time. 'Nobody who sees this wonderful and enthralling production can ever think of the *Ring* in the same way again', explained one critic and fan of the Jones-Lowery production. And this is what the whole century of Covent Garden *Ring* cycles demonstrates. Like the slowly acquired patina of fine furniture, each interpretation has extended and altered the way in which Wagner's seminal work is understood by each successive generation, and kept it a part of our living culture – and it would seem likely to continue so for some considerable time longer.

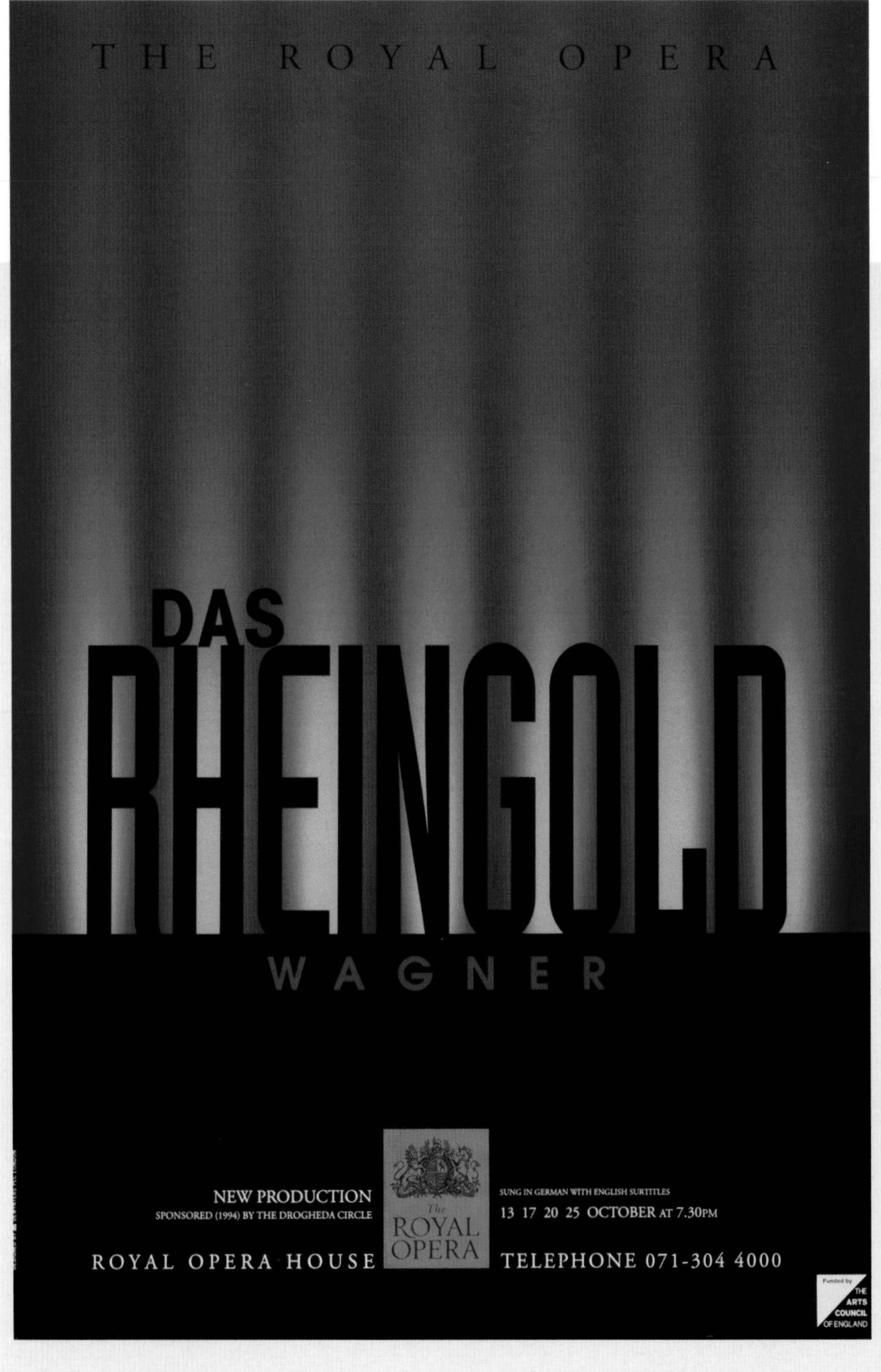

Posters for *Das Rheingold,* and *Die Walküre* (both 1994)

Original designs by Nigel Lowery for the frontcloths of *Siegfried,* Acts I and II.

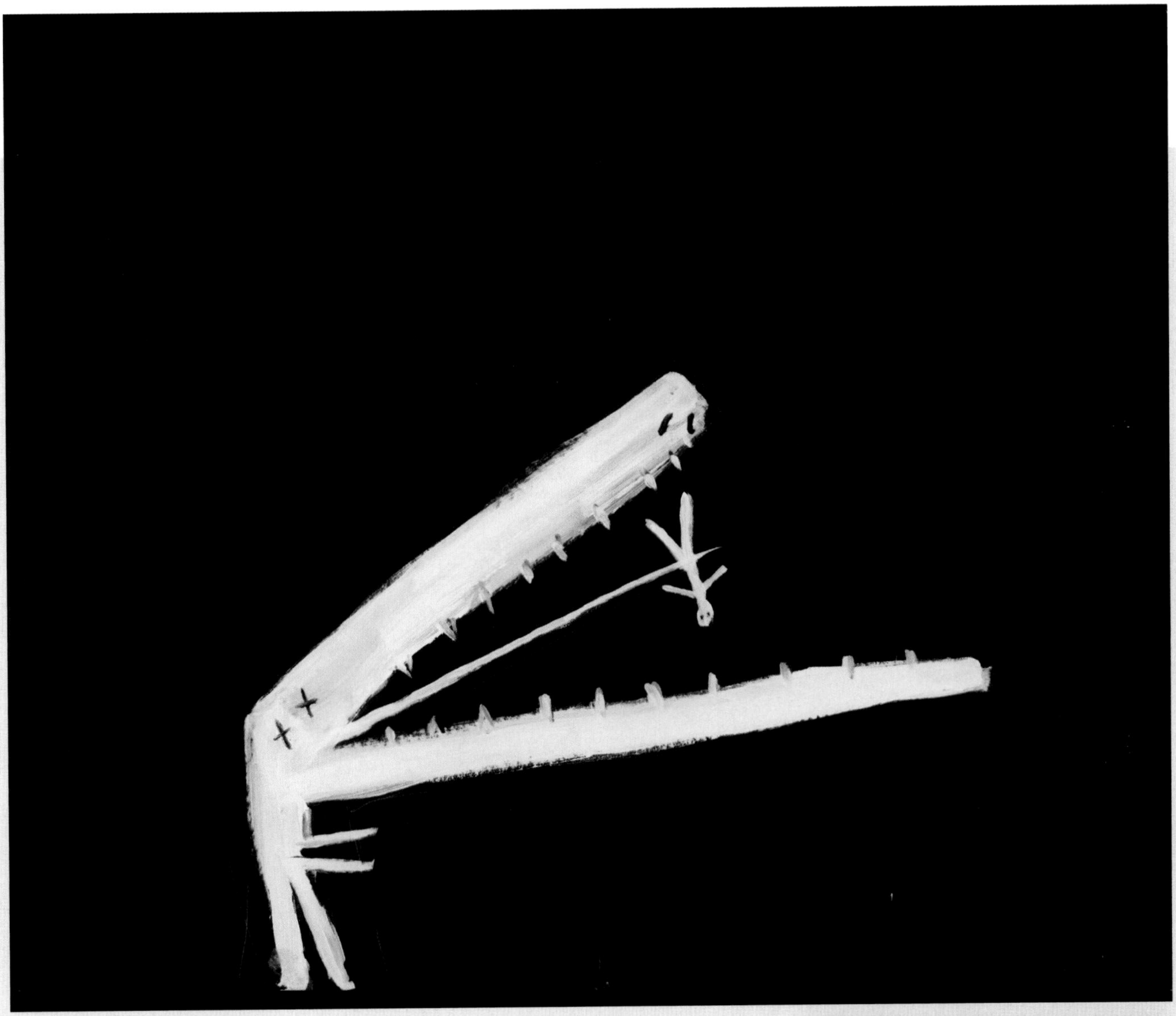

Das Rheingold (1996).
Ekkehard Wlaschiha as Alberich and Leah-Marian Jones as Flosshilde with her cavorting sisters behind her. The 'Beryl Cook' padded body suits designed by Nigel Lowery for the naked Rhinedaughters prompted a good deal of response, with their antics described as anything from 'an Andrews Sisters routine' to a re-creation of the Three Graces. Wlaschiha's Alberich, as Rodney Milnes described him, 'starts as a clown in tights and flippers, like Max Wall in one of his friskier moods, and ends as a wholly alienated, glittery-eyed monster'.

From left to right, Paul Charles Clarke as Froh, Gwynne Howell as Fasolt, John Tomlinson as Wotan and Carsten Stabell as Fafner (1994).

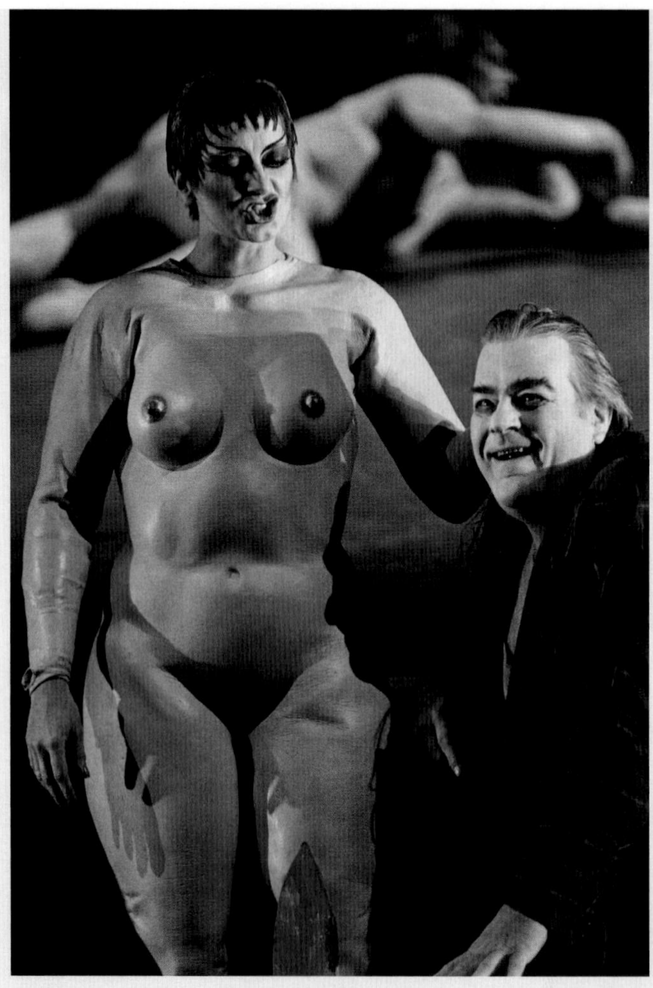

Robin Leggate (curled on the floor) as Mime in Nibelheim (1994).

Considering the giants' payment (1994). From left to right, Peter Sidhom (Donner), Robert Tear (Loge), Paul Charles Clarke (Froh), Gwynne Howell (Fasolt), Jane Henschel (Fricka), Carsten Stabell (Fafner), Rita Cullis (Freia) and John Tomlinson (Wotan). The mixture of characterizations and costumes caused the *Evening Standard* to report on 'Donner as a Keystone Cop with one hand in a boxing glove; Froh as a Club-Med barman; Wotan a surgeon; Fricka a Queen Victoria lookalike and Freia a twelve-inch plastic doll.'

The conjoined twin giants literally tear themselves apart as they argue over Freia (1994). Gwynne Howell as Fasolt (left) with Carsten Stabell as Fafner.

Die Walküre (1994).
Siegmund (Poul Elming) drawing Nothung from a figure with besoms for head and hands representing the World Ash Tree; opposite, the assembled Valkyries with Wotan (John Tomlinson).

Siegfried.
Acts I and II (1996): Siegfried Jerusalem as Siegfried (left) and Graham Clark as Mime; Graham Clark as Mime (behind) with John Tomlinson as the Traveller (the translated role name was used for this production); opposite, Act II, a fairytale pumpkin-headed 'dragon' from whom Siegfried does not learn fear.

Act III (1995): Brünnhilde (Anne Evans) and Siegfried (Siegfried Jerusalem).

Götterdämmerung.
Prologue (1996): Brünnhilde (Deborah Polaski) and Siegfried (Siegfried Jerusalem).

Act I (1996). From left to right, Siegfried Jerusalem as Siegfried, Alan Held as Gunther and Kurt Rydl as Hagen.

Act II (1995), with Brünnhilde (Deborah Polaski) paraded before Gunther (Alan Held) as Hagen (Kurt Rydl) looks on.

Brünnhilde (Deborah Polaski) brings about the end of the gods (1996).

APPENDIX I
PERFORMANCES AND CASTING

The appendices have been compiled primarily from programmes, change of cast slips and Duty Manager reports of the Royal Opera House; supplementary information has come from press reports, H. Rosenthal's *Two Centuries of Opera at Covent Garden* (1958) and J.P. Wearing's *The London Stage: a Calendar of Plays and Players* (1976–93). The listing of performances on the Royal Opera House stage is as complete as could be verified at the time of going to press.

Role abbreviations

ALB:	Alberich
BRH:	Brünnhilde
DON:	Donner
ED:	Erda
FAF:	Fafner
FAS:	Fasolt
FLH:	Flosshilde
FR:	Froh
FRE:	Freia
FRK:	Fricka
GEH:	Gerhilde
GRG:	Grimgerde
GTR:	Gutrune
GUN:	Gunther
HAG:	Hagen
HLW:	Helmwige
HUN:	Hunding
LG:	Loge
MM:	Mime
NN:	Norn(s) [roles unspecified]
NN1:	First Norn
NN2:	Second Norn
NN3:	Third Norn
OTL:	Ortlinde
RHD:	Rhinedaughter(s) [*aka* Rhinemaiden(s); roles unspecified]
RSW:	Rossweisse
SGF:	Siegfried
SGL:	Sieglinde
SGM:	Siegmund
SGR:	Siegrune
SWL:	Schwertleite
VLK:	Valkyrie(s) [roles unspecified]
WAN:	Wanderer [*aka* Traveller]
WDB:	Woodbird
WEL:	Wellgunde
WGL:	Woglinde
WLT:	Waltraute
WOT:	Wotan

All performances of ***Ring*** operas at the Royal Opera House are included; unless otherwise stated, performances were sung in German; new production details are given at their first occurrence only; minor name variants have been standardized on their most familiar forms.

Opera (date/dates): **Character abbreviation**: performer, (date) alternate performer**.** [supplementary information]

NP	New production
Name, (date) Name	Alternate performers, date(s) given
Name/(date) Name	Alternate performers in series, date(s) unconfirmed
?	Unconfirmed/unknown name
[Xxx]	Unknown forename; title as billed

1892

Conductor: Gustav Mahler; Director: Friedrich Heinrich Lissmann
Siegfried (8 June). **ALB:** Mathieu Lorent; **BRH:** Rosa Sucher; **ED:** Ernestine Schumann-Heink; **FAF:** Heinrich Wiegand; **MM:** Julius Lieban; **SGF:** Max Alvary; **WAN:** Karl Grengg; **WDB:** Sophie Traubmann

ONE CYCLE
Conductor: Gustav Mahler; Director: Friedrich Heinrich Lissmann
Das Rheingold (22 June). **ALB:** Friedrich Heinrich Lissmann; **DON:** Zoltan Dome; **ED:** Mathilde Fröhlich; **FAF:** Ferdinand Litter; **FAS:** Heinrich Wiegand; **FLH:** Ernestine Schumann-Heink; **FR:** Hugo Simon; **FRE:** Kathi Bettaque; **FRK:** Pelagie Ende-Andriessen; **LG:** Max Alvary; **MM:** Julius Lieban; **WEL:** Paula Ralph; **WGL:** Sophie Traubmann; **WOT:** Karl Grengg
Die Walküre (29 June). **BRH:** Pelagie Ende-Andriessen; **FRK:** Ernestine Schumann-Heink; **GEH:** Sophie Kollar; **GRG:** ? Simon; **HUN:** Heinrich Wiegand; **HLW:** Sophie Traubmann; **OTL:** Paula Ralph; **RSW:** ? Upleger; **SWL:** Louise Meisslinger; **SGL:** Kathi Bettaque; **SGM:** Max Alvary; **SGR:** Ernestine Schumann-Heink; **WLT:** Mathilde Fröhlich; **WOT:** Theodor Reichmann
Siegfried (6 July): **ALB:** Friedrich Heinrich Lissmann; **BRH:** Katharina Klafsky; **ED:** Ernestine Schumann-Heink; **FAF:** Heinrich Wiegand; **MM:** Julius Lieban; **SGF:** Max Alvary; **WAN:** Theodor Reichmann; **WDB:** Sophie Traubmann
Götterdämmerung (13 July): **ALB:** Friedrich Heinrich Lissmann; **BRH:** Katharina Klafsky; **FLH:** Mathilde Fröhlich; **GTR:** Kathi Bettaque; **GUN:** August Knapp; **HAG:** Heinrich Wiegand; **SGF:** Max Alvary; **WEL:** Paula Ralph; **WGL:** Sophie Traubmann; **WLT:** Ernestine Schumann-Heink. [Norns scene omitted]

1893

Conductor: Emil Steinbach
Die Walküre (5 July). **BRH:** Fanny Moran-Olden; **FRK:** Louise Meisslinger; **GEH:** Carla Dagmar; **GRG:** Luranah Aldridge; **HLW:** [Fräulein] Gherlsen; **HUN:** David Bispham; **OTL:** Mathilde Bauermeister; **RSW:** [Mlle] Wilmor; **SGL:** Luise Reuss-Belce; **SGM:** Max Alvary; **SGR:** Marie Brema; **SWL:** Louise Meisslinger; **WLT:** Cecile Brani; **WOT:** Heinrich Wiegand
Siegfried (19 July). **ALB:** David Bispham; **BRH:** Fanny Moran-Olden; **ED:** Rosa Olitzka; **FAF:** [Herr] Waldmann; **MM:** Julius Lieban; **SGF:** Max Alvary; **WAN:** Heinrich Wiegand; **WDB:** [Fräulein] Gherlsen;

1895

Conductor: George Henschel; Director: E.C. Hedmont
Language: English (translation by H. and F. Corder)
The Valkyrie (16, 21, 24, 26 October, 2, 9 November). **BRH:** Lillian Tree; **FRK:** Rosa Olitzka/I. Recoschwitz; **HUN:** Alex Bevan; **SGL:** Susan Strong; **SGM:** E.C. Hedmont, (9) Edwin Wareham; **VLK:** Ella Russell, Clarice Sinico, Mary Gray, [Mme] Trefelyn, Kate? Lee, Clare? Addison, Isa? McCusker, Rosa Olitzka; **WOT:** David Bispham

1896

Conductor: Luigi Mancinelli.
Language: French
Die Walküre (13, 19 June). **BRH:** Eugenia Mantelli; **FRK:** Fernanda Brazzi; **GEH:** Clare? Addison; **GRG:** ?; **HLW:** Ella Russell; **HUN:** Armand Castelmary; **OTL:** Mathilde Bauermeister; **RSW:** Cecile Brani; **SGL:** Lola Beeth; **SGM:** Albert Alvarez; **SGR:** Louise Kirkby Lunn; **SWL:** Rosa Olitzka; **WLT:** Louise Meisslinger; **WOT:** Henri Albers

1897

Conductor: Anton Seidl
Die Walküre (12, 16, 24 June). **BRH:** Marie Brema, (24) Ada Adiny; **FRK:** Ernestine Schumann-Heink; **GEH:** Maud Roudez; **GRG:** [Miss] Bartlett; **HUN:** Lemprière Pringle; **HLW:** Regina de Sales, (24) [Frau] Lieban; **OTL:** Mathilde Bauermeister; **RSW:** Jane de Vigne; **SWL:** Louise Meisslinger; **SGL:** Susan Strong; **SGM:** Ernest Van Dyck, (24) Andreas Dippel; **SGR:** Frances McCulloch; **WLT:** Ernestine Schumann-Heink; **WOT:** David Bispham
Siegfried (21, 26 June, 12, 23 July). **ALB:** David Bispham; **BRH:** Susan Strong, (26, 12, 23) Sophie Sedlmair; **ED:** Ernestine Schumann-Heink, (12, 23) Louise Meisslinger; **FAF:** Ludovico Viviani; **MM:** Julius Lieban; **SGF:** Jean de Reszke; **WAN:** Edouard de Reszke; **WDB:** Frances Saville, (12, 23) Marie Engle

1898

Conductor: Herman Zumpe
Die Walküre (11, 23 May). **BRH:** Marie Brema; **FRK:** Louise Meisslinger; **GEH:** Maud Roudez; **GRG:** [Miss] Bartlett; **HLW:** Regina de Sales; **HUN:** Lemprière Pringle; **OTL:** Mathilde Bauermeister; **RSW:** Agnes Janson; **SGL:** [Frau] Czuick; **SGM:** Franz Costa; **SGR:** Frances McCulloch; **SWL:** Luranah Aldridge; **WLT:** Louise Meisslinger; **WOT:** Anton van Rooy

Conductor: Felix Mottl
THREE CYCLES
Das Rheingold (6, 14, 27 June). **ALB:** Karl Nebe; **DON:** Hector Dufranne, (14, 27) Rudolf von Milde; **ED:** Ernestine Schumann-Heink; **FAF:** Mathieu Lorent, (14, 27) Lemprière Pringle; **FAS:** Rudolf Wittekopf; **FLH:** Ernestine Schumann-Heink; **FR:** Andreas Dippel; **FRE:** Marion Weed; **FRK:** Marie Brema; **LG:** Ernest Van Dyck; **MM:** Hans Breuer; **WEL:** Helene Hieser; **WGL:** Josefine von Artner; **WOT:** Anton van Rooy
Die Walküre (8, 17, 28 June). **BRH:** Marie Brema, (28) Milka Ternina; **FRK:** Ernestine Schumann-Heink; **GEH:** Josefine von Artner; **GRG:** Marion Weed; **HLW:** Regina de Sales, (24) [Frau] Lieban; **HUN:** Rudolf Wittekopf; **OTL:** Mathilde Bauermeister; **RSW:** Agnes Janson; **SGL:** Emma Eames, (17) Milka Ternina; **SGM:** Ernest Van Dyck; **SGR:** Helene Hieser; **SWL:** Louise Meisslinger; **WLT:** Ernestine Schumann-Heink; **WOT:** Anton van Rooy

Siegfried (9, 21, 30 June): **ALB:** Karl Nebe; **BRH:** Lillian Nordica; **ED:** Ernestine Schumann-Heink; **FAF:** Rudolf Wittekopf; **MM:** Hans Breuer; **SGF:** Jean de Reszke, (30) Andreas Dippel; **WAN:** Edouard de Reszke, (21, 30) Anton van Rooy; **WDB:** Josefine von Artner, (21) [Mlle] Christmann
Götterdämmerung (11 June, 2, 4 July). **ALB:** Karl Nebe; **BRH:** Lillian Nordica, (2) Milka Ternina; **FLH:** Ernestine Schumann-Heink, (4) Louise Meisslinger; **GTR:** Frances Saville, (4) [unsung]; **GUN:** Rudolf von Milde; **HAG:** Edouard de Reszke; **NN:** Josefine von Artner, Louise Meisslinger, Ernestine Schumann-Heink; **SGF:** Andreas Dippel, (2, 4) Jean de Reszke; **WEL:** Helene Hieser; **WGL:** Josefine von Artner; **WLT:** Ernestine Schumann-Heink. [11 June: Dippel replaced the indisposed Jean de Reszke as Siegfried. 4 July: Frances Saville indisposed and Gutrune was unsung. Advertised performance of 24 June cancelled as both Brünnhildes were indisposed; rescheduled to 5 July then changed to 4 July.]

1899
Conductor: Karl Muck
Die Walküre (18, 24 May, 6, 29 June). **BRH:** Félia Litvinne/Lillian Nordica/(29) Marie Brema; **FRK:** Ernestine Schumann-Heink/(29) Rosa Olitzka; **GEH:** Maud Roudez; **GRG:** ? Moika-Kellogg/(29) [Miss] Bartlett; **HLW:** Louise Sobrino; **HUN:** Lemprière Pringle; **OTL:** Mathilde Bauermeister; **RSW:** Maria Altona; **SGL:** (29) Johanna Gadski/Susan Strong/Lilli Lehmann; **SGM:** Ernest Van Dyck; **SGR:** Frances McCulloch; **SWL:** Ernestine Schumann-Heink/Rosa Olitzka/(29) Louise Homer; **WLT:** Ernestine Schumann-Heink/(29) Rosa Olitzka; **WOT:** Anton van Rooy/(29) David Bispham

1900
Conductor: Felix Mottl
Die Walküre (23 June). **BRH:** Milka Ternina; **FRK:** Rosa Olitzka; **GEH:** Louise Sobrino; **GRG:** Marie Delmar; **HLW:** Aurelie Révy; **HUN:** Victor Klopfer; **OTL:** Mathilde Bauermeister; **RSW:** Edyth Walker; **SGL:** Johanna Gadski; **SGM:** Ernst Kraus; **SGR:** Helene Hieser; **SWL:** Louise Homer; **WLT:** Rosa Olitzka; **WOT:** Anton van Rooy
Siegfried (2 July). **ALB:** Fritz Friedrichs; **BRH:** Ellen Gulbranson; **ED:** Edyth Walker; **FAF:** Victor Klopfer; **MM:** Hans Breuer; **SGF:** Ernst Kraus; **WAN:** Anton van Rooy; **WDB:** Fritzi Scheff

TWO CYCLES
Conductor: Felix Mottl
Das Rheingold (5, 25 June). **ALB:** Fritz Friedrichs; **DON:** Adolph Mühlmann; **ED:** Ernestine Schumann-Heink, (25) Edyth Walker; **FAF:** Lemprière Pringle; **FAS:** Robert Blass, (25) Victor Klopfer; **FLH:** Ernestine Schumann-Heink, (25) Rosa Olitzka; **FR:** Leo Slezak; **FRE:** Susan Strong; **FRK:** Luise Reuss-Belce; **LG:** Otto Briesemeister; **MM:** Hans Breuer; **WEL:** Helene Hieser; **WGL:** Louise Sobrino; **WOT:** Anton van Rooy
Die Walküre (6, 26 June). **BRH:** Milka Ternina, (26) Ellen Gulbranson; **FRK:** Ernestine Schumann-Heink, (26) Edyth Walker; **GEH:** Louise Sobrino; **GRG:** Marie Delmar; **HLW:** Aurelie Révy; **HUN:** Robert Blass, (26) Victor Klopfer; **OTL:** Mathilde Bauermeister, (26) [Mme] Cortesi; **RSW:** Edyth Walker; **SGL:** Johanna Gadski, (26) Milka Ternina; **SGM:** Ernst Kraus; **SGR:** Helene Hieser; **SWL:** Louise Homer; **WLT:** Ernestine Schumann-Heink, (26) Rosa Olitzka; **WOT:** Anton van Rooy

Siegfried (7, 27 June). **ALB:** Fritz Friedrichs; **BRH:** Milka Ternina, (27) Ellen Gulbranson; **ED:** Ernestine Schumann-Heink, (27) Edyth Walker; **FAF:** Robert Blass, (27) Victor Klopfer; **MM:** Hans Breuer; **SGF:** Andreas Dippel, (27) Leo Slezak; **WAN:** Anton van Rooy, (27) Theodor Bertram; **WDB:** Fritzi Scheff
Götterdämmerung (9, 29 June). **ALB:** Fritz Friedrichs; **BRH:** Milka Ternina, (29) Ellen Gulbranson; **FLH:** Rosa Olitzka; **GTR:** Luise Reuss-Belce; **GUN:** Adolph Mühlmann; **HAG:** Robert Blass; **NN:** Louise Sobrino, Rosa Olitzka, Ernestine Schumann-Heink; **SGF:** Ernst Kraus; **WEL:** Helene Hieser; **WGL:** Louise Sobrino; **WLT:** Ernestine Schumann-Heink, (29) Edyth Walker

1901
Conductor: Otto Lohse
Siegfried (23 May, 1 June). **ALB:** David Bispham; **BRH:** Wilhelmine Frankel Claus, (1) Milka Ternina; **ED:** Rosa Olitzka; **FAF:** Robert Blass; **MM:** Albert Reiss; **SGF:** Heinrich Knote; **WAN:** Hans Mohwinkel, (1) Anton van Rooy; **WDB:** Louise Sobrino. [Due to the illness of Ernest Van Dyck (Tristan), the performance of *Tristan und Isolde* scheduled for 1 June was replaced with *Siegfried*]

1902
Conductor: Otto Lohse
Die Walküre (15 May, 7 June). **BRH:** Lillian Nordica, (7) Marie Brema; **FRK:** Louise Kirkby Lunn, (7) Olive Fremstad; **GEH:** Louise Sobrino; **GRG:** Marie Delmar; **HLW:** Maria Altona; **HUN:** Robert Blass, (7) Victor Klopfer; **OTL:** Mathilde Bauermeister; **RSW:** Christine Helian; **SGL:** Magda Lohse; **SGM:** Aloys Pennarini, (7) Ernst Kraus; **SGR:** Frances McCulloch; **SWL:** [Miss] Turner; **WLT:** Louise Kirkby Lunn, (7) Olive Fremstad; **WOT:** Anton van Rooy
Siegfried (21, 26 May, 2 June). **ALB:** David Bispham; **BRH:** Lillian Nordica, (26, 2) Paula Doenges; **ED:** Ottilie Metzger; **FAF:** Robert Blass; **MM:** Albert Reiss; **SGF:** Aloys Pennarini; **WAN:** Anton van Rooy; **WDB:** Louise Sobrino

Conductor: Richard Eckhold.
Language: English
Siegfried (18 September): **ALB:** William Dever; **BRH:** Fanny Moody; **ED:** Lily Moody; **FAF:** Charles Manners; **MM:** Payne Clarke; **SGF:** Philip Brozel; **WAN:** Charles Magrath; **WDB:** Alice Boaden. [The programme misspelt 'Erda' as 'Freda']

1903
THREE CYCLES
Conductor: Hans Richter. Sets [partially new]: Harry Brooke/Bruce Smith/W. Telbin/Hawes Craven. Costumes: Attilio Comelli
Das Rheingold (27 April, 5, 11 May). **ALB:** Marcel Krasa; **DON:** Hans Mohwinkel; **ED:** Louise Kirkby Lunn; **FAF:** Victor Klopfer, (11) Robert Blass; **FAS:** Edgar Oberstetter; **FLH:** Marie Hertzer-Deppe; **FR:** Josef Lewandowski; **FRE:** Marie Zimmermann; **FRK:** Olive Fremstad; **LG:** Ernest Van Dyck; **MM:** Julius Lieban, (5, 11) Albert Reiss; **WEL:** Marie Knüpfer-Egli; **WGL:** Emilie Feuge-Gleiss; **WOT:** Theodor Bertram, (5) Edmund Müller, (11) Anton van Rooy
Die Walküre (29 April, 6, 12 May). **BRH:** Martha Leffler-Burkhardt, (6, 12) Milka Ternina; **FRK:** Olive Fremstad; **GEH:** Louise Sobrino; **GRG:** Louise Meisslinger; **HLW:** Emilie Feuge-Gleiss; **HUN:** Victor Klopfer, (12) Robert Blass; **OTL:** Mathilde Bauermeister, (6) Marie Knüpfer-Egli; **RSW:** Agnes Janson; **SGL:** Marie Knüpfer-Egli, (6) Adelaida Bolska; **SGM:** Ernest Van Dyck; **SGR:** Frances McCulloch; **SWL:** Marie Hertzer-Deppe; **WLT:** Louise Kirkby Lunn; **WOT:** Theodor Bertram, (6, 12) Anton van Rooy
Siegfried (30 April, 7, 15 May). **ALB:** Marcel Krasa; **BRH:** Martha Leffler-Burkhardt, (7) Milka Ternina, (15) Josephine Reinl; **ED:** Louise Kirkby Lunn; **FAF:** Victor Klopfer, (15) Robert Blass; **MM:** Julius Lieban, (7, 15) Albert Reiss; **SGF:** Ernst Kraus, (15) Georges Anthes; **WAN:** Theodor Bertram, (7, 15) Anton van Rooy; **WDB:** Emilie Feuge-Gleiss
Götterdämmerung (2, 9, 16 May). **ALB:** Marcel Krasa; **BRH:** Martha Leffler-Burkhardt, (9, 16) Milka Ternina; **FLH:** Marie Hertzer-Deppe; **GTR:** Marie Zimmermann, (16) Marie Knüpfer-Egli; **GUN:** Anton van Rooy, (9, 16) Edmund Müller; **HAG:** Theodor Bertram, (9, 16) Edgar Oberstetter; **NN:** Marie Hertzer-Deppe, Marie Knüpfer-Egli, Emilie Feuge-Gleiss; **SGF:** Ernst Kraus; **WEL:** Marie Knüpfer-Egli; **WGL:** Emilie Feuge-Gleiss; **WLT:** Louise Kirkby Lunn

Conductor: Otto Lohse
Die Walküre (22 May). **BRH:** Milka Ternina; **FRK:** Olive Fremstad; **GEH:** Louise Sobrino; **GRG:** Louise Meisslinger; **HLW:** Emilie Feuge-Gleiss; **HUN:** Victor Klopfer; **OTL:** Mathilde Bauermeister; **RSW:** Agnes Janson; **SGL:** Marie Knüpfer-Egli; **SGM:** Ernst Kraus; **SGR:** Frances McCulloch; **SWL:** Marie Hertzer-Deppe; **WLT:** Olive Fremstad; **WOT:** Anton van Rooy [indisposed during performance], Hans Mohwinkel

Conductor: Richard Eckhold
Language: English
Siegfried (8 September): **ALB:** William Dever; **BRH:** Fanny Moody; **ED:** Teify Davies; **FAF:** Frederick Clendon; **MM:** Payne Clarke; **SGF:** Louis Arens; **WAN:** Charles Magrath; **WDB:** Florence Easton. [The programme misspelt 'Erda' as 'Freda' again]

1905
TWO CYCLES
Conductor: Hans Richter
Das Rheingold (1, 10 May). **ALB:** Desider Zador; **DON:** Walter Soomer; **ED:** Louise Kirkby Lunn; **FAF:** Wilhelm Raboth; **FAS:** Allen Hinckley; **FLH:** Harriet Behnne; **FR:** Karl Wildbrunn; **FRE:** Marie Knüpfer-Egli; **FRK:** Josephine Reinl; **LG:** Carl Burrian; **MM:** Albert Reiss; **WEL:** Bella Alten; **WGL:** Hermine Bosetti; **WOT:** Clarence Whitehill, (10) Anton van Rooy
Die Walküre (2, 12 May). **BRH:** Marie Wittich, (12) Félia Litvinne; **FRK:** Josephine Reinl; **GEH:** Louise Sobrino; **GRG:** Luranah Aldridge; **HLW:** Agnes Nicholls; **HUN:** Allen Hinckley; **OTL:** Suzanne Metcalf; **RSW:** Winifred Ludlam; **SGL:** Katharina Fleischer-Edel, (12) Marie Wittich; **SGM:** Carl Burrian; **SGR:** Edna Thornton; **SWL:** Harriet Behnne; **WLT:** Louise Kirkby Lunn; **WOT:** Clarence Whitehill
Siegfried (4, 13 May). **ALB:** Desider Zador; **BRH:** Marie Wittich, (13) Félia Litvinne; **ED:** Louise Kirkby Lunn; **FAF:** Allen Hinckley; **MM:** Albert Reiss; **SGF:** Ernst Kraus; **WAN:** Clarence Whitehill, (13) Anton van Rooy; **WDB:** Hermine Bosetti
Götterdämmerung (6, 15 May). **ALB:** Desider Zador; **BRH:** Marie Wittich, (15) Félia Litvinne; **FLH:** Harriet Behnne; **GTR:** Marie Knüpfer-Egli; **GUN:** Clarence Whitehill; **HAG:** Allen Hinckley; **NN:** Edna Thornton, Marie Knüpfer-Egli, Agnes Nicholls; **SGF:** Ernst Kraus; **WEL:** Bella Alten; **WGL:** Agnes Nicholls; **WLT:** Louise Kirkby Lunn

1906

TWO CYCLES
Conductor: Hans Richter
Das Rheingold (4, 12 May). **ALB:** Desider Zador; **DON:** George Hüpeden, (12) Francis Braun; **ED:** Louise Kirkby Lunn; **FAF:** Wilhelm Raboth; **FAS:** Paul Knüpfer; **FLH:** Marie Grimm; **FR:** Hanns Nietan; **FRE:** Marie Knüpfer-Egli; **FRK:** Josephine Reinl; **LG:** Karl Jörn; **MM:** Julius Lieban; **WEL:** Marga Burchardt; **WGL:** Agnes Nicholls; **WOT:** Carl Braun, (12) Anton van Rooy. [4 May: Braun replaced the indisposed Clarence Whitehill]
Die Walküre (5, 14 May). **BRH:** Josephine Reinl, (14) Milka Ternina; **FRK:** Marie Grimm, (14) Josephine Reinl; **GEH:** Marga Burchardt; **GRG:** Edith Clegg; **HLW:** Agnes Nicholls; **HUN:** Paul Knüpfer; **OTL:** Cicely Gleeson-White; **RSW:** Winifred Ludlam; **SGL:** Marie Knüpfer-Egli, (14) Marie Wittich; **SGM:** Ernst Konrad; **SGR:** Edna Thornton; **SWL:** [Frl.] Wenner, (14) Marie Grimm; **WLT:** Alice Renard; **WOT:** Clarence Whitehill, (14) Anton van Rooy. [5 May: Reinl replaced the indisposed Wittich]
Siegfried (7, 16 May). **ALB:** Desider Zador; **BRH:** Marie Wittich, (16) Johanna Gadski; **ED:** Marie Grimm, (16) Louise Kirkby Lunn; **FAF:** Wilhelm Raboth; **MM:** Julius Lieban; **SGF:** Ernst Konrad, (16) Georges Anthes; **WAN:** Clarence Whitehill, (16) Anton van Rooy; **WDB:** Agnes Nicholls
Götterdämmerung (9, 18 May). **ALB:** Desider Zador; **BRH:** Marie Wittich, (18) Johanna Gadski; **FLH:** Marie Grimm; **GTR:** Marga Burchardt; **GUN:** Clarence Whitehill; **HAG:** Wilhelm Raboth; **NN1:** Marie Grimm; **NN2:** Marie Knüpfer-Egli; **NN3:** Agnes Nicholls; **SGF:** Anton Bürger, (18) Ernst Konrad; **WEL:** Marie Knüpfer-Egli; **WGL:** Agnes Nicholls; **WLT:** Louise Kirkby Lunn. [9 May: Konrad replaced the indisposed Bürger at very short notice]

Conductor: Hans Richter
Die Walküre (22 May). **BRH:** Johanna Gadski; **FRK:** Josephine Reinl; **GEH:** Marga Burchardt; **GRG:** Edith Clegg; **HLW:** Agnes Nicholls; **HUN:** Paul Knüpfer; **OTL:** Ciceley Gleeson-White; **RSW:** Winifred Ludlam; **SGL:** Milka Ternina; **SGM:** Georges Anthes; **SGR:** Edna Thornton; **SWL:** Marie Grimm; **WLT:** Alice Renard; **WOT:** Anton van Rooy

1907

Conductor: Franz Schalk
Die Walküre (22, 26 January, 1, 6 February). **BRH:** Félia Litvinne; **FRK:** Rosa Olitzka, (26, 6) Marie Brema; **GEH:** Pauline Cramer; **GRG:** Emmie Tatham; **HLW:** Agnes Nicholls, (6) Muriel Gough; **HUN:** Allen Hinckley, (6) David Bispham; **OTL:** Madeleine Friedheim; **RSW:** Winifred Ludlam; **SGL:** Ada von Westhoven, (26, 1) Ida Hiedler, (6) Agnes Nicholls; **SGM:** Ernst Kraus, (1, 6) Ernest Van Dyck; **SGR:** Mary Gray, (26) [Fräulein] von Bibow; **SWL:** Constance Webb Ware; **WLT:** Rosa Olitzka, (6) Adrienne von Kraus-Osborne; **WOT:** Fritz Feinhals, (26, 6) Theodor Bertram

TWO CYCLES
Conductor: Hans Richter
Das Rheingold (30 April, 8 May). **ALB:** Desider Zador; **DON:** [Herr] Stockhausen; **ED:** Edna Thornton; **FAF:** Wilhelm Raboth; **FAS:** Paul Knüpfer; **FLH:** Cilla Tolli; **FR:** Hanns Nietan; FRE: Marie Knüpfer-Egli; **FRK:** Louise Kirkby Lunn; **LG:** Karl Jörn; **MM:** Hans Bechstein; **WEL:** Erna Fiebiger; **WGL:** Agnes Nicholls; **WOT:** Clarence Whitehill, (8) Anton van Rooy
Die Walküre (1, 9 May). **BRH:** Ellen Gulbranson; **FRK:** Louise Kirkby Lunn; **GEH:** Erna Fiebiger; **GRG:** G. Lonsdale; **HLW:** Agnes Nicholls; **HUN:** Paul Knüpfer; **OTL:** Cicely Gleeson-White; **RSW:** Maud Santley; **SGL:** Katharina Fleischer-Edel; **SGM:** Ernst Kraus, (9) Peter Cornelius; **SGR:** Edna Thornton; **SWL:** Cilla Tolli; **WLT:** Louise Kirkby Lunn; **WOT:** Clarence Whitehill, (9) Anton van Rooy
Siegfried (3, 11 May): **ALB:** Desider Zador; **BRH:** Ellen Gulbranson; **ED:** Louise Kirkby Lunn; **FAF:** Wilhelm Raboth; **MM:** Hans Bechstein; **SGF:** Ernst Kraus; **WAN:** Clarence Whitehill, (11) Anton van Rooy; **WDB:** Agnes Nicholls
Götterdämmerung (6, 14 May). **ALB:** Desider Zador; **BRH:** Ellen Gulbranson; **FLH:** Cilla Tolli; **GTR:** Marie Knüpfer-Egli; **GUN:** [Herr] Stockhausen; **HAG:** Wilhelm Raboth; **NN1:** Cilla Tolli; **NN2:** Cicely Gleeson-White; **NN3:** Agnes Nicholls; **SGF:** Ernst Kraus; **WEL:** Erna Fiebiger; **WGL:** Agnes Nicholls; **WLT:** Louise Kirkby Lunn

Conductor: Hans Richter
Die Walküre (18 May). **BRH:** Ellen Gulbranson; **FRK:** Louise Kirkby Lunn; **GEH:** Erna Fiebiger; **GRG:** G. Lonsdale; **HLW:** Agnes Nicholls; **HUN:** Paul Knüpfer; **OTL:** Cicely Gleeson-White; **RSW:** Maud Santley; **SGL:** Katharina Fleischer-Edel; **SGM:** Peter Cornelius; **SGR:** Edna Thornton; **SWL:** Cilla Tolli; **WLT:** Louise Kirkby Lunn; **WOT:** Anton van Rooy

1908

TWO CYCLES
Conductor: Hans Richter. Producer: E.C. Hedmont (Assistant: H.G. Moore). Costumes: Attilio Comelli
Language: English
The Rhinegold (27 January, 3 February). **ALB:** Thomas Meux; **DON:** Charles Knowles; **ED:** Edna Thornton; **FAF:** Francis Harford; **FAS:** Robert Radford; **FLH:** Edna Thornton; **FR:** Walter Hyde; **FRE:** Christine d'Almayne; **FRK:** Borghild Bryhn-Langaard; **LG:** E.C. Hedmont; MM: Hans Bechstein; **WEL:** Caroline Hatchard; **WGL:** Leonora Sparkes; **WOT:** Clarence Whitehill. [Francis Archambault originally advertised as Donner]
The Valkyrie (28 January, 4 February). **BRH:** Borghild Bryhn-Langaard; **FRK:** Maud Santley, (4) Lily Crawforth; **GEH:** Caroline Hatchard; **GRG:** Phyllis Archibald; **HLW:** Leonora Sparkes; **HUN:** Robert Radford; **OTL:** Jenny Taggart; **RSW:** Dilys Jones; **SGL:** Agnes Nicholls; **SGM:** Walter Hyde; **SGR:** Edna Thornton; **SWL:** Maria Yelland; **WLT:** Maud Santley, (4) Alice Renard; **WOT:** Clarence Whitehill. [4 February, Crawforth and Renard replaced an indisposed Santley]
Siegfried (30 January, 6 February). **ALB:** Thomas Meux; **BRH:** Agnes Nicholls, (6) Perceval Allen; **ED:** Edna Thornton; **FAF:** Francis Harford; **MM:** Hans Bechstein; **SGF:** Peter Cornelius; **WAN:** Clarence Whitehill; **WDB:** Caroline Hatchard
The Twilight of the Gods (1, 8 February). **ALB:** Thomas Meux; **BRH:** Perceval Allen; **FLH:** Edna Thornton; **GTR:** Edith Evans; **GUN:** Frederic Austin; **HAG:** Charles Knowles; **NN1:** Edna Thornton; **NN2:** Caroline Hatchard; **NN3:** Leonora Sparkes; **SGF:** Peter Cornelius; **WEL:** Caroline Hatchard; **WGL:** Leonora Sparkes; **WLT:** [scene omitted], (8) Edna Thornton. [Francis Archambault originally advertised as Gunter; 1 February, Waltraute scene omitted when Maud Santley was suddenly taken ill]

Conductor: Hans Richter
Die Walküre (1, 9 May, 4 June). **BRH:** Ellen Gulbranson, (4) Edyth Walker; **FRK:** Louise Kirkby Lunn; **GEH:** Caroline Hatchard; **GRG:** Phyllis Archibald; **HLW:** Leonora Sparkes; **HUN:** Paul Knüpfer, (4) Karl Mang; **OTL:** Marie Knüpfer-Egli; **RSW:** Dilys Jones; **SGL:** Cäcilie Rüsche-Endorf, (4) Agnes Nicholls; **SGM:** Peter Cornelius; **SGR:** Edna Thornton; **SWL:** Florence Wickham; **WLT:** Louise Kirkby Lunn; **WOT:** Anton van Rooy
Götterdämmerung (5, 13 May). **ALB:** Desider Zador; **BRH:** Ellen Gulbranson; **FLH:** Florence Wickham, (13) Edna Thornton; **GTR:** Marie Knüpfer-Egli; **GUN:** Clarence Whitehill; HAG: Karl Mang; **NN1:** Florence Wickham, (13) Edna Thornton; **NN2:** Caroline Hatchard; **NN3:** Leonora Sparkes; **SGF:** Peter Cornelius; **WEL:** Caroline Hatchard; **WGL:** Leonora Sparkes; **WLT:** Louise Kirkby Lunn

1909

THREE CYCLES
Conductor: Hans Richter
Language: English
The Rhinegold (16, 26 January, 4 February). **ALB:** Thomas Meux; **DON:** Charles Knowles; **ED:** Edna Thornton; **FAF:** Francis Harford; **FAS:** Robert Radford; **FLH:** Edna Thornton; **FR:** Maurice D'Oisly; **FRE:** Edith Evans; **FRK:** Cicely Gleeson-White, (26) Marcia van Dresser; **LG:** Walter Hyde; **MM:** Hans Bechstein, (4) Denis Byndon-Ayres; **WEL:** Caroline Hatchard; **WGL:** Alice Prowse, (26) ?; **WOT:** Clarence Whitehill
The Valkyrie (18, 28 January, 6 February). **BRH:** Minnie Saltzmann-Stevens; **FRK:** Cicely Gleeson-White; **GEH:** Caroline Hatchard; **GRG:** Gwladys Roberts; **HLW:** Alice Prowse; **HUN:** Robert Radford; **OTL:** Edith Evans; **RSW:** Dilys Jones; **SGL:** Rachel Frease-Green; **SGM:** Walter Hyde; **SGR:** Edith Clegg; **SWL:** Maria Yelland; **WLT:** Marie Alexander; **WOT:** Clarence Whitehill
Siegfried (20, 30 January, 8 February). **ALB:** Thomas Meux; **BRH:** Minnie Saltzmann-Stevens; **ED:** Edna Thornton; **FAF:** Francis Harford; **MM:** Hans Bechstein; **SGF:** Peter Cornelius; **WAN:** Clarence Whitehill; **WDB:** Caroline Hatchard
The Twilight of the Gods (22 January, 1, 11 February). **ALB:** Thomas Meux; **BRH:** Minnie Saltzmann-Stevens; **FLH:** Edna Thornton; **GTR:** Edith Evans, (1, 11) Marcia van Dresser; **GUN:** Frederic Austin; **HAG:** Charles Knowles; **NN1:** Dilys Jones, (1, 11) Edna Thornton; **NN2:** Caroline Hatchard; **NN3:** Alice Prowse, (1, 11) ?; **SGF:** Peter Cornelius; **WEL:** Caroline Hatchard; **WGL:** Alice Prowse, (1, 11) ?; **WLT:** Edna Thornton

Conductor: Hans Richter
Die Walküre (16 February). **BRH:** Minnie Saltzmann-Stevens; **FRK:** Cicely Gleeson-White; **GEH:** Caroline Hatchard; **GRG:** Gwladys Roberts; **HLW:** Alice Prowse; **HUN:** Robert Radford; **OTL:** Edith Evans; **RSW:** Dilys Jones; **SGL:** Rachel Frease-Green; **SGM:** Francis Maclennan; **SGR:** Edith Clegg; **SWL:** [Miss] Twemlow; **WLT:** Marie Alexander; **WOT:** Clarence Whitehill

Conductor: Hans Richter
Die Walküre (29 April, 5 May). **BRH:** Minnie Saltzmann-Stevens; **FRK:** Louise Kirkby Lunn; **GEH:** Caroline Hatchard; **GRG:** Gwladys Roberts; **HLW:** Cicely Gleeson-White; **HUN:** Francis Harford; **OTL:** Edith Evans; **RSW:** Dilys Jones; **SGL:** Marcia van Dresser; **SGM:** Walter Hyde; **SGR:** Edith Clegg; **SWL:** [Miss] Moresta;

WLT: Marie Alexander; **WOT:** Alfons Schützendorf. [Harford replaced the indisposed Robert Radford]

1910

TWO CYCLES

Conductors: Hans Richter, (3, 4 May) Paul Drach, (6 May) Ludwig Rottenberg, (19 May) Alfred Hertz. [Illness caused the replacement of Richter for the second cycle]

Das Rheingold (25 April, 3 May). **ALB:** Desider Zador; **DON:** Alfons Schützendorf; **ED:** Edna Thornton; **FAF:** Johannes Fönss; **FAS:** Josef Schlembach; **FLH:** Edna Thornton; **FR:** Sydney Russell; **FRE:** Edith Evans; **FRK:** Louise Kirkby Lunn; **LG:** Johannes Sembach, (3) Carl Strätz; **MM:** Hans Bechstein; **WEL:** Marie Knüpfer-Egli; **WGL:** Elizabeth Amsden; **WOT:** Anton van Rooy

Die Walküre (26 April, 4 May). **BRH:** Minnie Saltzmann-Stevens, (4) Melanie Kurt; **FRK:** ?, (4) Louise Kirkby Lunn; **GEH:** Margery Baxter; **GRG:** Marie Wadia; **HLW:** Elizabeth Amsden; **HUN:** Johannes Fönss; **OTL:** Edith Evans; **RSW:** Edith Clegg; **SGL:** Melanie Kurt, (4) Marie Knüpfer-Egli; **SGM:** Johannes Sembach, (4) Peter Cornelius; **SGR:** Anna Hofmann; **SWL:** Alys Mutch; **WLT:** Edna Thornton; **WOT:** Anton van Rooy, (4) Alfons Schützendorf

Siegfried (28 April, 6 May). **ALB:** Desider Zador; **BRH:** Minnie Saltzmann-Stevens; **ED:** Louise Kirkby Lunn, (6) Edna Thornton; **FAF:** Johannes Fönss; **MM:** Hans Bechstein; **SGF:** Peter Cornelius; **WAN:** Anton van Rooy; **WDB:** Amy Evans

Götterdämmerung (30 April, 19 May). **ALB:** Desider Zador, (19) Thomas Meux; **BRH:** Minnie Saltzmann-Stevens, (19) Félia Litvinne; **FLH:** Edna Thornton; **GTR:** Elizabeth Amsden; **GUN:** Alfons Schützendorf; **HAG:** Johannes Fönss; **NN1:** Edna Thornton; **NN2:** Marie Knüpfer-Egli; **NN3:** Amy Evans; **SGF:** Carl Strätz, (19) Peter Cornelius; **WEL:** Marie Knüpfer-Egli; **WGL:** Amy Evans; **WLT:** Louise Kirkby Lunn. [The death of King Edward VII caused the second performance to be rescheduled from 9 May as advertised]

1911

THREE CYCLES

Conductor: Franz Schalk

Das Rheingold (19, 30 October, 8 November). **ALB:** August Kiess; **DON:** Erich Hunold; **ED:** Marion Beeley; **FAF:** Johannes Fönss; **FAS:** James H. Goddard; **FLH:** Ella Gmeiner; **FR:** Haigh Jackson; **FRE:** Clytie Hine; **FRK:** Elsa Bengell, (30, 8) Borghild Bryhn-Langaard; **LG:** Heinrich Hensel; **MM:** Hans Bechstein; **WEL:** Marie Knüpfer-Egli; **WGL:** Olga Kallensee; **WOT:** Anton van Rooy

Die Walküre (21, 31 October, 9 November). **BRH:** Cäcilie Rüsche-Endorf, (9) Minnie Saltzmann-Stevens; **FRK:** Elsa Bengell; **GEH:** Marie Knüpfer-Egli; **GRG:** Ella Gmeiner; **HLW:** Olga Kallensee; **HUN:** Johannes Fönss; **OTL:** Clytie Hine; **RSW:** Dilys Jones; **SGL:** Borghild Bryhn-Langaard; **SGM:** Heinrich Hensel, (31) Peter Cornelius; **SGR:** Marion Beeley; **SWL:** Alys Mutch; **WLT:** Elsa Bengell; **WOT:** Anton van Rooy

Siegfried (23 October, 2, 13 November). **ALB:** August Kiess; **BRH:** Minnie Saltzmann-Stevens, (2) Cäcilie Rüsche-Endorf; **ED:** Marion Beeley; **FAF:** Johannes Fönss; **MM:** Hans Bechstein; **SGF:** Peter Cornelius, (2) Heinrich Hensel; **WAN:** Anton van Rooy; **WDB:** Olga Kallensee, (13) Alice Wilna

Götterdämmerung (25 October, 4, 15 November). **ALB:** August Kiess; **BRH:** Cäcilie Rüsche-Endorf, (4, 15) Minnie Saltzmann-Stevens; **FLH:** Ella Gmeiner; **GTR:** Marie Knüpfer-Egli ; **GUN:** Erich Hunold; **HAG:** Johannes Fönss; **NN1:** Ella Gmeiner; **NN2:** Marie Knüpfer-Egli; **NN3:** Olga Kallensee; **SGF:** Peter Cornelius, (4, 15) Heinrich Hensel; **WEL:** Clytie Hine; **WGL:** Olga Kallensee; **WLT:** Elsa Bengell, (15) Frieda Langendorff

1912

TWO CYCLES

Conductor: Ludwig Rottenberg

Das Rheingold (23 April, 3 May). **ALB:** August Kiess; **DON:** Franz Kronen; **ED:** Gwladys Roberts; **FAF:** Johannes Fönss; **FAS:** James H. Goddard; **FLH:** [Mlle] Boberg; **FR:** Maurice D'Oisly; **FRE:** Marie Knüpfer-Egli; **FRK:** Louise Kirkby Lunn; **LG:** Heinrich Hensel; **MM:** Hans Bechstein; **WEL:** [Mme] Kacerowska; **WGL:** Rhoda von Glehn; **WOT:** Anton van Rooy

Die Walküre (25 April, 4 May). **BRH:** Gertrud Kappel; **FRK:** Louise Kirkby Lunn; **GEH:** [Mme] Kacerowska; **GRG:** Gwladys Roberts; **HLW:** Rhoda von Glehn; **HUN:** Johannes Fönss; **OTL:** Marie Knüpfer-Egli; **RSW:** Dilys Jones; **SGL:** Minnie Saltzmann-Stevens; **SGM:** Peter Cornelius, (4) Heinrich Hensel; **SGR:** Edith Clegg; **SWL:** Alys Mutch; **WLT:** [Mlle] Boberg; **WOT:** Anton van Rooy

Siegfried (27 April, 6 May). **ALB:** August Kiess; **BRH:** Minnie Saltzmann-Stevens; **ED:** Louise Kirkby Lunn; **FAF:** Johannes Fönss; **MM:** Hans Bechstein; **SGF:** Heinrich Hensel, (6) Peter Cornelius; **WAN:** Anton van Rooy; **WDB:** Amy Evans

Götterdämmerung (29 April, 8 May). **ALB:** August Kiess; **BRH:** Gertrud Kappel; **FLH:** [Mlle] Boberg; **GTR:** Marie Knüpfer-Egli; **GUN:** Franz Kronen; **HAG:** Johannes Fönss; **NN1:** [Mlle] Boberg; **NN2:** [Mme] Kacerowska; **NN3:** Rhoda von Glehn; **SGF:** Heinrich Hensel, (8) Peter Cornelius; **WEL:** [Mme] Kacerowska; **WGL:** Rhoda von Glehn; **WLT:** Louise Kirkby Lunn

1913

THREE CYCLES

Conductors: Paul Drach, (28 April) Arthur Nikisch. Producer: Herr Nowack

Das Rheingold (22, 30 April, 8 May). **ALB:** August Kiess; **DON:** Werner Engel; **ED:** Kathleen Howard, (8) Dilys Jones; **FAF:** Johannes Fönss; **FAS:** James H. Goddard; **FLH:** [Mlle] Schaeffer; **FR:** Knud Gerner, (30, 8) Peter Unkel; **FRE:** Greta Jonsson; **FRK:** Louise Kirkby Lunn; **LG:** Heinrich Hensel; **MM:** Hans Bechstein; **WEL:** [Miss] D'Arcy; **WGL:** Josephine Rourke; **WOT:** Anton van Rooy

Die Walküre (23 April, 1, 9 May). **BRH:** Gertrud Kappel; **FRK:** Louise Kirkby Lunn, (9) Kathleen Howard; **GEH:** Millicent Field, (1, 9) Greta Jonsson; **GRG:** [Mlle] Schaeffer; **HLW:** [Mlle] Chepkowska; **HUN:** Willy Bader; **OTL:** [Miss] D'Arcy; **RSW:** Dilys Jones; **SGL:** Minnie Saltzmann-Stevens; **SGM:** Peter Cornelius; **SGR:** Marion Beeley; **SWL:** Lily Crawforth; **WLT:** Kathleen Howard; **WOT:** Anton van Rooy, (1, 9) August Kiess

Siegfried (25 April, 3, 12 May). **ALB:** August Kiess; **BRH:** Minnie Saltzmann-Stevens; **ED:** Louise Kirkby Lunn, (12) Kathleen Howard; **FAF:** Willy Bader; **MM:** Hans Bechstein; **SGF:** Peter Cornelius; **WAN:** Anton van Rooy; **WDB:** Josephine Rourke

Götterdämmerung (28 April, 6, 14 May). **ALB:** August Kiess; **BRH:** Gertrud Kappel, (14) Minnie Saltzmann-Stevens; **FLH:** [Mlle] Schaeffer; **GTR:** Luise Perard-Petzl; **GUN:** Werner Engel; **HAG:** Johannes Fönss, (14) Putnam Griswold; **NN1:** [Mlle] Schaeffer; **NN2:** [Miss] D'Arcy; **NN3:** [Mlle] Chepkowska; **SGF:** Peter Cornelius, (6) Heinrich Hensel; **WEL:** [Miss] D'Arcy; **WGL:** Josephine Rourke; **WLT:** Louise Kirkby Lunn, (6) Kathleen Howard

1914

Conductor: Artur Bodanzky

Die Walküre (18, 26 February, 2 March). **BRH:** Cäcilie Rüsche-Endorf, (26) Berta Morena, (2) Marta Wittkowska; **FRK:** Franziska Bender-Schäfer; **GEH:** Annie Puchmayer; **GRG:** Elisabeth von Pandar; **HLW:** Rosina Buckman; **HUN:** Paul Knüpfer; **OTL:** Dora Gibson; **RSW:** Dilys Jones; **SGL:** Eva von der Osten, (26, 2) Melanie Kurt; **SGM:** Jacques Urlus; **SGR:** Ethel Fenton; **SWL:** Mabel Corran; **WLT:** Franziska Bender-Schäfer; **WOT:** Paul Bender, (2) August Kiess

TWO CYCLES

Conductor: Arthur Nikisch. Designs [partially new]: Oliver Bernard

Das Rheingold (21 April, 4 May). **ALB:** August Kiess; **DON:** Charles Mott; **ED:** Charlotte Dahmen; **FAF:** Johannes Fönns; **FAS:** Paul Knüpfer; **FLH:** Dilys Jones; **FR:** Jean Skrobisch; **FRE:** Greta Jonsson; **FRK:** Louise Kirkby Lunn; **LG:** Johannes Sembach; **MM:** Hans Bechstein; **WEL:** Bessie Jones; **WGL:** Sybil Vane; **WOT:** Paul Bender, (4) Robert Parker

Die Walküre (22 April, 5 May). **BRH:** Gertrud Kappel; **FRK:** Louise Kirkby Lunn, (5) Charlotte Dahmen; **GEH:** Greta Jonsson; **GRG:** Adelaide Gretton; **HLW:** Rosina Buckman; **HUN:** Johannes Fönss, (5) Paul Knüpfer; **OTL:** Dora Gibson; **RSW:** Dilys Jones; **SGL:** Maude Fay; **SGM:** Peter Cornelius; **SGR:** Ethel Fenton; **SWL:** Mabel Corran; **WLT:** Charlotte Dahmen; **WOT:** Paul Bender, (5) Clarence Whitehill

Siegfried (5 April, 7 May). **ALB:** August Kiess; **BRH:** Gertrud Kappel; **ED:** Louise Kirkby Lunn; **FAF:** Johannes Fönss; **MM:** Hans Bechstein; **SGF:** Peter Cornelius; **WAN:** Paul Bender, (7) Clarence Whitehill; **WDB:** Bessie Jones

Götterdämmerung (27 April, 9 May). **ALB:** August Kiess, (9) Jan Hemsing; **BRH:** Gertrud Kappel; **FLH:** Dilys Jones; **GTR:** Maude Fay; **GUN:** Charles Mott; **HAG:** Paul Knüpfer; **NN1:** Dilys Jones; **NN2:** Bessie Jones; **NN3:** Sybil Vane; **SGF:** Peter Cornelius; **WEL:** Bessie Jones; **WGL:** Sybil Vane; **WLT:** Louise Kirkby Lunn

1921

Language: English

Conductors: Eugene Goossens (2) Enriquez de la Fuente

The Valkyrie (24 October, 16 November, 2 December). **BRH:** Eva Turner; **FRK:** Doris Woodall; **HUN:** Harry Brindle; **SGL:** Hope Laurin; **SGM:** William Boland; **VLK:** Muriel McDougall, Winifred Geverding, Eva Colton, Ethel Earl, Gladys Parker, Evelyn Tay, Ethelreda Freegarde; **WOT:** Kingsley Lark, (16) Augustus Milner

Conductor: Eugene Goossens

The Rhinegold (7, 30 November). **ALB:** Frederick Clendon; **DON:** Booth Hitchin; **ED:** Doris Woodall; **FAF:** William Anderson; **FAS:** Harry Brindle; **FLH:** Gladys Parr; **FR:** Lisant Beardmore; **FRE:** May Malone; **FRK:** Eva Turner; **LG:** William Boland; **MM:** Horace Vincent; **WEL:** Doris Woodall; **WGL:** Gladys Cranston; **WOT:** Augustus Milner

Conductor: Eugene Goossens

Siegfried (25 November, 6 December). **ALB:** Henry Rabke; **BRH:** Eva Turner; **ED:** Doris Woodall; **FAF:** Harry Brindle; **MM:** Colin Tinley; **SGF:** John Perry; **WAN:** Augustus Milner; **WDB:** Maude Neilson

1922

TWO CYCLES

Conductors: Albert Coates, (1 June) Julius Harrison

Language: English

The Rhinegold (15, 29 May). **ALB**: William Michael; **DON**: Frederic Collier; **ED**: Phyllis Archibald; **FAF**: Norman Allin; **FAS**: Robert Radford; **FLH**: Edith Furmedge; **FR**: Tudor Davies; **FRE**: Anna Lindsey; **FRK**: Edna Thornton; **LG**: Walter Hyde; **MM**: Sydney Russell; **WEL**: May Blyth; **WGL**: Gertrude Johnson; **WOT**: Clarence Whitehill

The Valkyrie (16, 30 May). **BRH**: Florence Austral; **FRK**: Edna Thornton; **HUN**: Robert Radford; **SGL**: Agnes Nicholls; **SGM**: Walter Hyde; **VLK**: Phyllis Archibald, Evelyn Arden, Eda Bennie, May Blyth, Dorothy Chapman, Mary Edison, Edith Furmedge, Anna Lindsey; **WOT**: Clarence Whitehill

Siegfried (18 May, 1 June). **ALB**: William Michael; **BRH**: Florence Austral; **ED**: Edna Thornton; **FAF**: Norman Allin; **MM**: Sydney Russell; **SGF**: Arthur Jordan; **WAN**: Clarence Whitehill; **WDB**: Agnes Nicholls?, (1) Gertrude Johnson [18: the Woodbird was uncredited in the programme; several reviews identified Nicholls as the singer]

The Twilight of the Gods (22 May, 5 June). **ALB**: William Michael; **BRH**: Beatrice Miranda, (5) Florence Austral; **GTR**: Eda Bennie; **GUN**: Andrew Shanks; **HAG**: Robert Radford, (5) Norman Allin; **NN1**: Mary Edison; **NN2**: May Blyth; **NN3**: Gertrude Johnson; **RHD**: Gertrude Johnson/(5) Agnes Nicholls, May Blyth, Edith Furmedge; **SGF**: Frank Mullings; **WLT**: Edna Thornton

Conductor: Albert Coates

Language: English.

The Valkyrie (14 June). **BRH**: Florence Austral; **FRK**: Edna Thornton; **HUN**: Robert Radford; **SGL**: Beatrice Miranda; **SGM**: William Boland; **VLK**: Phyllis Archibald, Evelyn Arden, Eda Bennie, May Blyth, Mary Edison, Edith Furmedge, Anna Lindsey, Olive Townend; **WOT**: Clarence Whitehill

Conductor: Albert Coates

Language: English.

Siegfried (16, 20 June): **ALB**: William Michael; **BRH**: Florence Austral, (20) Agnes Nicholls; **ED**: Edna Thornton; **FAF**: Norman Allin; **MM**: Sydney Russell; **SGF**: Arthur Jordan; **WAN**: Clarence Whitehill, (20) Robert Parker; **WDB**: Gertrude Johnson

1923

Conductor: Percy Pitt

Language: English

The Valkyrie (4, 18 January). **BRH**: Florence Austral; **FRK**: Edna Thornton; **HUN**: Norman Allin, (18) William Anderson; **SGL**: Beatrice Miranda; **SGM**: Walter Hyde; **VLK**: Juliette Autran, Margery Baxter, Gladys Leathwood, May Blyth, Elsy Treweek, Dorothy Chapman, Muriel Brunskill, Hilda Fox; **WOT**: Robert Parker

Conductor: Eugene Goossens

Language: English

Siegfried (11 January). **ALB**: William Michael; **BRH**: Florence Austral; **ED**: Edna Thornton; **FAF**: William Anderson; **MM**: Sydney Russell; **SGF**: William Boland; **WAN**: Robert Parker; **WDB**: Doris Lemon

Conductor: Albert Coates. Producer: George King. Designer: Oliver P. Bernard Language: English

ONE CYCLE

The Rhinegold (15 May). **ALB**: William Michael; **DON**: Frederic Collier; **ED**: Muriel Brunskill; **FAF**: Norman Allin; **FAS**: Robert Radford; **FLH**: Muriel Brunskill; **FR**: Tudor Davies; **FRE**: Elsy Treweek; **FRK**: Edna Thornton; **LG**: Walter Hyde; **MM**: Sydney Russell; **WEL**: May Blyth; **WGL**: Doris Lemon; **WOT**: Robert Parker

The Valkyrie (17 May). **BRH**: Florence Austral; **FRK**: Enid Cruickshank; **HUN**: Robert Radford; **SGL**: Agnes Nicholls; **SGM**: Walter Hyde; **VLK**: Florence Ayre, Margery Baxter, Gladys Leathwood, May Blyth, Elsy Treweek, Dorothy Chapman, Muriel Brunskill, Hilda Fox; **WOT**: Robert Parker

Siegfried (22 May). **ALB**: William Michael; **BRH**: Florence Austral; **ED**: Muriel Brunskill; **FAF**: William Anderson; **MM**: Sydney Russell; **SGF**: Arthur Jordan; **WAN**: Robert Parker; **WDB**: Doris Lemon

The Twilight of the Gods (28 May). **ALB**: William Michael; **BRH**: Florence Austral; **GTR**: Elsy Treweek; **GUN**: Andrew Shanks; **HAG**: Robert Radford; **RHD**: Doris Lemon, May Blyth, Muriel Brunskill; **NN1**: Muriel Brunskill; **NN2**: May Blyth; **NN3**: Doris Lemon; **SGF**: Arthur Jordan; **WLT**: Edna Thornton

Conductor: Hamilton Harty

The Valkyrie (5 June). **BRH**: Florence Austral; **FRK**: Edna Thornton; **HUN**: Norman Allin; **SGL**: Agnes Nicholls; **SGM**: Walter Hyde; **VLK**: Florence Ayre, Margery Baxter, Gladys Leathwood, May Blyth, Florence Foote, Dorothy Chapman, Muriel Brunskill, Hilda Fox; **WOT**: Horace Stevens

Conductor: Eugene Goossens

Siegfried (8 June): **ALB**: William Michael; **BRH**: Florence Austral; **ED**: Edna Thornton; **FAF**: William Anderson; **MM**: Sydney Russell; **SGF**: John Perry; **WAN**: Joseph Farrington; **WDB**: Doris Lemon

1924

Conductor: Eugene Goossens

Language: English

The Valkyrie (1 February). **BRH**: Florence Austral; **FRK**: Edna Thornton; **HUN**: Norman Allin; **SGL**: Agnes Nicholls CBE; **SGM**: Walter Hyde; **VLK**: Florence Ayre, Margery Baxter, Gladys Leathwood, May Blyth, Florence Foote, Dorothy Chapman, Irene Milton, Hilda Fox; **WOT**: Robert Parker

Siegfried (25 January, 6 February). **ALB**: William Michael; **BRH**: Florence Austral; **ED**: Edna Thornton; **FAF**: William Anderson; **MM**: Sydney Russell; **SGF**: Walter Widdop; **WAN**: Joseph Farrington; **WDB**: Doris Lemon

TWO CYCLES

Conductor: Bruno Walter

Das Rheingold (5, 13 May). **ALB**: Eduard Habich, (13) Willy Paul; **DON**: Karl Renner; **ED**: Helene Jung; **FAF**: Nicola Zec; **FAS**: Hermann Marowski; **FLH**: Edith Furmedge; **FR**: Hans Clemens; **FRE**: Nellie Jaffary; **FRK**: Ernestine Färber-Strasser, (13) Maria Olczewska; **LG**: Walter Kirchhoff; **MM**: Albert Reiss; **WEL**: Margaret Duff; **WGL**: Rosel Landwehr; **WOT**: Friedrich Schorr

Die Walküre (6, 14 May). **BRH**: Gertrud Kappel, (14) Frida Leider; **FRK**: Ernestine Färber-Strasser, (14) Maria Olczewska; **GEH**: Margaret Duff; **GRG**: Edith Furmedge; **HLW**: Rosel Landwehr; **HUN**: Paul Bender, (14) Nicola Zec; **OTL**: May Busby; **RSW**: Evelyn Arden; **SGL**: Göta Ljungberg; **SGM**: Jacques Urlus, (14) Lauritz Melchior; **SGR**: Kathleen Burton; **SWL**: Helene Jung; **WLT**: Ernestine Färber-Strasser, (14) Maria Olczewska; **WOT**: Friedrich Schorr

Siegfried (7, 15 May). **ALB**: Eduard Habich; **BRH**: Gertrud Kappel; **ED**: Helene Jung; **FAF**: Nicola Zec; **MM**: Albert Reiss; **SGF**: Fritz Soot, (15) Nicolai Reinfeld; **WAN**: Wilhelm Buers, (15) Friedrich Schorr; **WDB**: Rosel Landwehr, (15) Katherine Arkandy. [7 May: at $2^1/_2$ hours' notice Soot replaced Reinfeld, who damaged his ankle during a rehearsal, necessitating a visit to Charing Cross Hospital.]

Götterdämmerung (9, 19 May). **ALB**: Eduard Habich; **BRH**: Gertrud Kappel, (19) Frida Leider; **FLH**: Edith Furmedge; **GTR**: Marcia van Dresser, (19) Göta Ljungberg; **GUN**: Karl Renner, (19) Friedrich Schorr; **HAG**: Paul Bender, (19) Nicola Zec; **NN1**: Edith Furmedge; **NN2**: Caroline Hatchard; **NN3**: Rosel Landwehr; **SGF**: Fritz Soot; **WEL**: Caroline Hatchard; **WGL**: Rosel Landwehr; **WLT**: Ernestine Färber-Strasser, (19) Maria Olczewska

Conductor: Karl Alwin

Siegfried Act III scene 2 only (16, 20 May). **BRH**: Florence Austral; **SGF**: Walter Kirchhoff [Given as the second part of a bill that began with Strauss's *Salome*]

Götterdämmerung (24 May). **ALB**: Willy Paul; **BRH**: Frida Leider; **FLH**: Edith Furmedge; **GTR**: Göta Ljungberg; **GUN**: Karl Renner; **HAG**: Paul Bender; **NN1**: Edith Furmedge; **NN2**: Caroline Hatchard; **NN3**: Rosel Landwehr; **SGF**: Fritz Soot; **WEL**: Caroline Hatchard; **WGL**: Rosel Landwehr; **WLT**: Maria Olczewska

Conductor: Bruno Walter

Die Walküre (30 May). **BRH**: Florence Austral; **FRK**: Maria Olczewska; **GEH**: Margaret Duff; **GRG**: Edith Furmedge; **HLW**: Rosel Landwehr; **HUN**: Hermann Marowski; **OTL**: May Busby; **RSW**: Evelyn Arden; **SGL**: Lotte Lehmann; **SGM**: Fritz Soot; **SGR**: Kathleen Burton; **SWL**: Helene Jung; **WLT**: Maria Olczewska; **WOT**: Wilhelm Buers

1925

Conductor: Robert Heger

Die Walküre (21, 29 May, 3 June). **BRH**: Gertrud Kappel, (29) Frida Leider; **FRK**: Bella Paalen, (29, 3) Maria Olczewska; **GEH**: Eda Bennie; **GRG**: Edith Furmedge; **HLW**: Rosel Landwehr; **HUN**: Emanuel List, (29) Otto Helgers; **OTL**: May Busby; **RSW**: Evelyn Arden; **SGL**: Delia Reinhardt; **SGM**: Fritz Soot, (3) Morgan Kingston; **SGR**: May Blyth; **SWL**: Marion Beeley; **WLT**: Bella Paalen; **WOT**: Friedrich Schorr, (3) Emil Schipper

1926

ONE CYCLE

Conductor: Bruno Walter

Das Rheingold (11 May). **ALB**: Eduard Habich; **DON**: Viktor Madin; **ED**: Luise Willer; **FAF**: Norman Allin; **FAS**: Otto Helgers; **FLH**: Gladys Palmer; **FR**: Barrington Hooper; **FRE**: May Busby; **FRK**: Maria Olczewska; **LG**: Hans Clemens; **MM**: Albert Reiss; **WEL**: May Blyth; **WGL**: Noel Eadie; **WOT**: Eduard Erhard

Die Walküre (14 May). **BRH**: Gertrud Kappel; **FRK**: Maria Olczewska; **GEH**: Maryan Almar; **GRG**: Enid Cruickshank; **HLW**: Noel Eadie; **HUN**: Norman Allin; **OTL**: May Busby; **RSW**: Evelyn Arden; **SGL**: Lotte

Lehmann; **SGM:** Lauritz Melchior; **SGR:** May Blyth; **SWL:** Marion Beeley; **WLT:** Gladys Palmer; **WOT:** Emil Schipper
Siegfried (17 May). **ALB:** Eduard Habich; **BRH:** Gertrud Kappel; **ED:** Maria Olczewska; **FAF:** Otto Helgers; **MM:** Albert Reiss; **SGF:** Lauritz Melchior; **WAN:** Emil Schipper; **WDB:** Katherine Arkandy
Götterdämmerung (19 May). **ALB:** Eduard Habich; **BRH:** Gertrud Kappel; **FLH:** Enid Cruickshank; **GTR:** Delia Reinhardt; **GUN:** Herbert Janssen; **HAG:** Otto Helgers; **NN:** Noel Eadie, May Blyth, Enid Cruickshank; **SGF:** Rudolf Laubenthal; **WEL:** May Blyth; **WGL:** Noel Eadie; **WLT:** Maria Olczewska

Conductor: Bruno Walter
Die Walküre (2 June). **BRH:** Gertrud Kappel; **FRK:** Luise Willer; **GEH:** Maryan Almar; **GRG:** Enid Cruickshank; **HLW:** Noel Eadie; **HUN:** Otto Helgers; **OTL:** May Busby; **RSW:** Evelyn Arden; **SGL:** Maria Jeritza; **SGM:** Lauritz Melchior; **SGR:** May Blyth; **SWL:** Marion Beeley; **WLT:** Gladys Palmer; **WOT:** Emil Schipper. [The audience's indulgence was craved on the part of Schipper 'who, suffering from a slight cold, is singing the role of *Wotan* rather than disappoint the public.']
Götterdämmerung (3 June). **ALB:** Eduard Habich; **BRH:** Frida Leider; **FLH:** Enid Cruickshank; **GTR:** Delia Reinhardt; **GUN:** Herbert Janssen; **HAG:** Otto Helgers; **SGF:** Rudolf Laubenthal; **WEL:** May Blyth; **WGL:** Noel Eadie; **WLT:** Maria Olczewska. [Norns omitted: 'Dawn on the Valkyrie's Rock. The scene opens at the point where Siegfried departs in search of adventure.' The performance started at 6.30pm, two hours later than the performance on 19 May]

1927

TWO CYCLES
Conductors: Bruno Walter, (20, 23, 26, 31 May) Robert Heger
Das Rheingold (5, 20 May). **ALB:** Eduard Habich; **DON:** Viktor Madin; **ED:** Clara Serena, (20) Gladys Palmer; **FAF:** Norman Allin; **FAS:** Otto Helgers; **FLH:** Gladys Palmer; **FR:** Henry Wendon; **FRE:** Liane Martiny, (20) Delia Reinhardt; **FRK:** Maria Olczewska; **LG:** Karl Erb, (20) Hans Clemens; **MM:** Albert Reiss; **WEL:** Kathlyn Hilliard; **WGL:** Noel Eadie; **WOT:** Friedrich Schorr
Die Walküre (6, 23 May). **BRH:** Frida Leider, (20) Nanny Larsén-Todsen; **FRK:** Sigrid Onegin; **GEH:** Alice Moxon; **GRG:** Enid Cruickshank; **HLW:** Liane Martiny; **HUN:** Norman Allin; **OTL:** May Busby; **RSW:** Evelyn Arden; **SGL:** Lotte Lehmann, (20) Göta Ljungberg; **SGM:** Lauritz Melchior; **SGR:** Gladys Palmer; **SWL:** Marion Beeley; **WLT:** Erna von Hoesslin; **WOT:** Friedrich Schorr
Siegfried (9, 26 May). **ALB:** Eduard Habich; **BRH:** Frida Leider, (26) Nanny Larsén-Todsen; **ED:** Maria Olczewska, (26) Sigrid Onegin; **FAF:** Otto Helgers; **MM:** Albert Reiss; **SGF:** Lauritz Melchior, (26) Rudolf Laubenthal; **WAN:** Friedrich Schorr; **WDB:** Katherine Arkandy
Götterdämmerung (11, 31 May). **ALB:** Eduard Habich; **BRH:** Frida Leider, (31) Nanny Larsén-Todsen; **FLH:** Clara Serena; **GTR:** Göta Ljungberg, (31) Delia Reinhardt; **GUN:** Herbert Janssen; **HAG:** Otto Helgers; **NN:** Marie Maltin/(31) Clara Serena, Gladys Palmer, Noel Eadie; **SGF:** Rudolf Laubenthal; **WEL:** Kathryn Hilliard; **WGL:** Noel Eadie; **WLT:** Maria Olczewska, (31) Sigrid Onegin

1928

TWO CYCLES
Conductors: Bruno Walter, (16, 18 May) Robert Heger
Das Rheingold (30 April, 11 May). **ALB:** Eduard Habich, (11) Viktor Madin; **DON:** Viktor Madin, (11) Roy Henderson; **ED:** Anny Andrassy; **FAF:** Ivar Andrésen; **FAS:** Otto Helgers; **FLH:** Gladys Palmer; **FR:** Henry Wendon; **FRE:** May Busby; **FRK:** Rosette Anday; **LG:** Hans Clemens; **MM:** Albert Reiss; **WEL:** Theresa Ambrose; **WGL:** Odette de Foras; **WOT:** Wilhelm Rode, (11) Hans Hermann Nissen
Die Walküre (2, 14 May). **BRH:** Elisabeth Ohms, (14) Frida Leider; **FRK:** Maria Olczewska; **GEH:** Theresa Ambrose; **GRG:** Enid Cruickshank; **HLW:** Odette de Foras; **HUN:** Otto Helgers, (14) Ivar Andrésen; **OTL:** May Busby; **RSW:** Evelyn Arden; **SGL:** Lotte Lehmann, (14) Göta Ljungberg; **SGM:** Lauritz Melchior; **SGR:** Gladys Palmer; **SWL:** Carys Davies; **WLT:** Anny Andrassy; **WOT:** Wilhelm Rode, (14) Emil Schipper
Siegfried (4, 16 May). **ALB:** Eduard Habich, (16) Viktor Madin; **BRH:** Elisabeth Ohms, (16) Frida Leider; **ED:** Maria Olczewska; **FAF:** Otto Helgers; **MM:** Albert Reiss; **SGF:** Rudolf Laubenthal, (16) Lauritz Melchior; **WAN:** Wilhelm Rode, (16) Hans Hermann Nissen; **WDB:** Marion McAfee, (16) Annette Blackwell
Götterdämmerung (8, 18 May). **ALB:** Eduard Habich; **BRH:** Elisabeth Ohms, (18) Frida Leider; **FLH:** Gladys Palmer; **GTR:** Göta Ljungberg, (18) Lotte Lehmann; **GUN:** Herbert Janssen; **HAG:** Otto Helgers, (18) Ivar Andrésen; **NN:** Gladys Palmer, Theresa Ambrose, Odette de Foras; **SGF:** Rudolf Laubenthal; **WEL:** Theresa Ambrose; **WGL:** Odette de Foras; **WLT:** Maria Olczewska, (18) Rosette Anday

1929

TWO CYCLES
Conductors: Bruno Walter, (6, 9, 13, 15 May) Robert Heger
Das Rheingold (23 April, 6 May). **ALB:** Viktor Madin, (6) Eduard Habich; **DON:** Roy Henderson; **ED:** Anny Andrassy; **FAF:** Ivar Andrésen; **FAS:** Alexander Kipnis; **FR:** Henry Wendon; **FLH:** Gladys Palmer; **FRE:** Josephine Wray; **FRK:** Rosette Anday, (6) Maria Olczewska; **LG:** Hans Clemens; **MM:** Albert Reiss; **WEL:** Betsy de la Porte; **WGL:** Odette de Foras; **WOT:** Friedrich Schorr, (6) Rudolf Bockelmann
Die Walküre (26 April, 9 May). **BRH:** Frida Leider; **FRK:** Rosette Anday, (9) Maria Olczewska; **GEH:** Gladys Cole; **GRG:** Mary Jarred; **HLW:** Odette de Foras; **HUN:** Alexander Kipnis; **OTL:** May Busby; **RSW:** Evelyn Arden; **SGL:** Lotte Lehmann, (9) Meta Seinemeyer; **SGM:** Lauritz Melchior; **SGR:** Gladys Palmer; **SWL:** Constance Willis; **WLT:** Anny Andrassy; **WOT:** Friedrich Schorr, (9) Wilhelm Fassbinder
Siegfried (30 April, 13 May). **ALB:** Eduard Habich, (13) Viktor Madin; **BRH:** Elisabeth Ohms; **ED:** Rosette Anday; **FAF:** William Anderson; **MM:** Albert Reiss; **SGF:** Lauritz Melchior; **WAN:** Rudolf Bockelmann, (13) Friedrich Schorr; **WDB:** Nora Gruhn
Götterdämmerung (3, 15 May). **ALB:** Eduard Habich; **BRH:** Frida Leider; **FLH:** Gladys Palmer; **GTR:** Delia Reinhardt, (15) Miriam Licette; **GUN:** Herbert Janssen; **HAG:** Alexander Kipnis, (15) Ivar Andrésen; **NN:** Gladys Palmer, Gladys Cole, Odette de Foras; **SGF:** Lauritz Melchior; **WEL:** Ina Souez; **WGL:** Odette de Foras; **WLT:** Maria Olczewska

Conductor: Albert Coates
Die Walküre (21 May). **BRH:** Florence Austral; **FRK:** Maria Olczewska; **GEH:** Gladys Cole; **GRG:** Mary Jarred; **HLW:** Odette de Foras; **HUN:** Alexander Kipnis; **OTL:** May Busby; **RSW:** Evelyn Arden; **SGL:** Meta Seinemeyer; **SGM:** Walter Widdop; **SGR:** Gladys Palmer; **SWL:** Constance Willis; **WLT:** Anny Andrassy; **WOT:** Rudolf Bockelmann. ['The indulgence of the Audience is asked on behalf of Madame Austral; she has just returned from an American tour for these performances, and, although not yet fully recovered from severe ear trouble, is singing to-night rather than cause disappointment.']

Conductor: Robert Heger
Götterdämmerung (23 May). **ALB:** Viktor Madin; **BRH:** Elisabeth Ohms; **FLH:** Gladys Palmer; **GTR:** Miriam Licette; **GUN:** Herbert Janssen; **HAG:** Ivar Andrésen; **NN:** Gladys Palmer, Gladys Cole, Odette de Foras; **SGF:** Lauritz Melchior; **WEL:** Ina Souez; **WGL:** Odette de Foras; **WLT:** Maria Olczewska

1930

TWO CYCLES
Conductors: Bruno Walter, (12, 15, 20, 22 May) Robert Heger
Das Rheingold (29 April, 12 May). **ALB:** Viktor Madin, (12) Eduard Habich; **DON:** Arthur Fear; **ED:** Anna Tibell; **FAF:** Ivar Andrésen; **FAS:** Otto Helgers; **FLH:** Gladys Palmer; **FR:** Edward Leer; **FRE:** Josephine Wray; **FRK:** Maria Olczewska; **LG:** Fritz Wolff; **MM:** Heinrich Tessmer, (12) Octave Dua; **WEL:** Betty Thompson; **WGL:** Odette de Foras; **WOT:** Rudolf Bockelmann, (12) Friedrich Schorr
Die Walküre (2, 15 May). **BRH:** Frida Leider; **FRK:** Maria Olczewska, (15) Constance Willis; **GEH:** Gladys Cole; **GRG:** May Keene; **HLW:** Thea Philips; **HUN:** Ivar Andrésen; **OTL:** Josephine Wray; **RSW:** Evelyn Arden; **SGL:** Lotte Lehmann, (15) Eva Turner; **SGM:** Lauritz Melchior; **SGR:** Gladys Palmer; **SWL:** Margaret McArthur; **WLT:** Anna Tibell; **WOT:** Friedrich Schorr, (15) Rudolf Bockelmann
Siegfried (5, 20 May). **ALB:** Viktor Madin; **BRH:** Frida Leider, (20) Nanny Larsén-Todsen; **ED:** Anna Tibell; **FAF:** Philip Bertram; **MM:** Heinrich Tessmer; **SGF:** Lauritz Melchior, (20) Rudolf Laubenthal; **WAN:** Friedrich Schorr, (20) Rudolf Bockelmann; **WDB:** Nora Gruhn
Götterdämmerung (9, 22 May). **ALB:** Eduard Habich, (22) Viktor Madin; **BRH:** Frida Leider, (22) Nanny Larsén-Todsen; **FLH:** Gladys Palmer; **GTR:** Odette de Foras; **GUN:** Herbert Janssen, (22) Arthur Fear; **HAG:** Otto Helgers, (22) Ivar Andrésen; **NN:** Gladys Palmer, Gladys Cole, Thea Philips; **SGF:** Lauritz Melchior, (22) Rudolf Laubenthal; **WEL:** Betty Thompson; **WGL:** Thea Philips; **WLT:** Maria Olczewska

1931

TWO CYCLES
Conductors: Bruno Walter, (8, 15, 19, 22, 25 May) Robert Heger
Das Rheingold (29 April, 15 May). **ALB:** Eduard Habich; **DON:** Viktor Madin; **ED:** Anna Tibell; **FAF:** Ivar Andrésen; **FAS:** Otto Helgers; **FLH:** Gladys Palmer; **FR:** Edward Leer; **FRE:** Josephine Wray; **FRK:** Maria Olczewska, (15) Luise Willer; **LG:** Fritz Wolff; **MM:** Heinrich Tessmer; **WEL:** Betty Thompson; **WGL:** Odette de Foras; **WOT:** Friedrich Schorr
Die Walküre (30 April, 19 May). **BRH:** Frida Leider;

FRK: Maria Olczewska, (19) Luise Willer; **GEH:** Gladys Cole; **GRG:** May Keene; **HLW:** Thea Philips; **HUN:** Otto Helgers, (19) Ivar Andrésen; **OTL:** Josephine Wray; **RSW:** Evelyn Arden; **SGL:** Lotte Lehmann, (19) Juliette Lippe; **SGM:** Lauritz Melchior; **SGR:** Gladys Palmer; **SWL:** Gabriele Joachim; **WLT:** Anna Tibell; **WOT:** Friedrich Schorr
Siegfried (4, 22 May). **ALB:** Eduard Habich; **BRH:** Juliette Lippe; **ED:** Luise Willer; **FAF:** Edward Delfosse; **MM:** Heinrich Tessmer; **SGF:** Lauritz Melchior; **WAN:** Friedrich Schorr; **WDB:** Nora Gruhn
Götterdämmerung (8, 25 May). **ALB:** Viktor Madin; **BRH:** Juliette Lippe, (25) Frida Leider; **FLH:** Gladys Palmer; **GTR:** Odette de Foras; **GUN:** Herbert Janssen; **HAG:** Ivar Andrésen; **NN:** Gladys Palmer, Gladys Cole, Thea Philips; **SGF:** Lauritz Melchior; **WEL:** Betty Thompson; **WGL:** Thea Philips; **WLT:** Maria Olczewska, (25) Luise Willer

Conductor: Adrian Boult
Language: English.
The Valkyrie (16 September, 2, 12 October). **BRH:** Monica Warner; **FRK:** Enid Cruickshank, (2, 12) Astra Desmond; **GEH:** Marjorie Parry; **GRG:** Vanwy Davies; **HLW:** Nora Gruhn; **HUN:** Norman Allin; **OTL:** Patricia Guest; **RSW:** Molly Street; **SGL:** Josephine Wray, (12) Odette de Foras; **SGM:** Francis Russell, (2) Parry Jones; **SGR:** Frances Maude; **SWL:** Evelyn Tay; **WLT:** Rispah Goodacre; **WOT:** Horace Stevens, (2) Robert Parker. [Boult appeared 'By permission of the B.B.C.']

1932
TWO CYCLES
Conductors: Robert Heger, (19 May, 3 June) Thomas Beecham
Das Rheingold (10, 25 May). **ALB:** Eduard Habich; **DON:** William Michael; **ED:** Rispah Goodacre; **FAF:** Norman Allin; **FAS:** Otto Helgers; **FLH:** Gladys Palmer; **FR:** Edward Leer; **FRE:** Josephine Wray; **FRK:** Maria Olczewska; **LG:** Fritz Wolff; **MM:** Heinrich Tessmer; **WEL:** Betty Thompson; **WGL:** Ina Souez; **WOT:** Ludwig Hofmann
Die Walküre (13, 30 May). **BRH:** Frida Leider; **FRK:** Maria Olczewska; **GEH:** Gladys Cole; **GRG:** May Keene; **HLW:** Thea Philips; **HUN:** Norman Allin; **OTL:** Josephine Wray; **RSW:** Evelyn Arden; **SGL:** Lotte Lehmann; **SGM:** Lauritz Melchior, (30) Walter Widdop; **SGR:** Gladys Palmer; **SWL:** Gabriele Joachim; **WLT:** Rispah Goodacre; **WOT:** Friedrich Schorr
Siegfried (16 May, 1 June). **ALB:** Eduard Habich; **BRH:** Frida Leider, (1) Florence Easton; **ED:** Rispah Goodacre; **FAF:** Edward Delfosse; **MM:** Heinrich Tessmer; **SGF:** Lauritz Melchior; **WAN:** Friedrich Schorr, (1) Ludwig Hofmann; **WDB:** Nora Gruhn
Götterdämmerung (19 May, 3 June). **ALB:** Eduard Habich; **BRH:** Frida Leider; **FLH:** Gladys Palmer; **GTR:** Odette de Foras; **GUN:** Herbert Janssen; **HAG:** Otto Helgers; **NN:** Gladys Palmer, Gladys Cole, Thea Philips; **SGF:** Lauritz Melchior; **WEL:** Betty Thompson; **WGL:** Thea Philips; **WLT:** Maria Olczewska

1933
TWO CYCLES
Conductor: Robert Heger
Das Rheingold (2, 10 May). **ALB:** Eduard Habich; **DON:** Samuel Worthington; **ED:** Mary Jarred; **FAF:** Norman Allin; **FAS:** Otto Helgers; **FLH:** Gladys Palmer; **FR:** Ben Williams; **FRE:** Josephine Wray; **FRK:** Maria Olczewska; **LG:** Fritz Wolff; **MM:** Hanns Fleischer; **WEL:** Betty Thompson; **WGL:** Odette de Foras; **WOT:** Friedrich Schorr
Die Walküre (3, 12 May). **BRH:** Frida Leider, (12) Florence Austral; **FRK:** Maria Olczewska, (12) Mary Jarred; **GEH:** Gladys Cole; **GRG:** May Keene; **HLW:** Thea Philips; **HUN:** Philip Bertram; **OTL:** Josephine Wray; **RSW:** Evelyn Arden; **SGL:** Lotte Lehmann; **SGM:** Fritz Wolff; **SGR:** Gladys Palmer; **SWL:** Gabriele Joachim; **WLT:** Rispah Goodacre; **WOT:** Friedrich Schorr
Siegfried (5, 17 May). **ALB:** Eduard Habich; **BRH:** Frida Leider, (17) Florence Austral; **ED:** Mary Jarred; **FAF:** Leslie Horsman; **MM:** Hanns Fleischer; **SGF:** Lauritz Melchior; **WAN:** Friedrich Schorr; **WDB:** Adele Kern, (17) Eugénia Triguez
Götterdämmerung (8, 19 May). **ALB:** Eduard Habich; **BRH:** Frida Leider; **FLH:** Gladys Palmer; **GTR:** Odette de Foras; **GUN:** Herbert Janssen, (19) Friedrich Schorr; **HAG:** Otto Helgers; **NN:** Thea Philips, Gladys Cole, Gladys Palmer; **SGF:** Lauritz Melchior; **WEL:** Betty Thompson; **WGL:** Thea Philips; **WLT:** Maria Olczewska

1934
TWO CYCLES
Conductor: Thomas Beecham. Producer: Dr Otto Erhardt. Technical adviser: Max Hasait
Das Rheingold (1, 9 May). **ALB:** Eduard Habich; **DON:** Paul Schoeffler; **ED:** Mary Jarred; **FAF:** Berthold Sterneck; **FAS:** Alexander Kipnis; **FLH:** Ruth Berglund; **FR:** Henry Wendon; **FRE:** Angela Kolniak; **FRK:** Gertrude Rünger; **LG:** Martin Kremer; **MM:** Erich Zimmermann; **WEL:** Betsy de la Porte; **WGL:** Erna Berger; **WOT:** Rudolf Bockelmann, (9) Hans Hermann Nissen
Die Walküre (2, 14 May). **BRH:** Frida Leider; **FRK:** Gertrude Rünger; **GEH:** Irene Morden; **GRG:** Maud Heaton; **HLW:** Frances Martin; **HUN:** Alexander Kipnis; **OTL:** Thelma Bardsley; **RSW:** Mahry Dawes; **SGL:** Lotte Lehmann; **SGM:** Franz Völker; **SGR:** Betsy de la Porte; **SWL:** Gladys Ripley; **WLT:** Angela Kolniak; **WOT:** Rudolf Bockelmann, (14) Hans Hermann Nissen
Siegfried (4, 16 May). **ALB:** Eduard Habich; **BRH:** Frida Leider; **ED:** Mary Jarred; **FAF:** Robert Easton; **MM:** Erich Zimmermann; **SGF:** Lauritz Melchior; **WAN:** Rudolf Bockelmann, (16) Hans Hermann Nissen; **WDB:** Erna Berger, (16) Ellice Illiard
Götterdämmerung (7, 18 May). **ALB:** Eduard Habich; **BRH:** Frida Leider; **FLH:** Ruth Berglund; **GTR:** Käte Heidersbach; **GUN:** Herbert Janssen; **HAG:** Emanuel List; **NN:** Mary Jarred, Ruth Berglund, Gertrude Rünger; **SGF:** Lauritz Melchior; **WEL:** Betty Thompson; **WGL:** Erna Berger, (18) Ellice Illiard; **WLT:** Gertrude Rünger

1935
TWO CYCLES
Conductor: Thomas Beecham
Das Rheingold (3, 15 May). **ALB:** Eduard Habich; **DON:** Arnold Matters; **ED:** Edith Furmedge; **FAF:** Robert Easton; **FAS:** Alexander Kipnis; **FLH:** Constance Willis; **FR:** Henry Wendon; **FRE:** Josephine Wray; **FRK:** Sabine Kalter; **LG:** Hans Clemens; **MM:** Hanns Fleischer; **WEL:** Betsy de la Porte; **WGL:** Erna Berger; **WOT:** Rudolf Bockelmann
Die Walküre (6, 17 May). **BRH:** Frida Leider, (17) Anny Konetzni; **FRK:** Sabine Kalter; **GEH:** Mae Craven; **GRG:** Maud Heaton; **HLW:** Renee Flynn; **HUN:** Emanuel List; **OTL:** Thelma Bardsley; **RSW:** Mahry Dawes; **SGL:** Lotte Lehmann; **SGM:** Lauritz Melchior; **SGR:** Joyce Newton; **SWL:** Gladys Ripley; **WLT:** Betsy de la Porte; **WOT:** Rudolf Bockelmann
Siegfried (9, 22 May). **ALB:** Eduard Habich; **BRH:** Frida Leider, (22) Anny Konetzni; **ED:** Edith Furmedge; **FAF:** Robert Easton; **MM:** Hanns Fleischer; **SGF:** Lauritz Melchior; **WAN:** Rudolf Bockelmann; **WDB:** Erna Berger
Götterdämmerung (13, 28 May). **ALB:** Eduard Habich; **BRH:** Frida Leider, (28) Anny Konetzni; **FLH:** Constance Willis; **GTR:** Rosalind von Schirach, (28) Maria Nezadal; **GUN:** Herbert Janssen, (28) Paul Schoeffler; **HAG:** Emanuel List; **NN:** Mary Jarred, Constance Willis, Mae Craven; **SGF:** Lauritz Melchior; **WEL:** Betty Thompson; **WGL:** Erna Berger; **WLT:** Sabine Kalter

Conductor: Albert Coates (with the LPO). Stage director: Charles Moor.
Language: English
Siegfried (4 September, 2 October). **ALB:** Percy Heming; **BRH:** Eva Turner; **ED:** Edith Furmedge; **FAF:** Robert Easton; **MM:** Octave Dua, (2) Roy Devereux; **SGF:** Walter Widdop; **WAN:** Robert Parker, (2) Arthur Fear; **WDB:** Stella Andreva, (2) Barbara Lane

1936
TWO CYCLES
Conductor: Thomas Beecham
Das Rheingold (6, 21 May). **ALB:** Eduard Habich; **DON:** Paul Schoeffler; **ED:** Edith Furmedge, (21) Enid Szantho; **FAF:** Robert Easton; **FAS:** Ludwig Weber; **FLH:** Margery Booth; **FR:** Henry Wendon; **FRE:** Josephine Wray; **FRK:** Kerstin Thorborg; **LG:** Martin Kremer; **MM:** Hanns Fleischer; **WEL:** Betsy de la Porte; **WGL:** Stella Andreva; **WOT:** Rudolf Bockelmann
Die Walküre (8, 25 May). **BRH:** Frida Leider, (25) Kirsten Flagstad; **FRK:** Kerstin Thorborg, (25) Enid Szantho; **GEH:** Mae Craven; **GRG:** Gwladys Garside; **HLW:** Elsa Stenning; **HUN:** Emanuel List, (25) Ludwig Weber; **OTL:** Thelma Bardsley; **RSW:** Mahry Dawes; **SGL:** Elisabeth Rethberg; **SGM:** Lauritz Melchior; **SGR:** Joyce Newton; **SWL:** Gladys Ripley; **WLT:** Betsy de la Porte; **WOT:** Rudolf Bockelmann [25 May: Bockelmann asked the audience's indulgence as he had a cold]
Siegfried (12, 27 May). **ALB:** Eduard Habich; **BRH:** Frida Leider, (27) Kirsten Flagstad; **ED:** Edith Furmedge, (27) Enid Szantho; **FAF:** Robert Easton; **MM:** Hanns Fleischer; **SGF:** Lauritz Melchior; **WAN:** Rudolf Bockelmann, (27) Max Roth; **WDB:** Stella Andreva
Götterdämmerung (14, 29 May). **ALB:** Eduard Habich; **BRH:** Frida Leider, (29) Kirsten Flagstad; **FLH:** Margery Booth; **GTR:** Maria Nezadal; **GUN:** Herbert Janssen; **HAG:** Emanuel List, (29) Ludwig Weber; **NN:** Mary Jarred, Constance Willis, Mae Craven; **SGF:** Lauritz Melchior; **WEL:** Jose Malone; **WGL:** Stella Andreva; **WLT:** Kerstin Thorborg, (29) Enid Szantho

1937
TWO CYCLES
Conductor: Wilhelm Furtwängler
Das Rheingold (13, 24 May). **ALB:** Eugen Fuchs; **DON:** Paul Schoeffler; **ED:** Edith Furmedge; **FAF:** Robert Easton; **FAS:** Ludwig Weber; **FLH:** Edith Furmedge; **FR:** Henry Wendon; **FRE:** Josephine Wray; **FRK:** Margarete Klose, (24) Kerstin Thorborg; **LG:** Fritz Wolff; **MM:** Erich Zimmermann; **WEL:** Edith Coates; **WGL:** Stella Andreva; **WOT:** Rudolf Bockelmann
Die Walküre (17, 26 May). **BRH:** Frida Leider, (26) Kirsten Flagstad; **FRK:** Margarete Klose, (26) Kerstin

Thorborg; **GEH:** Mae Craven; **GRG:** Gwladys Garside; **HLW:** Elsa Stenning; **HUN:** Ludwig Weber; **OTL:** Thelma Bardsley; **RSW:** Evelyn Arden; **SGL:** Maria Müller; **SGM:** Franz Völker; **SGR:** Edith Coates; **SWL:** Gladys Ripley; **WLT:** Linda Seymour; **WOT:** Rudolf Bockelmann
Siegfried (19, 28 May). **ALB:** Eugen Fuchs; **BRH:** Frida Leider, (28) Kirsten Flagstad; **ED:** Edith Furmedge; **FAF:** Robert Easton; **MM:** Erich Zimmermann; **SGF:** Max Lorenz, (28) Lauritz Melchior; **WAN:** Rudolf Bockelmann; **WDB:** Stella Andreva
Götterdämmerung (21 May, 1 June). **ALB:** Eugen Fuchs; **BRH:** Frida Leider, (1) Kirsten Flagstad; **FLH:** Linda Seymour; **GTR:** Maria Nezadal; **GUN:** Herbert Janssen; **HAG:** Ludwig Weber; **NN:** Mary Jarred, Constance Willis, Mae Craven; **SGF:** Max Lorenz, (1) Lauritz Melchior; **WEL:** Jose Malone; **WGL:** Stella Andreva; **WLT:** Margarete Klose, (1) Kerstin Thorborg

1938
TWO CYCLES
Conductor: Wilhelm Furtwängler
Das Rheingold (18, 30 May). **ALB:** Adolf Vogel; **DON:** Herbert Janssen; **ED:** Mary Jarred; **FAF:** Norman Allin; **FAS:** Ludwig Weber; **FLH:** Edith Furmedge; **FR:** Henry Wendon; **FRE:** Anny von Stosch; **FRK:** Kerstin Thorborg, (30) Karin Branzell; **LG:** Fritz Wolff; **MM:** Erich Zimmermann, (30) Karl Laufkötter; **WEL:** Edith Coates; **WGL:** Stella Andreva; **WOT:** Rudolf Bockelmann, (30) Karl Kamann
Die Walküre (20 May, 1 June). **BRH:** Anny Konetzni, (1) Frida Leider; **FRK:** Kerstin Thorborg; **GEH:** Mae Craven; **GRG:** Maud Heaton; **HLW:** Elsa Stenning; **HUN:** Ludwig Weber, (1) Wilhelm Schirp; **OTL:** Anita Oberländer; **RSW:** Monica Warner; **SGL:** Hilde Konetzni, (1) Tiana Lemnitz; **SGM:** Lauritz Melchior; **SGR:** Edith Coates; **SWL:** Gladys Ripley; **WLT:** Erika Storm; **WOT:** Rudolf Bockelmann, (1) Karl Kamann
Siegfried (24 May, 3 June). **ALB:** Adolf Vogel; **BRH:** Anny Konetzni, (3) Frida Leider; **ED:** Edith Furmedge; **FAF:** Wilhelm Strienz; **MM:** Erich Zimmermann, (3) Karl Laufkötter; **SGF:** Lauritz Melchior; **WAN:** Rudolf Bockelmann, (3) Karl Kamann; **WDB:** Stella Andreva
Götterdämmerung (27 May, 7 June). **ALB:** Adolf Vogel; **BRH:** Anny Konetzni, (7) Frida Leider; **FLH:** Freda Townson; **GTR:** Anny von Stosch; **GUN:** Herbert Janssen; **HAG:** Ludwig Weber, (7) Wilhelm Schirp; **NN:** Mary Jarred, Constance Willis, Mae Craven; **SGF:** Lauritz Melchior; **WEL:** Betty Thompson; **WGL:** Stella Andreva; **WLT:** Kerstin Thorborg

1939
ONE CYCLE
Conductor: Thomas Beecham
Das Rheingold (6 June). **ALB:** Jean Stern; **DON:** Arnold Matters; **ED:** Mary Jarred; **FAF:** Robert Easton; **FAS:** Ludwig Weber; **FLH:** Edith Furmedge; **FR:** Henry Wendon; **FRE:** Josephine Wray; **FRK:** Kerstin Thorborg; **LG:** Adolf Fischer; **MM:** Karl Laufkötter; **WEL:** Edith Coates; **WGL:** Stella Andreva; **WOT:** Paul Schoeffler
Die Walküre (9 June). **BRH:** Anny Konetzni; **FRK:** Kerstin Thorborg; **GEH:** Mae Craven; **GRG:** Maud Heaton; **HLW:** Ruth Packer; **HUN:** Ludwig Weber; **OTL:** Anita Oberländer; **RSW:** Nancy Evans; **SGL:** Hilde Konetzni; **SGM:** Lauritz Melchior; **SGR:** Edith Coates; **SWL:** Freda Townson; **WLT:** Gwladys Garside; **WOT:** Emil Treskow
Siegfried (12 June). **ALB:** Jean Stern; **BRH:** Anny Konetzni; **ED:** Edith Furmedge; **FAF:** Norman Walker; **MM:** Karl Laufkötter; **SGF:** Lauritz Melchior; **WAN:** Emil Treskow; **WDB:** Stella Andreva
Götterdämmerung (14 June). **ALB:** Jean Stern; **BRH:** Anny Konetzni; **FLH:** Freda Townson; **GTR:** Maria Nezadal; **GUN:** Herbert Janssen; **HAG:** Ludwig Weber; **NN:** Mary Jarred, Edith Furmedge, Mae Craven; **SGF:** Lauritz Melchior; **WEL:** Betty Thompson; **WGL:** Stella Andreva; **WLT:** Kerstin Thorborg

1948
Conductor: Karl Rankl. Producer: Friedrich Schramm. Designer: Reece Pemberton (Act I)
Language: English

The Valkyrie (3, 8, 13, 18, 23, 30 March). **BRH:** Kirsten Flagstad; **FRK:** Edith Coates; **GEH:** Elizabeth Abercrombie; **GRG:** Constance Shacklock; **HLW:** Audrey Bowman; **HUN:** David Franklin; **OTL:** Muriel Rae; **RSW:** Rosina Raisbeck; **SGL:** Doris Doree; **SGM:** Arthur Carron; **SGR:** Denise Francis-Sirou; **SWL:** Elisabeth Harbutt; **WLT:** Edith Coates; **WOT:** Hans Hotter
Siegfried (11, 20, 30 November). **ALB:** Grahame Clifford; **BRH:** Astrid Varnay; **ED:** Edith Furmedge; **FAF:** Norman Walker; **MM:** Peter Klein; **SGF:** Set Svanholm; **WAN:** Hans Hotter; **WDB:** Shirley Russell
The Valkyrie (13, 17 November). **BRH:** Astrid Varnay; **FRK:** Edith Coates; **GEH:** Elizabeth Abercrombie; **GRG:** Constance Shacklock; **HLW:** Audrey Bowman; **HUN:** David Franklin, (17) Trevor Anthony; **OTL:** Muriel Rae; **RSW:** Rosina Raisbeck; **SGL:** Doris Doree; **SGM:** Set Svanholm; **SGR:** Denise Francis-Sirou; **SWL:** Valetta Iacopi; **WOT:** Hans Hotter; **WLT:** Edith Coates

1949
TWO CYCLES
Conductor: Karl Rankl
Das Rheingold (12, 30 May). **ALB:** Grahame Clifford; **DON:** Rhydderch Davies; **ED:** Edith Furmedge; **FAF:** David Franklin, (30) Norman Walker; **FAS:** Marian Nowakowski, (19) Ludwig Weber; **FLH:** Jean Watson, (30) Monica Sinclair; **FR:** Edgar Evans; **FRE:** Blanche Turner; **FRK:** Edith Coates; **LG:** Set Svanholm; **MM:** Peter Klein, (30) Peter Markwort; **WEL:** Rosina Raisbeck; **WGL:** Muriel Rae; **WOT:** Hans Hotter
Die Walküre (16, 31 May). **BRH:** Kirsten Flagstad; **FRK:** Edith Coates; **GEH:** Elizabeth Abercrombie; **GRG:** Constance Shacklock; **HLW:** Audrey Bowman; **HUN:** David Franklin, (31) Trevor Anthony; **OTL:** Muriel Rae; **RSW:** Rosina Raisbeck; **SGL:** Doris Doree; **SGM:** Set Svanholm; **SGR:** Denise Francis-Sirou; **SWL:** Jean Watson; **WLT:** Edith Coates; **WOT:** Hans Hotter, (31) Kenneth Schon. [Schon replaced at short notice the indisposed Hotter}
Siegfried (19 May, 2 June). **ALB:** Grahame Clifford; **BRH:** Kirsten Flagstad; **ED:** Jean Watson; **FAF:** Norman Walker; **MM:** Peter Klein, (2) Peter Markwort; **SGF:** Set Svanholm; **WAN:** Hans Hotter; **WDB:** Shirley Russell
Götterdämmerung (25 May, 8 June). **ALB:** Grahame Clifford; **BRH:** Kirsten Flagstad; **FLH:** Constance Shacklock; **GTR:** Doris Doree; **GUN:** Hans Hotter, (8) Paul Schoeffler; **HAG:** Deszoe Ernster; **NN1:** Constance Shacklock; **NN2:** Rosina Raisbeck; **NN3:** Sylvia Fisher; **SGF:** Set Svanholm; **WEL:** Elizabeth Abercrombie; **WGL:** Audrey Bowman; **WLT:** Edith Coates

1950
TWO CYCLES
Conductor: Karl Rankl
Das Rheingold (8, 19 June). **ALB:** Grahame Clifford; **DON:** Rhydderch Davies; **ED:** Jean Watson; **FAF:** Marian Nowakowski; **FAS:** Ludwig Weber; **FLH:** Monica Sinclair; **FR:** Edgar Evans; **FRE:** Blanche Turner; **FRK:** Edith Coates, (19) Constance Shacklock; **LG:** Set Svanholm; **MM:** Erich Zimmermann, (19) Peter Klein; **WEL:** Rosina Raisbeck; **WGL:** Audrey Bowman; **WOT:** Andreas Boehm
Die Walküre (10, 21 June). **BRH:** Kirsten Flagstad; **FRK:** Edith Coates, (21) Constance Shacklock; **GEH:** Elizabeth Abercrombie; **GRG:** Constance Shacklock; **HLW:** Audrey Bowman; **HUN:** Ludwig Weber; **OTL:** Blanche Turner; **RSW:** Rosina Raisbeck; **SGL:** Sylvia Fisher; **SGM:** Set Svanholm; **SGR:** Monica Sinclair; **SWL:** Jean Watson; **WLT:** Edith Coates; **WOT:** Andreas Boehm
Siegfried (14, 23 June). **ALB:** Grahame Clifford; **BRH:** Kirsten Flagstad; **ED:** Jean Watson; **FAF:** Norman Walker; **MM:** Erich Zimmermann, (23) Peter Klein; **SGF:** Set Svanholm; **WAN:** Andreas Boehm; **WDB:** Audrey Bowman
Götterdämmerung (17, 26 June). **ALB:** Grahame Clifford; **BRH:** Kirsten Flagstad; **FLH:** Constance Shacklock; **GTR:** Doris Doree; **GUN:** Paul Schoeffler; **HAG:** Ludwig Weber; **NN1:** Constance Shacklock; **NN2:** Rosina Raisbeck; **NN3:** Sylvia Fisher; **SGF:** Set Svanholm; **WEL:** Elizabeth Abercrombie; **WGL:** Audrey Bowman; **WLT:** Edith Coates

1951
TWO CYCLES
Conductor: Karl Rankl
Das Rheingold (4, 7 May). **ALB:** Otakar Kraus; DON: Rhydderch Davies; **ED:** Jean Watson; **FAF:** Gottlob Frick; **FAS:** Marian Nowakowski; **FLH:** Monica Sinclair; **FR:** Edgar Evans; **FRE:** Blanche Turner; **FRK:** Edith Coates; **LG:** Set Svanholm; **MM:** Peter Klein; **WEL:** Rosina Raisbeck; **WGL:** Audrey Bowman; **WOT:** Hans Hotter
Die Walküre (10, 14 May). **BRH:** Anny Konetzni; **FRK:** Edith Coates; **GEH:** Elizabeth Abercrombie; **GRG:** Constance Shacklock; **HLW:** Audrey Bowman; **HUN:** Gottlob Frick; **OTL:** Blanche Turner; **RSW:** Rosina Raisbeck; **SGL:** Sylvia Fisher; **SGM:** Set Svanholm; **SGR:** Monica Sinclair; **SWL:** Jean Watson; **WLT:** Edith Coates; **WOT:** Hans Hotter
Siegfried (18, 22 May). **ALB:** Otakar Kraus; **BRH:** Astrid Varnay; **ED:** Jean Watson; **FAF:** Norman Walker; **MM:** Peter Klein; **SGF:** Set Svanholm; **WAN:** Hans Hotter; **WDB:** Audrey Bowman
Götterdämmerung (24, 26 May). **ALB:** Grahame Clifford; **BRH:** Kirsten Flagstad; **FLH:** Constance Shacklock; **GTR:** Sylvia Fisher; **GUN:** Marko Rothmüller; **HAG:** Gottlob Frick; **NN1:** Constance Shacklock; **NN2:** Barbara Howitt; **NN3:** Sylvia Fisher; **SGF:** Set Svanholm; **WEL:** Elizabeth Abercrombie; **WGL:** Audrey Bowman; **WLT:** Edith Coates

Conductor: Karl Rankl
Die Walküre (31 May). **BRH:** Astrid Varnay; **FRK:** Edith Coates; **GEH:** Elizabeth Abercrombie; **GRG:** Constance Shacklock; **HLW:** Audrey Bowman; **HUN:** Gottlob Frick; **OTL:** Blanche Turner; **RSW:** Rosina Raisbeck; **SGL:** Kirsten Flagstad; **SGM:** Set Svanholm; **SGR:** Monica Sinclair; **SWL:** Jean Watson; **WLT:** Edith Coates; **WOT:** Sigurd Björling

1953

Conductor: Fritz Stiedry
Die Walküre (19, 24, 26, 30 October). **BRH:** Margaret Harshaw; **FRK:** Edith Coates; **GEH:** Emelie Hooke; **GRG:** Constance Shacklock; **HLW:** Joan Sutherland; **HUN:** Frederick Dalberg; **OTL:** Blanche Turner; **RSW:** Barbara Howitt; **SGL:** Sylvia Fisher; **SGM:** Ramón Vinay; **SGR:** Monica Sinclair; **SWL:** Jean Watson; **WLT:** Edith Coates; **WOT:** Hans Hotter, (30) Karl Kamann

Conductor: Karl Rankl
Siegfried (22, 28 October). **ALB:** Otakar Kraus; **BRH:** Astrid Varnay; **ED:** Jean Watson; **FAF:** Norman Walker; **SGF:** Set Svanholm, (28) Günther Treptow; **MM:** Paul Kuen; **WAN:** Hans Hotter, (28) Karl Kamann; **WDB:** Mattiwilda Dobbs

1954

TWO CYCLES
Conductor: Fritz Stiedry. Producer: Rudolf Hartmann. Designer: Leslie Hurry. Lighting: John Sullivan
Das Rheingold (NP. 27 May, 21 June). **ALB:** Otakar Kraus; **DON:** Rhydderch Davies; **ED:** Constance Shacklock; **FAF:** Michael Langdon; **FAS:** Frederick Dalberg; **FLH:** Marjorie Thomas; **FR:** Edgar Evans; **FRE:** Eleanor Houston; **FRK:** Maria von Ilosvay; **LG:** Erich Witte; **MM:** Peter Markwort, (21) Paul Kuen; **WEL:** Rosina Raisbeck; **WGL:** Joan Sutherland; **WOT:** Ferdinand Frantz
Die Walküre (NP. 2, 23 June). **BRH:** Margaret Harshaw; **FRK:** Maria von Ilosvay; **GEH:** Rosina Raisbeck; **GRG:** Constance Shacklock; **HLW:** Joan Sutherland; **HUN:** Frederick Dalberg; **OTL:** Hella Toros; **RSW:** Gita Denise; **SGL:** Sylvia Fisher; **SGM:** Hans Beirer, (23) Set Svanholm; **SGR:** Patricia Johnson; **SWL:** Valetta Iacopi; **WLT:** Janet Howe; **WOT:** Ferdinand Frantz
Siegfried (NP. 8, 25 June). **ALB:** Otakar Kraus; **BRH:** Margaret Harshaw; **ED:** Constance Shacklock; **FAF:** Michael Langdon; **MM:** Paul Kuen; **SGF:** Set Svanholm; **WAN:** Ferdinand Frantz; **WDB:** Joan Sutherland
Götterdämmerung (NP. 17, 29 June). **ALB:** Otakar Kraus; **BRH:** Margaret Harshaw; **FLH:** Marjorie Thomas; **GTR:** Elfriede Wasserthal; **GUN:** Hermann Uhde; **HAG:** Deszoe Ernster; **NN1:** Maria von Ilosvay; **NN2:** Constance Shacklock; **NN3:** Sylvia Fisher; **SGF:** Set Svanholm; **WEL:** Rosina Raisbeck; **WGL:** Joan Sutherland; **WLT:** Maria von Ilosvay

1955

TWO CYCLES
Conductor: Rudolf Kempe
Das Rheingold (10 May, 8 June). **ALB:** Otakar Kraus; **DON:** Rhydderch Davies; **ED:** Jean Madeira; **FAF:** Frederick Dalberg; **FAS:** Ludwig Hofmann; **FLH:** Glenice Halliday; **FR:** Edgar Evans; **FRE:** Amy Shuard; **FRK:** Maria von Ilosvay; **LG:** Erich Witte; **MM:** Peter Klein; **WEL:** Una Hale; **WGL:** Joan Sutherland; **WOT:** Hans Hotter, (8) Paul Schoeffler
Die Walküre (14 May, 10 June). **BRH:** Margaret Harshaw; **FRK:** Maria von Ilosvay; **GEH:** Amy Shuard; **GRG:** Constance Shacklock; **HLW:** Joan Sutherland; **HUN:** Frederick Dalberg; **OTL:** Hella Toros, (10) Una Hale; **RSW:** Janet Howe; **SGL:** Leonie Rysanek, (10) Hilde Konetzni; **SGM:** Ramón Vinay; **SGR:** Noreen Berry; **SWL:** Valetta Iacopi; **WLT:** Edith Coates; **WOT:** Hans Hotter, (10) James Pease
Siegfried (19 May, 14 June). **ALB:** Otakar Kraus; **BRH:** Margaret Harshaw; **ED:** Jean Madeira; **FAF:** Frederick Dalberg; **MM:** Peter Klein; **SGF:** Set Svanholm; **WAN:** Hans Hotter, (14) James Pease; **WDB:** Adèle Leigh
Götterdämmerung (27 May, 17 June). **ALB:** Otakar Kraus; **BRH:** Margaret Harshaw; **FLH:** Glenice Halliday; **GTR:** Hilde Konetzni; **GUN:** Marko Rothmüller; **HAG:** Ludwig Hofmann; **NN1:** Maria von Ilosvay; **NN2:** Constance Shacklock; **NN3:** Amy Shuard; **SGF:** Set Svanholm; **WEL:** Una Hale; **WGL:** Joan Sutherland; **WLT:** Maria von Ilosvay

1956

TWO CYCLES
Conductor: Rudolf Kempe. Producer: Hartmann, rehearsed by Peter Potter
Das Rheingold (24 May, 11 June). **ALB:** Otakar Kraus; **DON:** Robert Allman; **ED:** Jean Madeira; **FAF:** Frederick Dalberg; **FAS:** Kurt Boehme; **FLH:** Glenice Halliday; **FR:** Edgar Evans; **FRE:** Una Hale; **FRK:** Maria von Ilosvay; **LG:** Erich Witte; **MM:** Peter Klein; **WEL:** Rosina Raisbeck; **WGL:** Joan Sutherland; **WOT:** Hans Hotter, (11) James Pease
Die Walküre (28 May, 12 June). **BRH:** Margaret Harshaw; **FRK:** Maria von Ilosvay; **GEH:** Amy Shuard; **GRG:** Constance Shacklock; **HLW:** Joan Sutherland; **HUN:** Frederick Dalberg; **OTL:** Una Hale; **RSW:** Marjorie Thomas; **SGL:** Sylvia Fisher; **SGM:** Ramón Vinay; **SGR:** Noreen Berry; **SWL:** Valetta Iacopi; **WLT:** Edith Coates; **WOT:** Hans Hotter, (12) James Pease
Siegfried (31 May, 14 June). **ALB:** Otakar Kraus; **BRH:** Margaret Harshaw; **ED:** Jean Madeira; **FAF:** Frederick Dalberg; **MM:** Peter Klein; **SGF:** Wolfgang Windgassen; **WAN:** Hans Hotter, (14) James Pease; **WDB:** Adèle Leigh
Götterdämmerung (6, 16 June). **ALB:** Otakar Kraus; **BRH:** Margaret Harshaw; **FLH:** Marjorie Thomas; **GTR:** Sylvia Fisher; **GUN:** Hermann Uhde; **HAG:** Kurt Boehme; **NN1:** Maria von Ilosvay; **NN2:** Constance Shacklock; **NN3:** Sylvia Fisher; **SGF:** Wolfgang Windgassen; **WEL:** Una Hale; **WGL:** Joan Sutherland; **WLT:** Maria von Ilosvay

1957

TWO CYCLES
Conductor: Rudolf Kempe
Das Rheingold (25 September, 1 October). **ALB:** Otakar Kraus ; **DON:** Robert Allman; **ED:** Maria von Ilosvay; **FAF:** Frederick Dalberg; **FAS:** Kurt Boehme; **FLH:** Marjorie Thomas; **FR:** Edgar Evans; **FRE:** Elisabeth Lindermeier; **FRK:** Georgine von Milinkovič; **LG:** Erich Witte; **MM:** Peter Klein; **WEL:** Una Hale; **WGL:** Joan Sutherland; **WOT:** Hans Hotter
Die Walküre (27 September, 8 October). **BRH:** Birgit Nilsson; **FRK:** Georgine von Milinkovič; **GEH:** Amy Shuard; **GRG:** Barbara Howitt; **HLW:** June Grant; **HUN:** Frederick Dalberg; **OTL:** Una Hale; **RSW:** Marjorie Thomas; **SGL:** Sylvia Fisher; **SGM:** Ramón Vinay, (8, Act II) Walter Geisler; **SGR:** Noreen Berry; **SWL:** Jean Watson; **WLT:** Edith Coates; **WOT:** Hans Hotter
Siegfried (1, 10 October). **ALB:** Otakar Kraus; **BRH:** Birgit Nilsson; **ED:** Maria von Ilosvay; **FAF:** Frederick Dalberg; **MM:** Peter Klein; **SGF:** Wolfgang Windgassen; **WAN:** Hans Hotter; **WDB:** Jeanette Sinclair
Götterdämmerung (4, 12 October). **ALB:** Otakar Kraus; **BRH:** Birgit Nilsson; **FLH:** Marjorie Thomas; **GTR:** Elisabeth Lindermeier; **GUN:** Hermann Uhde; **HAG:** Kurt Boehme; **NN1:** Maria von Ilosvay; **NN2:** Constance Shacklock; **NN3:** Amy Shuard, (12) Sylvia Fisher; **SGF:** Wolfgang Windgassen; **WEL:** Una Hale; **WGL:** Joan Sutherland; **WLT:** Maria von Ilosvay

Conductor: Rudolf Kempe
Götterdämmerung (14, 17 October). **ALB:** Otakar Kraus; **BRH:** Birgit Nilsson; **FLH:** Marjorie Thomas; **GTR:** Elisabeth Lindermeier; **GUN:** Hermann Uhde; **HAG:** Gottlob Frick, (17) Kurt Boehme; **NN1:** Maria von Ilosvay; **NN2:** Constance Shacklock; **NN3:** Amy Shuard; **SGF:** Set Svanholm, (17) Bernd Aldenhoff; **WEL:** Una Hale; **WGL:** Joan Sutherland; **WLT:** Maria von Ilosvay. [Svanholm and Aldenhoff replaced the indisposed Windgassen]
Die Walküre (19 October). **BRH:** Sylvia Fisher; **FRK:** Georgine von Milinkovič; **GEH:** Amy Shuard; **GRG:** Barbara Howitt; **HLW:** June Grant; **HUN:** Frederick Dalberg; **OTL:** Una Hale; **RSW:** Marjorie Thomas; **SGL:** Marianne Schech; **SGM:** Ramón Vinay; **SGR:** Noreen Berry; **SWL:** Jean Watson; **WLT:** Edith Coates; **WOT:** Hans Hotter

1958

TWO CYCLES
Conductor: Rudolf Kempe
Das Rheingold (19 September, 6 October). **ALB:** Otakar Kraus; **DON:** David Kelly; **ED:** Rut Siewert; **FAF:** Gottlob Frick; **FAS:** Kurt Boehme; **FLH:** Marjorie Thomas; **FR:** Edgar Evans; **FRE:** Una Hale; **FRK:** Maria von Ilosvay; **LG:** Richard Holm; **MM:** Peter Klein; **WEL:** Una Hale; **WGL:** Joan Sutherland; **WOT:** Hans Hotter
Die Walküre (24 September, 7 October). **BRH:** Astrid Varnay; **FRK:** Maria von Ilosvay; **GEH:** Amy Shuard; **GRG:** Lauris Elms; **HLW:** Judith Pierce; **HUN:** Kurt Boehme; **OTL:** Una Hale; **RSW:** Marjorie Thomas; **SGL:** Marianne Schech; **SGM:** Jon Vickers; **SGR:** Noreen Berry; **SWL:** Jean Watson; **WLT:** Margreta Elkins; **WOT:** Hans Hotter
Siegfried (29 September, 9 October). **ALB:** Otakar Kraus; **BRH:** Astrid Varnay; **ED:** Rut Siewert; **FAF:** Michael Langdon; **MM:** Peter Klein; **SGF:** Wolfgang Windgassen, (9, Acts II and III) Karl Liebl; **WAN:** Hans Hotter; **WDB:** Joan Sutherland
Götterdämmerung (3, 11 October). **ALB:** Otakar Kraus; **BRH:** Astrid Varnay; **FLH:** Marjorie Thomas; **GTR:** Hilde Konetzni; **GUN:** Hans Hotter; **HAG:** Gottlob Frick; **NN1:** Maria von Ilosvay; **NN2:** Marjorie Thomas; **NN3:** Amy Shuard; **SGF:** Wolfgang Windgassen; **WEL:** Una Hale; **WGL:** Joan Sutherland; **WLT:** Maria von Ilosvay

1959

TWO CYCLES
Conductors: Franz Konwitschny, (6) Reginald Goodall
Das Rheingold (18 September, 5 October). **ALB:** Otakar Kraus; **DON:** David Kelly; **ED:** Marga Höffgen; **FAF:** Michael Langdon; **FAS:** Kurt Boehme; **FLH:** Marjorie Thomas; **FR:** Edgar Evans; **FRE:** Una Hale; **FRK:** Ursula Böse; **LG:** Richard Holm; **MM:** Peter Klein; **WEL:** Josephine Veasey, (5) Una Hale; **WGL:** Joan Carlyle; **WOT:** Hans Hotter
Die Walküre (23 September, 6 October). **BRH:** Astrid Varnay, (6) Martha Mödl; **FRK:** Ursula Böse; **GEH:** Joyce Barker; **GRG:** Heather Begg; **HLW:** Judith Pierce; **HUN:** Kurt Boehme; **OTL:** Una Hale; **RSW:** Josephine Veasey; **SGL:** Amy Shuard; **SGM:** Ramón Vinay; **SGR:** Noreen Berry; **SWL:** Jean Watson; **WLT:** Margreta Elkins; **WOT:** Hans Hotter

Siegfried (28 September, 8 October). **ALB:** Otakar Kraus; **BRH:** Astrid Varnay, (8) Martha Mödl; **ED:** Marga Höffgen; **FAF:** Michael Langdon; **MM:** Peter Klein; **SGF:** Wolfgang Windgassen; **WAN:** Hans Hotter; **WDB:** Jeanette Sinclair
Götterdämmerung (2, 10 October). ALB: Otakar Kraus; **BRH:** Astrid Varnay, (10) Martha Mödl; **FLH:** Marjorie Thomas; **GTR:** Amy Shuard; **GUN:** Hermann Uhde; **HAG:** Gottlob Frick; **NN1:** Marjorie Thomas; **NN2:** Monica Sinclair; **NN3:** Amy Shuard; **SGF:** Wolfgang Windgassen; **WEL:** Una Hale, (10) Josephine Veasey; **WGL:** Joan Carlyle; **WLT:** Ursula Böse

1960

TWO CYCLES
Conductor: Rudolph Kempe. Production: Rehearsed by Witte
Das Rheingold (16 September, 3 October). **ALB:** Otakar Kraus; **DON:** Forbes Robinson; **ED:** Marga Höffgen; **FAF:** Michael Langdon; **FAS:** David Ward; **FLH:** Marjorie Thomas; **FR:** Edgar Evans; **FRE:** Una Hale; **FRK:** Ursula Böse; **LG:** Richard Holm; **MM:** Gerhard Stolze; **WEL:** Josephine Veasey; **WGL:** Joan Carlyle; **WOT** Hermann Uhde
Die Walküre (21 September, 4 October). **BRH:** Margaret Harshaw; **FRK:** Ursula Böse; **GEH:** Rosina Raisbeck; **GRG:** Heather Begg; **HLW:** Judith Pierce; **HUN:** David Ward; **OTL:** Una Hale; **RSW:** Josephine Veasey; **SGL:** Amy Shuard; **SGM:** Wolfgang Windgassen; **SGR:** Noreen Berry; **SWL:** Monica Sinclair; **WLT:** Margreta Elkins; **WOT:** Hans Hotter
Siegfried (26 September, 6 October). **ALB:** Otakar Kraus; **BRH:** Margaret Harshaw, (6) Birgit Nilsson; **ED:** Marga Höffgen; **FAF:** Michael Langdon; **MM:** Gerhard Stolze; **SGF:** Wolfgang Windgassen; **WAN:** Hans Hotter; **WDB:** Joan Carlyle
Götterdämmerung (30 September, 8 October). **ALB:** Otakar Kraus; **BRH:** Margaret Harshaw, (8) Birgit Nilsson; **FLH:** Marjorie Thomas; **GTR:** Amy Shuard; **GUN:** Hermann Uhde; **HAG:** Gottlob Frick; **NN1:** Marjorie Thomas; **NN2:** Constance Shacklock, (8) Monica Sinclair; **NN3:** Una Hale; **SGF:** Wolfgang Windgassen; **WEL:** Josephine Veasey; **WGL:** Joan Carlyle; **WLT:** Ursula Böse

1961

Conductor: Georg Solti. Producer: Hans Hotter. Designer: Herbert Kern
Die Walküre (NP. 29 September, 2, 5, 9 October). **BRH:** Anita Välkki; **FRK:** Rita Gorr; **GEH:** Marie Collier; **GRG:** Maureen Guy; **HLW:** Judith Pierce; **HUN:** Michael Langdon; **OTL:** Julia Malyon; **RSW:** Josephine Veasey; **SGL:** Claire Watson; **SGM:** Jon Vickers; **SGR:** Noreen Berry; **SWL:** Joan Edwards; **WLT:** Margreta Elkins; **WOT:** Hans Hotter

1962

Conductor: Georg Solti. Producer: Hans Hotter. Designer: Günther Schneider-Siemssen. Lighting: William Bundy and Günther Schneider-Siemssen
Siegfried (NP. 7, 11, 14, 17 September). **ALB:** Otakar Kraus; **BRH:** Birgit Nilsson; **ED:** Rut Siewert; **FAF:** Joseph Rouleau; **MM:** Gerhard Stolze; **SGF:** Wolfgang Windgassen; **WAN:** David Ward; **WDB:** Barbara Holt

Conductor: Georg Solti.
Die Walküre (7, 11, 14 December). **BRH:** Amy Shuard; **FRK:** Grace Hoffman; **GEH:** Ava June; **GRG:** Maureen Guy; **HLW:** Judith Pierce; HUN: Michael Langdon; **OTL:** Una Hale; **RSW:** Josephine Veasey; **SGL:** Claire Watson; **SGM:** Ernst Kozub; **SGR:** Noreen Berry; **SWL:** Monica Sinclair; **WLT:** Margreta Elkins; **WOT:** Hans Hotter

1963

Conductor: Georg Solti. Producer: Hans Hotter. Designer: Günther Schneider-Siemssen. Lighting: William Bundy and Günther Schneider-Siemssen.
Götterdämmerung (NP. 11, 14, 16, 19 September). **ALB:** Otakar Kraus; **BRH:** Birgit Nilsson; **FLH:** Maureen Guy; **GTR:** Marie Collier; **GUN:** Thomas Stewart; **HAG:** Gottlob Frick; **NN1:** Monica Sinclair; **NN2:** Margreta Elkins; **NN3:** Rita Hunter; **SGF:** Wolfgang Windgassen; **WEL:** Gwyneth Jones; **WGL:** Barbara Holt; **WLT:** Josephine Veasey

1964

TWO CYCLES
Conductor: Georg Solti. Producer: Hans Hotter (*Siegfried* revival rehearsed by Anderson). Designer: Günther Schneider-Siemssen. Lighting: William Bundy and Günther Schneider-Siemssen
Das Rheingold (NP. 3, 21 September). **ALB:** Frans Andersson; **DON:** Peter Glossop; **ED:** Maureen Guy; **FAF:** Michael Langdon; **FAS:** Forbes Robinson; **FLH:** Maureen Guy; **FR:** John Dobson; **FRE:** Marie Collier; **FRK:** Josephine Veasey; **LG:** Richard Holm; **MM:** John Lanigan; **WEL:** Gwyneth Jones; **WGL:** Joan Carlyle; **WOT:** David Ward
Die Walküre (NP. 5, 22 September). **BRH:** Anita Välkki; **FRK:** Grace Hoffman; **GEH:** Marie Collier; **GRG:** Maureen Guy; **HLW:** Judith Pierce; **HUN:** Michael Langdon; **OTL:** Gwyneth Jones; **RSW:** Elizabeth Bainbridge; **SGL:** Claire Watson; **SGM:** Ernst Kozub; **SGR:** Noreen Berry; **SWL:** Monica Sinclair; **WLT:** Josephine Veasey; **WOT:** David Ward
Siegfried (12, 24 September). **ALB:** Otakar Kraus; **BRH:** Amy Shuard; **ED:** Marga Höffgen; **FAF:** Michael Langdon; **MM:** Gerhard Stolze; **SGF:** Wolfgang Windgassen; **WAN:** David Ward; **WDB:** Joan Carlyle
Götterdämmerung (19, 26 September). **ALB:** Otakar Kraus; **BRH:** Amy Shuard; **FLH:** Maureen Guy; **GTR:** Marie Collier; **GUN:** Thomas Stewart; **HAG:** Gottlob Frick; **NN1:** Marga Höffgen; **NN2:** Maureen Guy; **NN3:** Gwyneth Jones; **SGF:** Wolfgang Windgassen; **WEL:** Gwyneth Jones; **WGL:** Joan Carlyle; **WLT:** Josephine Veasey

1965

TWO CYCLES
Conductor: Georg Solti
Das Rheingold (22 September, 11 October). **ALB:** Gustav Neidlinger, (11) Otakar Kraus; **DON:** Victor Godfrey; **ED:** Maureen Guy; **FAF:** Michael Langdon; **FAS:** Forbes Robinson, (11) Arnold van Mill; **FLH:** Maureen Guy; **FR:** John Dobson; **FRE:** Elizabeth Vaughan; **FRK:** Josephine Veasey; **LG:** Gerhard Stolze; **MM:** John Lanigan; **WEL:** Elizabeth Robson; **WGL:** Joan Carlyle; **WOT:** David Ward, (11) Hans Hotter
Die Walküre (23 September, 12 October). **BRH:** Amy Shuard; **FRK:** Josephine Veasey; **GEH:** Anne Edwards; **GRG:** Maureen Guy; **HLW:** Rae Woodland; **HUN:** Michael Langdon; **OTL:** Margaret Kingsley; **RSW:** Elizabeth Bainbridge; **SGL:** Claire Watson; **SGM:** Ernst Kozub; **SGR:** Noreen Berry; **SWL:** Yvonne Minton; **WLT:** Ann Howard; **WOT:** David Ward, (12) Hans Hotter
Siegfried (29 September, 14 October). **ALB:** Gustav Neidlinger, (14) Otakar Kraus; **BRH:** Amy Shuard; **ED:** Maureen Guy; **FAF:** Michael Langdon; **MM:** Gerhard Stolze; **SGF:** Wolfgang Windgassen; **WAN:** David Ward, (14) Hans Hotter; **WDB:** Elizabeth Vaughan, (14) Joan Carlyle
Götterdämmerung (8, 16 October). **ALB:** Gustav Neidlinger, (16) Otakar Kraus; **BRH:** Amy Shuard; **FLH:** Maureen Guy; **GTR:** Heather Harper; **GUN:** John Shaw; **HAG:** Gottlob Frick; **NN1:** Helen Watts; **NN2:** Maureen Guy; **NN3:** Gwyneth Jones; **SGF:** Wolfgang Windgassen; **WEL:** Elizabeth Robson; **WGL:** Joan Carlyle; **WLT:** Josephine Veasey

Conductor: Edward Downes
Das Rheingold (18 October). **ALB:** Otakar Kraus; **DON:** Victor Godfrey; **ED:** Maureen Guy; **FAF:** Michael Langdon; **FAS:** Forbes Robinson; **FLH:** Maureen Guy; **FR:** John Dobson; **FRE:** Elizabeth Vaughan; **FRK:** Josephine Veasey; **LG:** Richard Holm; **MM:** John Lanigan; **WEL:** Elizabeth Robson; **WGL:** Joan Carlyle; **WOT:** David Ward
Die Walküre (1, 4 November). **BRH:** Marijke van der Lugt; **FRK:** Josephine Veasey, (4) Grace Hoffman; **GEH:** Anne Edwards; **GRG:** Maureen Guy; **HLW:** Rae Woodland; **HUN:** Michael Langdon; **OTL:** Margaret Kingsley; **RSW:** Elizabeth Bainbridge; **SGL:** Claire Watson; **SGM:** Ernst Kozub; **SGR:** Noreen Berry; **SWL:** Yvonne Minton; **WLT:** Ann Howard; **WOT:** David Ward
Götterdämmerung (5, 6 November). **ALB:** Otakar Kraus; **BRH:** Amy Shuard; **FLH:** Maureen Guy; **GTR:** Heather Harper; **GUN:** John Shaw; **HAG:** Gottlob Frick; **NN1:** Helen Watts; **NN2:** Maureen Guy; **NN3:** Rita Hunter; **SGF:** Wolfgang Windgassen; **WEL:** Elizabeth Robson; **WGL:** Joan Carlyle; **WLT:** Josephine Veasey

1966

TWO CYCLES
Conductors: Georg Solti
Das Rheingold (12, 31 October). **ALB:** Gustav Neidlinger; **DON:** Napoléon Bisson; **ED:** Maureen Guy; FAF: Michael Langdon; **FAS:** Forbes Robinson; **FLH:** Maureen Guy; **FR:** John Dobson; **FRE:** Elizabeth Vaughan; **FRK:** Josephine Veasey; **LG:** Richard Holm; **MM:** John Lanigan; **WEL:** Yvonne Minton; **WGL:** Elizabeth Robson; **WOT:** David Ward
Die Walküre (13 October, 1 November). **BRH:** Ludmila Dvoraková, (1) Amy Shuard; **FRK:** Josephine Veasey; **GEH:** Marie Hayward; **GRG:** Maureen Guy; **HLW:** Rae Woodland; **HUN:** Michael Langdon; **OTL:** Margaret Kingsley; **RSW:** Elizabeth Bainbridge; **SGL:** Gwyneth Jones; **SGM:** Ernst Kozub; **SGR:** Anna Reynolds; **SWL:** Monica Sinclair; **WLT:** Yvonne Minton; **WOT:** David Ward
Siegfried (21 October, 3 November). **ALB:** Gustav Neidlinger; **BRH:** Ludmila Dvoraková, (3) Amy Shuard; **ED:** Maureen Guy; **FAF:** Michael Langdon; **MM:** Gerhard Stolze, (3) John Lanigan; **SGF:** Ticho Parly; **WAN:** David Ward; **WDB:** Elizabeth Vaughan
Götterdämmerung (28 October, 5 November). **ALB:** Gustav Neidlinger; **BRH:** Ludmila Dvoraková, (5) Amy Shuard; **FLH:** Maureen Guy, (5) Elizabeth Bainbridge; **GTR:** Gwyneth Jones; **GUN:** John Shaw; **HAG:** Michael Langdon; **NN1:** Helen Watts; **NN2:** Maureen Guy, (5) Yvonne Minton; **NN3:** Elizabeth Fretwell; **SGF:** Karl-Josef Hering; **WEL:** Yvonne Minton; **WGL:** Elizabeth Robson; **WLT:** Josephine Veasey

1967

2 CYCLES

Conductors: Georg Solti, (2, 3, 5, 7) Edward Downes

Das Rheingold (13 September, 2 October). **ALB:** Gwyn Griffiths, (2) Otakar Kraus; **DON:** Donald McIntyre; **ED:** Helen Watts; **FAF:** Kurt Boehme; **FAS:** Forbes Robinson; **FLH:** Elizabeth Bainbridge; **FR:** Jon Andrew; **FRE:** Elizabeth Vaughan; **FRK:** Josephine Veasey; **LG:** John Dobson; **MM:** John Lanigan; **WEL:** Yvonne Minton; **WGL:** Elizabeth Robson; **WOT:** Theo Adam, (2) Hans Hotter

Die Walküre (14 September, 3 October). **BRH:** Amy Shuard, (3) Ludmila Dvoraková; **FRK:** Josephine Veasey; **GEH:** Ava June; **GRG:** Patricia Purcell; **HLW:** Vivien Townley; **HUN:** Kurt Boehme; **OTL:** Margaret Kingsley; **RSW:** Elizabeth Bainbridge; **SGL:** Ingrid Bjoner; **SGM:** Ernst Kozub; **SGR:** Noreen Berry; **SWL:** Monica Sinclair; **WLT:** Yvonne Minton; **WOT:** Theo Adam, (3) Herbert Fliether. [3 October: Fliether replaced the indisposed Hans Hotter]

Siegfried (22 September, 7 October). **ALB:** Napoléon Bisson; **BRH:** Amy Shuard, (7) Ludmila Dvoraková; **ED:** Helen Watts; **FAF:** Kurt Boehme; **MM:** John Lanigan; **SGF:** Ticho Parly; **WAN:** Theo Adam, (7) Herbert Fliether; **WDB:** Joan Carlyle, (7) Elizabeth Vaughan. [7 October: the performance of *Siegfried* scheduled for 5 October was switched with *Götterdämmerung* due to the indisposition of Hotter as Wotan and the unavailability of Fliether to replace him on 5 October]

Götterdämmerung (29 September, 5 October). **ALB:** Napoléon Bisson; **BRH:** Amy Shuard, (5) Ludmila Dvoraková; **FLH:** Elizabeth Bainbridge; **GTR:** Heather Harper, (5: Act II) Sylvia Fisher; **GUN:** John Shaw; **HAG:** Kurt Boehme; **NN1:** Helen Watts; **NN2:** Yvonne Minton; **NN3:** Elizabeth Fretwell; **SGF:** Ticho Parly; **WEL:** Yvonne Minton; **WGL:** Elizabeth Robson; **WLT:** Josephine Veasey. [5 October: the rescheduling of this performance created a clash for Harper; hence, Fisher sang Gutrune for Act II, allowing Harper to complete her pre-existing engagement and still sing most of Gutrune]

1968

TWO CYCLES

Conductors: Georg Solti, (30, 1, 3, 5) Edward Downes

Das Rheingold (11, 30 September). **ALB:** Gwyn Griffiths, (30) Otakar Kraus; **DON:** Donald McIntyre; **ED:** Helen Watts; **FAF:** Michael Langdon; **FAS:** Kurt Boehme; **FLH:** Elizabeth Bainbridge; **FR:** Jon Andrew; **FRE:** Elizabeth Vaughan; **FRK:** Josephine Veasey; **LG:** John Dobson; **MM:** John Lanigan; **WEL:** Yvonne Minton; **WGL:** Elizabeth Robson; **WOT:** Theo Adam, (30) David Ward

Die Walküre (12 September, 1 October). **BRH:** Amy Shuard, (1) Ludmila Dvoraková; **FRK:** Josephine Veasey; **GEH:** Ava June; **GRG:** Patricia Purcell; **HLW:** Vivien Townley; **HUN:** Michael Langdon; **OTL:** Margaret Kingsley; **RSW:** Heather Begg; **SGL:** Gwyneth Jones; **SGM:** James King; **SGR:** Noreen Berry; **SWL:** Elizabeth Bainbridge; **WLT:** Yvonne Minton; **WOT:** Theo Adam

Siegfried (20 September, 3 October). **ALB:** Gwyn Griffiths, (3) Otakar Kraus; **BRH:** Amy Shuard, (3) Ludmila Dvoraková; **ED:** Helen Watts; **FAF:** Michael Langdon; **MM:** John Lanigan; **SGF:** Karl-Josef Hering; **WAN:** David Ward; **WDB:** Elizabeth Vaughan

Götterdämmerung (28 September, 5 October). **ALB:** Gwyn Griffiths, (5) Otakar Kraus; **BRH:** Amy Shuard, (5) Ludmila Dvoraková; **FLH:** Elizabeth Bainbridge; **GTR:** Heather Harper; **GUN:** John Shaw; **HAG:** Michael Langdon; **NN1:** Helen Watts; **NN2:** Yvonne Minton; **NN3:** Rita Hunter; **SGF:** Karl-Josef Hering; **WEL:** Yvonne Minton; **WGL:** Elizabeth Robson; **WLT:** Josephine Veasey

1970

TWO CYCLES

Conductors: Georg Solti, (28, 29, 1, 3) Edward Downes

Das Rheingold (9, 28 September). **ALB:** Zoltán Kélémen; **DON:** John Shaw; **ED:** Helen Watts; **FAF:** Michael Langdon; **FAS:** Martti Talvela; **FLH:** Elizabeth Bainbridge; **FR:** Ermanno Mauro; **FRE:** Ava June; **FRK:** Josephine Veasey; **LG:** John Dobson; **MM:** John Lanigan; **WEL:** Anne Howells; **WGL:** Elizabeth Robson; **WOT:** David Ward, (28) Donald McIntyre

Die Walküre (10, 29 September). **BRH:** Ludmila Dvoraková, (29) Amy Shuard; **FRK:** Josephine Veasey; **GEH:** Ava June; **GRG:** Jean Temperley; **HLW:** Catherine Duval; **HUN:** Martti Talvela, (29) Michael Langdon; **OTL:** Margaret Kingsley; **RSW:** Heather Begg; **SGL:** Helga Dernesch; **SGM:** James King, (29) Helge Brilioth; **SGR:** Noreen Berry; **SWL:** Elizabeth Bainbridge; **WLT:** Patricia Purcell; **WOT:** David Ward, (29) Donald McIntyre

Siegfried (18 September, 1 October). **ALB:** Zoltán Kélémen; **BRH:** Ludmila Dvoraková, (1) Amy Shuard; **ED:** Helen Watts; **FAF:** Michael Langdon; **MM:** John Lanigan; **SGF:** Karl-Josef Hering; **WAN:** David Ward; **WDB:** Helen Lawrence

Götterdämmerung (26 September, 3 October). **ALB:** John Modenos; **BRH:** Ludmila Dvoraková, (3) Amy Shuard; **FLH:** Elizabeth Bainbridge; **GTR:** Heather Harper; **GUN:** John Shaw; **HAG:** Martti Talvela, (3) Michael Langdon; **NN1:** Helen Watts; **NN2:** Maureen Guy; **NN3:** Margaret Kingsley; **SGF:** Karl-Josef Hering; **WEL:** Anne Howells; **WGL:** Elizabeth Robson; **WLT:** Josephine Veasey

1971

TWO CYCLES

Conductor: Edward Downes

Das Rheingold (8, 27 September). **ALB:** Marius Rintzler; **DON:** John Shaw; **ED:** Helen Watts; **FAF:** Michael Langdon; **FAS:** Karl Ridderbusch; **FLH:** Elizabeth Bainbridge; **FR:** Alberto Remedios; **FRE:** Ava June; **FRK:** Ruth Hesse; **LG:** John Lanigan; **MM:** John Dobson; **WEL:** Gillian Knight; **WGL:** Elizabeth Robson; **WOT:** Donald McIntyre, (27) David Ward

Die Walküre (9, 28 September). **BRH:** Amy Shuard, (28) Ludmila Dvoraková; **FRK:** Ruth Hesse; **GEH:** Ava June; **GRG:** Gillian Knight; **HLW:** Catherine Duval; **HUN:** Karl Ridderbusch; **OTL:** Margaret Kingsley; **RSW:** Heather Begg; **SGL:** Helga Dernesch; **SGM:** Richard Cassilly; **SGR:** Noreen Berry; **SWL:** Elizabeth Bainbridge; **WLT:** Patricia Purcell; **WOT:** Donald McIntyre, (28) David Ward

Siegfried (17, 30 September). **ALB:** Marius Rintzler; **BRH:** Amy Shuard, (30) Ludmila Dvoraková; **ED:** Helen Watts; **FAF:** Dennis Wicks; **MM:** John Dobson; **SGF:** Helge Brilioth; **WAN:** Donald McIntyre, (30) David Ward; **WDB:** Teresa Cahill

Götterdämmerung (25 September, 2 October). **ALB:** Marius Rintzler; **BRH:** Amy Shuard, (2) Ludmila Dvoraková; **FLH:** Elizabeth Bainbridge; **GTR:** Wendy Fine; **GUN:** John Shaw; **HAG:** Karl Ridderbusch; **NN1:** Helen Watts; **NN2:** Gillian Knight; **NN3:** Margaret Kingsley; **SGF:** Helge Brilioth; **WEL:** Gillian Knight; **WGL:** Elizabeth Robson; **WLT:** Ruth Hesse

1974

Conductor: Colin Davis. Producer: Götz Friedrich. Sets: Josef Svoboda. Costumes: Ingrid Rosell. Lighting: William Bundy. Movement: Eleanor Fazan

Das Rheingold (NP. 30 September, 4, 8, 10 October). **ALB:** Zoltán Kélémen; **DON:** Norman Bailey; **ED:** Elizabeth Bainbridge; **FAF:** Donald Shanks; **FAS:** Matti Salminen; **FLH:** Gillian Knight; **FR:** Robert Tear; **FRE:** Ava June; **FRK:** Josephine Veasey; **LG:** George Shirley; **MM:** Ragnar Ulfung; **WEL:** Eiddwen Harrhy; **WGL:** Valerie Masterson; **WOT:** Donald McIntyre

Die Walküre (NP. 1, 5, 9, 12 October). **BRH:** Berit Lindholm, (9) Katalina Kasza; **FRK:** Josephine Veasey; **GEH:** Ava June; **GRG:** Anne Wilkens; **HLW:** Pauline Tinsley; **HUN:** Hans Sotin; **OTL:** Margaret Kingsley; **RSW:** Elizabeth Bainbridge; **SGL:** Marita Napier; **SGM:** Richard Cassilly; **SGR:** Gillian Knight; **SWL:** Patricia Payne; **WLT:** Heather Begg; **WOT:** Donald McIntyre, (9) Norman Bailey

1975

Conductors: Colin Davis, (9) Reginald Goodall. Producer: Götz Friedrich. Sets: Josef Svoboda. Costumes: Ingrid Rosell. Lighting: William Bundy. Movement: Eleanor Fazan

Siegfried (NP. 17 September, 1, 6, 11 October). **ALB:** Zoltán Kélémen; **BRH:** Berit Lindholm, (11) Katalina Kasza; **ED:** Elizabeth Bainbridge, (11) Patricia Payne; **FAF:** Matti Salminen; **MM:** Ragnar Ulfung; **SGF:** Helge Brilioth, (1, 11) Jean Cox; **WAN:** Donald McIntyre, (11) David Ward; **WDB:** Norma Burrowes

Das Rheingold (26 September, 3, 8 October). **ALB:** Zoltán Kélémen; **DON:** Raymond Herincx; **ED:** Elizabeth Bainbridge, (8) Patricia Payne; **FAF:** Matti Salminen; **FAS:** David Ward, (8) Robert Lloyd; **FLH:** Gillian Knight; **FR:** Robert Tear; **FRE:** Jeannine Altmeyer; **FRK:** Josephine Veasey; **LG:** George Shirley; **MM:** Ragnar Ulfung, (8) John Dobson; **WEL:** Eiddwen Harrhy; **WGL:** Valerie Masterson; **WOT:** Donald McIntyre, (8) David Ward

Die Walküre (29 September, 4, 9 October). **BRH:** Berit Lindholm, (9) Katalina Kasza; **FRK:** Josephine Veasey; **GEH:** Milla Andrew; **GRG:** Anne Collins; **HLW:** Katie Clarke; **HUN:** Aage Haugland; **OTL:** Margaret Kingsley; **RSW:** Elizabeth Bainbridge; **SGL:** Esther Kovacs; **SGM:** Richard Cassilly; **SGR:** Gillian Knight; **SWL:** Patricia Payne; **WLT:** Anne Wilkens; **WOT:** Donald McIntyre

1976

Conductor: Colin Davis. Producer: Götz Friedrich. Sets: Josef Svoboda. Costumes: Ingrid Rosell. Lighting: William Bundy. Movement: Eleanor Fazan.

Götterdämmerung (NP. 16 September). **ALB:** Zoltán Kélémen; **BRH:** Berit Lindholm; **FLH:** Gillian Knight; **GTR:** Hanna Lisowska; **GUN:** Siegmund Nimsgern; **HAG:** Bengt Rundgren; **NN1:** Patricia Payne; **NN2:** Elizabeth Connell; **NN3:** Pauline Tinsley; **SGF:** Jean Cox; **WEL:** Eiddwen Harrhy; **WGL:** Valerie Masterson; **WLT:** Yvonne Minton

TWO CYCLES

Conductor: Colin Davis.

Das Rheingold (21 September, 4 October). **ALB:** Zoltán Kélémen; **DON:** Raymond Herincx; **ED:** Elizabeth Bainbridge; **FAF:** Matti Salminen; **FAS:** Robert Lloyd; **FLH:** Gillian Knight; **FR:** Robert Tear; **FRE:** Joan Carlyle; **FRK:** Josephine Veasey; **LG:** George Shirley; **MM:** Ragnar

Ulfung; **WEL:** Eiddwen Harrhy; **WGL:** Valerie Masterson; **WOT:** Donald McIntyre, (4) Norman Bailey
Die Walküre (25 September, 5 October). **BRH:** Berit Lindholm, (5) Katalina Kasza; **FRK:** Josephine Veasey; **GEH:** Milla Andrew; **GRG:** Anne Collins; **HLW:** Lorna Haywood; **HUN:** Aage Haugland; **OTL:** Margaret Kingsley; **RSW:** Elizabeth Bainbridge; **SGL:** Marita Napier; **SGM:** René Kollo, (5) Peter Hofmann; **SGR:** Gillian Knight; **SWL:** Patricia Payne; **WLT:** Anne Wilkens; **WOT:** Donald McIntyre, (5) Norman Bailey
Siegfried (29 September, 7 October). **ALB:** Zoltán Kélémen; **BRH:** Berit Lindholm, (7) Katalina Kasza; **ED:** Elizabeth Bainbridge, (7) Patricia Payne; **FAF:** Matti Salminen; **MM:** Ragnar Ulfung; **SGF:** Jean Cox; **WAN:** Donald McIntyre, (7) Norman Bailey; **WDB:** Norma Burrowes, (7) Teresa Cahill
Götterdämmerung (1, 9 October). **ALB:** Zoltán Kélémen; **BRH:** Berit Lindholm; **FLH:** Gillian Knight; **GTR:** Hanna Lisowska; **GUN:** Siegmund Nimsgern; **HAG:** Bengt Rundgren; **NN1:** Patricia Payne; **NN2:** Elizabeth Connell; **NN3:** Pauline Tinsley; **SGF:** Jean Cox; **WEL:** Eiddwen Harrhy; **WGL:** Valerie Masterson; **WLT:** Yvonne Minton, (9) Gillian Knight

1978

THREE CYCLES
Conductor: Colin Davis
Das Rheingold (11 September, 2, 9 October). **ALB:** Zoltán Kélémen; **DON:** Hermann Becht; **ED:** Patricia Payne, (9) Elizabeth Bainbridge; **FAF:** Matti Salminen; **FAS:** Robert Lloyd; **FLH:** Gillian Knight; **FR:** Robert Tear; **FRE:** Rachel Yakar; **FRK:** Josephine Veasey; **LG:** George Shirley; **MM:** Paul Crook, (9) John Dobson; **WEL:** Eiddwen Harrhy; **WGL:** Teresa Cahill; **WOT:** Donald McIntyre
Die Walküre (12 September, 3, 10 October). **BRH:** Gwyneth Jones, (3) Berit Lindholm; **FRK:** Josephine Veasey; **GEH:** Margaret Curphey; **GRG:** Linda Finnie; **HLW:** Pauline Tinsley; **HUN:** Aage Haugland; **OTL:** Angela Bostock; **RSW:** Elizabeth Bainbridge; **SGL:** Helga Dernesch; **SGM:** Peter Hofmann, (3) Richard Cassilly; **SGR:** Gillian Knight; **SWL:** Patricia Payne; **WLT:** Anne Wilkens; **WOT:** Donald McIntyre
Siegfried (22 September, 5, 12 October). **ALB:** Zoltán Kélémen; **BRH:** Gwyneth Jones, (5) Berit Lindholm; **ED:** Elizabeth Bainbridge, (12) Patricia Payne; **FAF:** Matti Salminen; **MM:** Paul Crook, (12) John Dobson; **SGF:** Jean Cox; **WAN:** Donald McIntyre; **WDB:** Yvonne Kenny
Götterdämmerung (30 September, 7, 14 October). **ALB:** Zoltán Kélémen; **BRH:** Gwyneth Jones, (7) Berit Lindholm; **FLH:** Gillian Knight; **GTR:** Helena Döse; **GUN:** Jerker Arvidson; **HAG:** Bengt Rundgren; **NN1:** Patricia Payne; **NN2:** Linda Finnie; **NN3:** Pauline Tinsley; **SGF:** Jean Cox; **WEL:** Eiddwen Harrhy; **WGL:** Teresa Cahill; **WLT:** Yvonne Minton, (14) Ortrun Wenkel

1980

TWO CYCLES
Conductor: Colin Davis
Das Rheingold (11, 29 September). **ALB:** Rolf Kühne; **DON:** Barry Mora; **ED:** Elizabeth Bainbridge, (29) Patricia Payne; **FAF:** Matti Salminen; **FAS:** Robert Lloyd; **FLH:** Gillian Knight; **FR:** John Treleaven; **FRE:** Uta-Maria Flake; **FRK:** Yvonne Minton; **LG:** Robert Tear; **MM:** John Dobson, (29) Paul Crook; **WEL:** Phyllis Cannan; **WGL:** Elizabeth Robson; **WOT:** Donald McIntyre, (29) Norman Bailey
Die Walküre (12, 30 September). **BRH:** Berit Lindholm, (30) Gwyneth Jones; **FRK:** Yvonne Minton; **GEH:** Milla Andrew; **GRG:** Linda Finnie; **HLW:** Lorna Haywood; **HUN:** Franz Hübner; **OTL:** Rosalind Plowright; **RSW:** Elizabeth Bainbridge; **SGL:** Jeannine Altmeyer; **SGM:** Peter Hofmann; **SGR:** Gillian Knight; **SWL:** Patricia Payne; **WLT:** Phyllis Cannan; **WOT:** Donald McIntyre, (30) Norman Bailey
Siegfried (19 September, 2 October). **ALB:** Rolf Kühne; **BRH:** Berit Lindholm, (2) Gwyneth Jones; **ED:** Elizabeth Bainbridge, (2) Patricia Payne; **FAF:** Matti Salminen; **MM:** John Dobson, (2) Paul Crook; **SGF:** Alberto Remedios; **WAN:** Donald McIntyre, (2) Norman Bailey; **WDB:** Elaine Mary Hall
Götterdämmerung (27 September, 4 October). **ALB:** Rolf Kühne; **BRH:** Berit Lindholm, (4) Gwyneth Jones; **FLH:** Gillian Knight; **GTR:** Linda Esther Gray; **GUN:** Rudolf Constantin; **HAG:** Franz Hübner; **NN1:** Patricia Payne; **NN2:** Linda Finnie; **NN3:** Milla Andrew; **SGF:** Alberto Remedios; **WEL:** Phyllis Cannan; **WGL:** Elizabeth Robson; **WLT:** Hanna Schwarz

1982

THREE CYCLES
Conductor: Colin Davis
Das Rheingold (6, 27 September, 4 October). **ALB:** John Gibbs, (27, 4) Rolf Kühne; **DON:** Phillip Joll; **ED:** Marta Szirmay, (27, 4) Elizabeth Bainbridge; **FAF:** Helmut Berger-Tuna; **FAS:** Robert Lloyd; **FLH:** Gillian Knight; **FR:** John Treleaven; **FRE:** Anne Evans; **FRK:** Yvonne Minton; **LG:** Robert Tear; **MM:** Paul Crook, (27, 4) John Dobson; **WEL:** Diana Montague; WGL: Elizabeth Robson; **WOT:** Donald McIntyre
Die Walküre (11, 28 September, 5 October). **BRH:** Gwyneth Jones, (5) Berit Lindholm; **FRK:** Yvonne Minton; **GEH:** Milla Andrew; **GRG:** Linda Finnie; **HLW:** Anne Evans; **HUN:** Franz Hübner; **OTL:** Elizabeth Robson; **RSW:** Elizabeth Bainbridge; **SGL:** Linda Esther Gray, (5) Gwyneth Jones; **SGM:** Richard Cassilly; **SGR:** Gillian Knight; **SWL:** Marta Szirmay; **WLT:** Phyllis Cannan; **WOT:** Donald McIntyre
Siegfried (17, 30 September, 7 October). **ALB:** John Gibbs, (30, 7) Rolf Kühne; **BRH:** Gwyneth Jones, (7) Berit Lindholm; **ED:** Marta Szirmay, (30, 7) Elizabeth Bainbridge; **FAF:** Helmut Berger-Tuna; **MM:** Paul Crook, (30, 7) John Dobson; **SGF:** Alberto Remedios; **WAN:** Donald McIntyre; **WDB:** Lillian Watson
Götterdämmerung (25 September, 2, 9 October). **ALB:** John Gibbs, (2, 9) Rolf Kühne; **BRH:** Gwyneth Jones, (9) Berit Lindholm; **FLH:** Gillian Knight; **GTR:** Anne Evans; **GUN:** Barry Mora; **HAG:** Franz Hübner; **NN1:** Marta Szirmay; **NN2:** Linda Finnie; **NN3:** Elizabeth Vaughan; **SGF:** Alberto Remedios; **WEL:** Diana Montague; **WGL:** Elizabeth Robson; **WLT:** Hanna Schwarz, (9) Linda Finnie

1986

ONE CYCLE [Welsh National Opera]
Conductor: Richard Armstrong. Producer: Göran Järvefelt. Designer: Carl Friedrich Oberle. Lighting: Robert Bryan
Language: English
The Rhinegold (25 September). **ALB:** Nicholas Folwell; **DON:** Barry Mora; **ED:** Anne Collins; **FAF:** Sean Rea; **FAS:** William Mackie; **FLH:** Patricia Bardon; **FR:** Richard Morton; **FRE:** Anne Williams-King; **FRK:** Penelope Walker; **LG:** Graham Clark; **MM:** John Harris; **WEL:** Deborah Stuart-Roberts; **WGL:** Eirian Davies; **WOT:** Phillip Joll
The Valkyrie (27 September). **BRH:** Anne Evans; **FRK:** Penelope Walker; **GEH:** Mary Lloyd-Davies; **GRG:** Caroline Baker; **HLW:** Christine Teare; **HUN:** John Tranter; **OTL:** Eirian Davies; **RSW:** Wendy Verco; **SGL:** Kathryn Harries; **SGM:** Warren Ellsworth; **SGR:** Helen Willis; **SWL:** Christine Bryan; **WLT:** Mary Hamilton; **WOT:** Phillip Joll
Siegfried (30 September). **ALB:** Nicholas Folwell; **BRH:** Anne Evans; **ED:** Anne Collins; **FAF:** John Tranter; **MM:** John Harris; **SGF:** Jeffrey Lawton; **WAN:** Phillip Joll; **WDB:** Simon Pike
The Twilight of the Gods (2 October). **ALB:** Nicholas Folwell; **BRH:** Anne Evans; **FLH:** Patricia Bardon; **GTR:** Kathryn Harries; **GUN:** Barry Mora; **HAG:** John Tranter; **NN1:** Anne Collins; **NN2:** Caroline Baker; **NN3:** Christine Teare; **SGF:** Jeffrey Lawton; **WEL:** Deborah Stuart-Roberts; **WGL:** Eirian Davies; **WLT:** Patricia Payne

1988

Conductor: Bernard Haitink. Producer: Yuri Lyubimov. Designer: Paul Hernon. Lighting: Robert Bryan
Das Rheingold (NP. 29 September, 1, 5, 8, 11, 13 October). **ALB:** Ekkehard Wlaschiha; **DON:** Phillip Joll; **ED:** Jadwiga Rappé; **FAF:** Willard White; **FAS:** Roderick Kennedy; **FLH:** Jane Turner; **FR:** Kim Begley; **FRE:** Nancy Gustafson; **FRK:** Helga Dernesch; **LG:** Kenneth Riegel; **MM:** John Dobson; **WEL:** Anne Mason; **WGL:** Judith Howarth; **WOT:** James Morris

1989

Conductor: Bernard Haitink. Director: Götz Friedrich. Designer: Peter Sykora. Lighting: John B. Read
Die Walküre (NP. 27 September, 2, 7, 10, 14, 20, 24 October). **BRH:** Gwyneth Jones; **FRK:** Helga Dernesch; **GEH:** Phyllis Cannan; **GRG:** Gillian Knight, (10, 14, 20) Anna Cooper; **HLW:** Penelope Daner, (24) Penelope Chalmers; **HUN:** John Tomlinson; **OTL:** Christine Teare; **RSW:** Anne-Marie Owens; **SGL:** Gabriele Schnaut; **SGM:** René Kollo, (24) Warren Ellsworth; **SGR:** Jane Turner; **SWL:** Catherine Wyn-Rogers; **WLT:** Anne Mason; **WOT:** James Morris

1990

Conductor: Bernard Haitink. Director: Götz Friedrich. Designer: Peter Sykora. Lighting: John B. Read
Siegfried (NP. 4, 9, 12, 16, 20 October). **ALB:** Ekkehard Wlaschiha, (20) Roderick Earle; **BRH:** Gwyneth Jones; **ED:** Birgitta Svendén; **FAF:** Willard White, (16) John Tranter; **MM:** Alexander Oliver, (16, 20) John Dobson; **SGF:** René Kollo; **WAN:** James Morris; **WDB:** Judith Howarth

1991

Conductor: Bernard Haitink. Director: Götz Friedrich. Designer: Peter Sykora. Lighting: John B. Read
Götterdämmerung (NP. 4, 9, 12, 16, 19 February). **ALB:** Roderick Earle; **BRH:** Gwyneth Jones; **FLH:** Jane Turner; **GTR:** Kathryn Harries; **GUN:** Donald Maxwell; **HAG:** John Tomlinson; **NN1:** Elizabeth Bainbridge; **NN2:** Phyllis Cannan; **NN3:** Christine Teare; **SGF:** René Kollo, (12) Spas Wenkoff, (16, 19) Reiner Goldberg; **WEL:** Anne Mason; **WGL:** Judith Howarth; **WLT:** Hanna Schwarz
Das Rheingold (NP. 16 September, 5 October). **ALB:** Ekkehard Wlaschiha; **DON:** Donald Maxwell; **ED:** Anne Gjevang, (5) Gillian Knight; **FAF:** Franz-Josef Selig; **FAS:** Gwynne Howell; **FLH:** Jane Turner; **FR:** Kim

Begley; **FRE:** Deborah Riedel; **FRK:** Helga Dernesch; **LG:** Kenneth Riegel; **MM:** Alexander Oliver, (5) John Dobson; **WEL:** Monica Groop; **WGL:** Gillian Webster, (5) Martha Sharp; **WOT:** James Morris

TWO CYCLES
Conductors: Bernard Haitink, (21) Edward Downes
Das Rheingold (21 September, 10 October).
ALB: Ekkehard Wlaschiha; **DON:** Donald Maxwell; **ED:** Anne Gjevang; **FAF:** Franz-Josef Selig; **FAS:** Gwynne Howell; **FLH:** Jane Turner; **FR:** Kim Begley; **FRE:** Deborah Riedel; **FRK:** Helga Dernesch; **LG:** Kenneth Riegel; **MM:** Alexander Oliver, (10) John Dobson; **WEL:** Monica Groop; **WGL:** Gillian Webster; **WOT:** John Tomlinson, (10) James Morris
Die Walküre (23 September, 11 October). **BRH:** Gwyneth Jones; **FRK:** Helga Dernesch; **GEH:** Phyllis Cannan; **GRG:** Gillian Knight; **HLW:** Christine Teare; **HUN:** John Tomlinson; **OTL:** Penelope Chalmers; **RSW:** Anne-Marie Owens; **SGL:** Karan Armstrong; **SGM:** Poul Elming; **SGR:** Jane Turner, (11) Karen Shelby; **SWL:** Catherine Wyn-Rogers; **WLT:** Monica Groop; **WOT:** James Morris
Siegfried (30 September, 14 October). **ALB:** Ekkehard Wlaschiha; **BRH:** Gwyneth Jones; **ED:** Anne Gjevang; **FAF:** Franz-Josef Selig; **MM:** John Dobson; **SGF:** René Kollo, (14) Reiner Goldberg; **WAN:** James Morris, (14) John Tomlinson; **WDB:** Elizabeth Gale
Götterdämmerung (8, 17 October). **ALB:** Ekkehard Wlaschiha; **BRH:** Gwyneth Jones; **FLH:** Jane Turner; **GTR:** Karan Armstrong; **GUN:** Donald Maxwell; **HAG:** John Tomlinson; **NN1:** Elizabeth Bainbridge; **NN2:** Phyllis Cannan; **NN3:** Christine Teare; **SGF:** René Kollo, (17) Reiner Goldberg; **WEL:** Monica Groop; **WGL:** Gillian Webster; **WLT:** Linda Finnie

1994

Conductor: Bernard Haitink. Director: Richard Jones. Designs: Nigel Lowery. Lighting: Pat Collins. Movement: Matthew Hamilton
Das Rheingold (NP. 13, 17, 20, 25 October).
ALB: Ekkehard Wlaschiha; **DON:** Peter Sidhom; **ED:** Birgitta Svendén; **FAF:** Carsten Stabell; **FAS:** Gwynne Howell; **FLH:** Leah-Marian Jones; **FR:** Paul Charles Clarke; **FRE:** Rita Cullis; **FRK:** Jane Henschel; **LG:** Robert Tear; **MM:** Robin Leggate; **WEL:** Gillian Webster; **WGL:** Judith Howarth; **WOT:** John Tomlinson
Die Walküre (NP. 14, 18, 22, 29 October).
BRH: Deborah Polaski; **FRK:** Jane Henschel; **GEH:** Penelope Chalmers; **GRG:** Gillian Knight; **HLW:** Rita Cullis; **HUN:** Matthias Hölle; **OTL:** Virginia Kerr; **RSW:** Penelope Walker; **SGL:** Ulla Gustafsson; **SGM:** Poul Elming; **SGR:** Clare Shearer; **SWL:** Catherine Wyn-Rogers; **WLT:** Anne Wilkens; **WOT:** John Tomlinson

1995

Conductor: Bernard Haitink. Director: Richard Jones. Designs: Nigel Lowery. Lighting: Pat Collins. Movement: Matthew Hamilton
Siegfried (NP. 27 March, 1, 4 April). **ALB:** Ekkehard Wlaschiha; **BRH:** Anne Evans; **ED:** Birgitta Svendén; **FAF:** Carsten Stabell; **MM:** Graham Clark; **SGF:** Siegfried Jerusalem; **WAN:** John Tomlinson; **WDB:** Linda Kitchen
Götterdämmerung (NP. 14, 19, 23, 28, 31 October).
ALB: Ekkehard Wlaschiha; **BRH:** Deborah Polaski; **FLH:** Leah-Marian Jones; **GTR:** Vivian Tierney; **GUN:** Alan Held; **HAG:** Kurt Rydl; **NN1:** Catherine Wyn-Rogers; **NN2:** Jane Irwin; **NN3:** Rita Cullis; **SGF:** Siegfried Jerusalem; **WEL:** Daniela Bechly; **WGL:** Judith Howarth; **WLT:** Jane Henschel

1996

Conductors: Bernard Haitink, (5) Jun Märkl
Götterdämmerung (27 February, 2, 5 March).
ALB: Roderick Earle; **BRH:** Anne Evans; **FLH:** Christine Botes; **GTR:** Vivian Tierney; **GUN:** Donald Maxwell; **HAG:** Kurt Rydl; **NN1:** Catherine Wyn-Rogers; **NN2:** Jane Irwin; **NN3:** Rita Cullis; **SGF:** Wolfgang Fassler; **WEL:** Sarah Pring; **WGL:** Judith Howarth; **WLT:** Jane Henschel

THREE CYCLES
Conductor: Bernard Haitink
Das Rheingold (21 September, 2, 24 October).
ALB: Ekkehard Wlaschiha; **DON:** Peter Sidhom; **ED:** Catherine Wyn-Rogers; FAF: Matthias Hölle; **FAS:** Peter Rose; **FLH:** Leah-Marian Jones; **FR:** Peter Evans; **FRE:** Rita Cullis; **FRK:** Jane Henschel; **LG:** Philip Langridge; **MM:** Robin Leggate; **WEL:** Gillian Webster; **WGL:** Rosemary Joshua; **WOT:** John Tomlinson
Die Walküre (30 September, 5, 25 October).
BRH: Deborah Polaski, (25: Act II) Anne Evans, (25: Act III) Penelope Chalmers; **FRK:** Jane Henschel; **GEH:** Penelope Chalmers, (25) Patricia Cameron; **GRG:** Gillian Knight; **HLW:** Rita Cullis; **HUN:** Matthias Hölle; **OTL:** Virginia Kerr, (5) Beth Michael; **RSW:** Penelope Walker; **SGL:** Ulla Gustafsson; **SGM:** Poul Elming; **SGR:** Jane Irwin; **SWL:** Catherine Wyn-Rogers; **WLT:** Anne Wilkens; **WOT:** John Tomlinson. [5: Polaski replaced the indisposed Evans; Michael replaced the advertised Kerr. 25: the continued indisposition of Evans required the cast changes for Act III]
Siegfried (7, 16, 28 October). **ALB:** Ekkehard Wlaschiha; **BRH:** Deborah Polaski, (16) Anne Evans, (28) Carla Pohl; **ED:** Catherine Wyn-Rogers; **FAF:** Matthias Hölle; **MM:** Graham Clark; **SGF:** Siegfried Jerusalem; **WAN:** John Tomlinson; **WDB:** Rosemary Joshua. [28: Pohl replaced the indisposed Evans]
Götterdämmerung (12, 19 October, 2 November).
ALB: Ekkehard Wlaschiha; **BRH:** Deborah Polaski, (2) Anne Evans; **FLH:** Leah-Marian Jones; **GTR:** Vivian Tierney; **GUN:** Alan Held; **HAG:** Kurt Rydl; **NN1:** Catherine Wyn-Rogers; **NN2:** Jane Irwin; **NN3:** Rita Cullis; **SGF:** Siegfried Jerusalem, (19: Acts II and III; 2) Wolfgang Fassler; **WEL:** Gillian Webster; **WGL:** Rosemary Joshua; **WLT:** Ann Murray. [19 and 2: Fassler took over from the indisposed Jerusalem]

Conductor: Simone Young
Die Walküre (6 December). **BRH:** Deborah Polaski; **FRK:** Jane Henschel; **GEH:** Penelope Chalmers; **GRG:** Gillian Knight; **HLW:** Rita Cullis; **HUN:** Matthias Hölle; **OTL:** Virginia Kerr; **RSW:** Penelope Walker; **SGL:** Karen Huffstodt; **SGM:** Plácido Domingo; **SGR:** Jane Irwin; **SWL:** Catherine Wyn-Rogers; **WLT:** Anne Wilkens; **WOT:** John Tomlinson. [Domingo celebrated his Silver Jubilee at Covent Garden with his British debut in Wagner; Huffstodt replaced the indisposed Anne Evans]

APPENDIX II
PERFORMERS AND ROLES

Unless combined where years of performance are the same, roles are listed alphabetically and performances within a given year of all roles for a character in the cycle are listed before partial role performances. For the latter (e.g. Brünnhilde in *Die Walküre* and *Siegfried* but not in *Götterdämmerung*), role names are listed in opera order, qualified by the relevant opera abbreviations:

(R) *Das Rheingold*
(W) *Die Walküre*
(S) *Siegfried*
(G) *Götterdämmerung*

A

Abercrombie, Elizabeth: GEH 1948–51; WEL(G) 1949–51
Adam, Theo: WAN 1967; WOT 1967–8
Addison, Clare?: GEH: 1896; VLK 1895
Adiny, Ada: BRH(W) 1897
Albers, Henri: WOT(W) 1896
Aldenhoff, Bernd: SGF(G) 1957
Aldridge, Luranah: GRG 1893, 1905; SWL 1898
Alexander, Marie: WLT(W) 1909
Allen, Perceval: BRH(G) 1908
Allin, Norman: FAF 1922; FAF(R) 1923, 1926–7, 1932–3, 1938; HAG: 1922; HUN 1923–4, 1926–7, 1931–2
Allman, Robert: DON 1956–7
Almar, Maryan: GEH 1926
Altmeyer, Jeannine: FRE 1975; SGL 1980
Alten, Bella: WEL 1905
Altona, Maria: HLW 1902; RSW 1899
Alvarez, Albert: SGM 1896
Alvary, Max: LG, SGF 1892; SGF(S) 1893; SGM 1892–3
Ambrose, Theresa: NN, GEH, WEL 1928
Amsden, Elizabeth: GTR, HLW, WGL 1910
Anday, Rosette: ED(S), FRK 1929; FRK(R), WLT(G) 1928
Anderson, William: FAF(R) 1921; FAF(S) 1923–4, 1929
Andersson, Frans: ALB(R) 1964
Andrassy, Anny: ED(R), WLT(W) 1928–9
Andrésen, Ivar: FAF(R), HAG 1928–31; HUN 1928, 1930–31
Andreva, Stella: WDB 1935–9; WGL 1936–9
Andrew, Jon: FR 1967–8
Andrew, Milla: GEH 1975–6, 1980, 1982; NN3 1980
Anthes, Georges: SGF(S) 1903, 1906; SGM 1906
Anthony, Trevor: HUN 1948–9
Archibald, Phyllis: ED(R), VLK 1922; GRG 1908
Arden, Evelyn: RSW: 1924–33, 1937; VLK 1922
Arens, Louis: SGF(S) 1903
Arkandy, Katherine: WDB 1924, 1926–7
Armstrong, Karan: GTR, SGL 1991
Artner, Josefine von: GEH, NN, WDB, WGL 1898
Arvidson, Jerker: GUN 1978
Austin, Frederic; GUN 1908–9
Austral, Florence: BRH 1922–4; BRH(W) 1929, 1933; BRH(S) 1933
Autran, Juliette: VLK 1923
Ayre, Florence: VLK 1923–4

B

Bader, Willy: FAF(S), HUN 1913
Bailey, Norman: DON 1974; WAN, WOT 1976, 1980; WOT(W) 1974
Bainbridge, Elizabeth: ED 1975–6, 1978, 1980, 1982; ED(R) 1974; FLH 1967–8, 1970–71; NN1 1991; RSW 1964–7, 1974–6, 1978, 1980, 1982; SWL 1968, 1970–71
Baker, Caroline: GRG, NN2 1986
Bardon, Patricia: FLH 1986
Bardsley, Thelma: OTL 1934–7
Barker, Joyce: GEH 1959
Bartlett, [Miss]: GRG 1897–9
Bauermeister, Mathilde: OTL 1893, 1896–1900, 1902–3
Baxter, Margery: GEH 1910; VLK 1923–4
Beardmore, Lisant: FR 1921
Bechly, Daniela: WEL 1995
Bechstein, Hans: MM 1907–14
Becht, Hermann: DON 1978
Beeley, Marion: ED 1911; SGR 1911, 1913; SWL 1925–7
Beeth, Lola: SGL 1896
Begg, Heather: GRG 1959–60; RSW 1968, 1970–71; WLT(W) 1974
Begley, Kim: FR 1988, 1991
Behnne, Harriet: FLH, SWL 1905
Beirer, Hans: SGM 1954
Bender, Paul: HAG, HUN 1924; WAN, WOT 1914
Bender-Schäfer, Franziska: FRK(W), WLT(W) 1914
Bengell, Elsa [Else]: FRK, WLT 1911
Bennie, Eda: GEH 1925; GTR, VLK 1922
Berger, Erna: WGL, WDB 1934–5
Berger-Tuna, Helmut: FAF 1982
Berglund, Ruth: NN, FLH 1934
Berry, Noreen: SGR 1955–62, 1964–5, 1967–8, 1970–71
Bertram, Philip: FAF(S) 1930; HUN 1933
Bertram, Theodor: WAN 1900, 1903; WOT 1903; WOT(W) 1907
Bettaque, Kathi: FRE, GTR, SGL 1892
Bevan, Alex: HUN 1895
Bibow, [Fräulein] von: SGR 1907
Bispham, David: ALB(S) 1893, 1897, 1901–2; HUN 1893–4, 1907; WOT(W) 1895, 1897, 1899
Bisson, Napoléon: ALB(G, S) 1967; DON 1966
Bjoner, Ingrid: SGL 1967
Björling, Sigurd: WOT(W) 1951
Blackwell, Annette: WDB 1928
Blass, Robert: FAF 1903; FAF(S) 1900–02; FAS, HAG 1900; HUN 1900, 1902–3
Blyth, May: NN2 1922–3; NN 1926; OTL 1924–6; RHD(G) 1922–3; VLK 1922–3; WEL 1926; WEL(R) 1922–3
Boaden, Alice: WBD 1902
Boberg, [Mlle]: FLH, NN1, WLT(W) 1912
Bockelmann, Rudolf: WAN, WOT 1929–30, 1934–8
Boehm, Andreas: WAN, WOT 1950
Boehme, Kurt: FAF 1967; FAS 1956–9, 1968; HAG 1956–7, 1967; HUN 1958–9, 1967
Böse, Ursula: FRK, WLT(G) 1959–60
Boland, William: LG 1921; SGF(S) 1923; SGM 1921–2
Bolska, Adelaida: SGL 1903
Booth, Margery: FLH 1936
Bosetti, Hermine: WGL(R), WDB 1905
Bostock, Angela: OTL 1978
Botes, Christine: FLH(G) 1996
Bowman, Audrey: HLW 1948–51; WDB, WGL 1950–51; WGL(G) 1949
Brani, Cecile: RSW 1896; WLT(W) 1893
Branzell, Karin: FRK(R) 1938
Braun, Carl: WOT(R) 1906
Braun, Francis: DON 1906
Brazzi Fernanda: FRK 1896
Brema, Marie: BRH(W) 1897–9, 1902; FRK(R) 1898; FRK(W) 1907; SGR 1893
Breuer, Hans: MM 1898, 1900
Briesemeister, Otto: LG 1900
Brilioth, Helge: SGF 1971; SGF(S) 1975; SGM 1970
Brindle, Harry: FAF(S), FAS, HUN 1921
Brozel, Philip: SGF(S) 1902
Brunskill, Muriel: ED, FLH(R), NN1, RHD(G), VLK 1923
Bryan, Christine: SWL 1986
Bryhn[-Langaard], Borghild: BRH(W), 1908; FRK(R), 1908, 1911; SGL 1911
Buckman, Rosina: HLW 1914
Buers, Wilhelm: WAN, WOT(W) 1924
Bürger, Anton: SGF 1906
Busby, May: FRE 1926, 1928; OTL 1924–9;
Burchardt, Marga: GEH, GTR, WEL(R) 1906
Burrian, Carl: LG, SGM 1905
Burrowes, Norma: WDB 1975–6
Burton, Kathleen: SGR 1924
Byndon-Ayres, Denis: MM 1909

C

Cahill, Teresa: WDB 1971, 1976; WGL 1978
Cameron, Patricia: GEH 1996
Cannan, Phyllis: GEH 1989, 1991; NN2 1991; WEL 1980; WLT(W) 1980, 1982
Carlyle, Joan: FRE 1976; WDB 1960, 1964–5, 1967; WGL 1959–60, 1964–5
Carron, Arthur: SGM 1948
Cassilly, Richard: SGM 1971, 1974–5, 1978, 1982
Castelmary, Armand: HUN 1896
Chalmers, Penelope: BRH(W, Act III only) 1996; GEH 1994, 1996; HLW 1989; OTL 1991
Chapman, Dorothy: VLK 1922–4
Chepkowska, [Mlle]: HLW, NN3 1913
Christmann, [Mlle]: WDB 1898
Clark, Graham: LG: 1986; MM(S) 1995–6
Clarke, Katie: HLW 1975
Clarke, Payne: MM(S) 1902–3
Clarke, Paul Charles: FR 1994
Clegg, Edith: GRG 1906; RSW 1910; SGR 1909, 1912
Clemens, Hans: FR 1924; LG 1926–9, 1935
Clendon, Frederick: ALB(R) 1921; FAF(S) 1903
Clifford, Grahame: ALB 1949–50; ALB(S)1948; ALB(G) 1951
Coates, Edith: FRK 1949–51; FRK(W) 1948, 1953; SGR, WEL(R) 1937–9; WLT 1949–51; WLT(W) 1948, 1953, 1955–7
Cole, Gladys: GEH, NN 1929–33
Collier, Frederic: DON 1922–3
Collier, Marie: FRE 1964; GEH 1961, 1964; GTR 1963–4
Collins, Anne: ED, NN1 1986; GRG 1975–6
Colton, Eva: VLK 1921
Connell, Elizabeth: NN2 1976
Constantin, Rudolf: GUN 1980
Cooper, Anna: GRG 1989
Cornelius, Peter: SGF 1908–14; SGM 1907–8, 1910–14
Corran, Mabel: SWL 1914
Cortesi, [Mme]: OTL 1900
Costa, Franz: SGM 1898
Cox, Jean: SGF 1976, 1978; SGF(S) 1975
Cramer, Pauline: GEH 1907
Cranston, Gladys: WGL(R) 1921
Craven, Mae: GEH, NN 1935–9
Crawforth, Lily: FRK(W) 1908; SWL 1913
Crook, Paul: MM 1978, 1980, 1982
Cruickshank, Enid: NN 1935–9; FRK(W) 1923, 1931; GRG 1926–8; NN 1926
Cullis, Rita: FRE, HLW 1994, 1996; NN3 1995–6
Curphey, Margaret: GEH 1978
Czuick, [Frau]: SGL 1898

D

Dagmar, Carla: GEH 1893
Dahmen, Charlotte: ED(R), FRK(W), WLT(W) 1914
Dalberg, Frederick: FAF 1955–7; FAS 1954; HUN 1953–7

Daner, Penelope: HLW 1989
Davies, Carys: SWL 1928
Davies, Eirian: OTL, WGL 1986
Davies, Rhydderch: DON 1949–51, 1954–5
Davies, Teify: ED(S) 1903
Davies, Tudor: FR 1922–3
Davies, Vanwy: GRG 1931
Dawes, Mahry: RSW 1934–6
D'Almayne, Christine: FRE 1908
D'Arcy, [Miss]: NN2, OTL, WEL 1913
Delfosse, Edward: FAF(S) 1931–2
Delmar, Marie: GRG 1900, 1902
Denise, Gita: RSW 1954
D'Oisly, Maurice: FR 1909, 1912
Dernesch, Helga: FRK 1991; FRK(R) 1988; FRK(W) 1989; SGL 1970–71, 1978
Desmond, Astra: FRK(W) 1931
Dever, William: ALB(S) 1902–3
Devereux, Roy: MM(S) 1935
Dippel, Andreas: FR, SGF 1898; SGF(S) 1900; SGM 1897
Dobbs, Mattiwilda: WDB 1953
Dobson, John: FR 1964–6; LG 1967–8, 1970; MM 1971, 1978, 1980, 1982, 1991; MM(R) 1975, 1988; MM(S) 1990
Doenges, Paula: BRH(S) 1902
Domingo, Plácido: SGM 1996
Dome, Zoltan: DON 1892
Doree, Doris: GTR 1949–50; SGL 1948–9
Döse, Helena: GTR 1978
Dresser, Marcia van: FRK(R), SGL 1909; GTR 1909, 1924
Dua, Octave: MM(S) 1930, 1935
Duff, Margaret: GEH, WEL(R) 1924
Dufranne, Hector: DON 1898
Duval, Catherine: HLW 1970–71
Dvoraková, Ludmila: BRH 1966–8, 1970–71
Dyck, Ernest van: LG 1898, 1903; SGM 1897–9, 1903, 1907

E

Eadie, Noel: HLW 1926; NN 1927; WGL 1926–7
Eames, Emma: SGL 1898
Earl, Ethel: VLK 1921
Earle, Roderick: ALB(S) 1990; ALB(G) 1991, 1996
Easton, Florence: BRH(S) 1932; WDB 1903
Easton, Robert: FAF 1935–7; FAF(R) 1939; FAF(S) 1934
Edison, Mary: NN1, VLK 1922
Edwards, Anne: GEH 1965
Edwards, Joan: SWL 1961
Elkins, Margreta: NN2: 1963; WLT(W) 1958–62
Ellsworth, Warren: SGM 1986, 1989
Elming, Poul: SGM 1991, 1994, 1996
Elms, Lauris: GRG 1958
Ende-Andriessen, Pelagie: BRH(W), FRK(R) 1892
Engel, Werner: DON, GUN 1913
Engle, Marie: WDB 1897
Erb, Karl: LG 1927
Erhard, Eduard: WOT(R) 1926
Ernster, Deszoe: HAG 1949, 1954
Evans, Anne: BRH 1986, 1995–6; FRE, GTR, HLW 1982
Evans, Amy: NN3, WGL(G) 1910; WDB 1910, 1912
Evans, Edgar: FR 1949–51, 1954–60
Evans, Edith: FRE, OTL 1909–10; GTR 1908
Evans, Nancy: RSW 1939
Evans, Peter: FR 1996

F

Färber-Strasser, Ernestine: FRK, WLT 1924
Farrington, Joseph: WAN 1923–4
Fassbinder, Wilhelm: WOT(W) 1929
Fassler, Wolfgang: SGF(G) 1996
Fay, Maude: GTR, SGL 1914
Fear, Arthur: DON, GUN 1930; WAN 1935
Feinhals, Fritz: WOT(W) 1907
Fenton, Ethel: SGR 1914
Feuge-Gleiss, Emilie: HLW, NN, WDB, WGL 1903
Fiebiger, Erna: GEH, WEL 1907
Field, Millicent: GEH 1913
Fine, Wendy: GTR 1971
Finnie, Linda: GRG, NN2 1978, 1980, 1982; WLT(G) 1982, 1991
Fischer, Adolf: LG 1939
Fisher, Sylvia: BRH(W) 1957; GTR 1951, 1956, 1967; NN3 1949–51, 1954, 1956–7; SGL 1950–51, 1953–4, 1956–7
Flagstad, Kirsten: BRH 1936–7, 1949–50; BRH(W) 1948; BRH(G) 1951
Flake, Uta-Maria: FRE 1980
Fleischer, Hanns: MM 1933, 1935–6
Fleischer-Edel, Katharina: SGL 1905, 1907
Fliether, Herbert: WAN, WOT(W) 1967
Flynn, Renee: HLW 1935
Folwell, Nicholas: ALB 1986
Fönss, Johannes: FAF, HUN 1910–12, 1914; FAF(R) 1913; HAG 1910–13
Foote, Florence: VLK 1923–4
Foras, Odette de: GTR 1930–33; HLW, NN, WGL 1928–9; SGL 1931; WGL(R) 1930–31, 1933
Fox, Hilda: VLK 1923–4
Francis-Sirou, Denise: SGR 1948–9
Frankel Claus, Wilhelmine: BRH(S) 1901
Franklin, David: FAF(R) 1949; HUN 1948–9
Frantz, Ferdinand: WAN, WOT 1954
Frease-Green, Rachel: SGL 1909
Freegarde, Ethelreda: VLK 1921
Fremstad, Olive: FRK 1903; FRK(W) 1902; WLT(W) 1902–3
Fretwell, Elizabeth: NN3 1966–7
Frick, Gottlob: FAF(R) 1951, 1958; HAG 1951, 1957–60, 1963–5; HUN 1951
Friedheim, Madeleine: OTL 1907
Friedrichs, Fritz: ALB 1900
Fröhlich, Mathilde: ED(R), FLH(G), WLT(W) 1892
Fuchs, Eugen: ALB 1937
Furmedge, Edith: ED 1935–7; ED(R) 1949; ED(S) 1938–9, 1948; FLH(G) 1924; FLH(R) 1922, 1924, 1937–9; GRG 1924–5; NN1 1924; NN 1939; RHD(G), VLK 1922

G

Gadski, Johanna: BRH 1906; SGL 1899–1900
Gale, Elizabeth: WDB 1991
Garside, Gwladys: GRG 1936–7; WLT(W) 1939
Geisler, Walter: SGM 1957
Gerner, Knud: FR 1913
Geverding, Winifred: VLK 1921
Gherlsen, [Fräulein]: HLW 1893
Gibbs, John: ALB 1982
Gibson, Dora: OTL 1914
Gjevang, Anne: ED 1991
Gleeson-White, Cicely: FRK, HLW 1909; NN2 1907; OTL 1906–7
Glehn, Rhoda von: HLW, NN3, WGL 1912
Glossop, Peter: DON 1964
Gmeiner, Ella: FLH, GRG, NN1 1911
Goddard, James H.: FAS 1911–13
Godfrey, Victor: DON 1965
Goldberg, Reiner: SGF 1991
Goodacre, Rispah: ED 1932; WLT(W) 1931–3
Gorr, Rita: FRK(W) 1961
Gough, Muriel: HLW 1907
Grant, June: HLW 1957
Gray, Linda Esther: GTR 1980; SGL 1982
Gray, Mary: SGR 1907; VLK 1895
Grengg, Karl: WAN, WOT(R) 1892
Gretton, Adelaide: GRG 1914
Griffiths, Gwyn: ALB 1968; ALB(R) 1967
Grimm, Marie: ED(S), FLH, FRK(W), NN1, SWL 1906
Griswold, Putnam: HAG 1913
Groop, Monica: WEL, WLT(W) 1991
Gruhn, Nora: HLW 1931; WDB 1929–32
Guest, Patricia: OTL 1931
Gulbranson, Ellen: BRH 1900, 1907; BRH(W, G) 1908
Gustafson, Nancy: FRE 1988
Gustafsson, Ulla: SGL 1994, 1996
Guy, Maureen: ED 1965–6; ED(R) 1964; FLH 1964–6; FLH(R) 1963; GRG 1961–2, 1964–6; NN2 1964–6, 1970

H

Habich, Eduard: ALB 1924, 1926–36
Hale, Una: FRE 1956, 1958–60; NN3 1960; OTL 1955–60, 1962; WEL 1955, 1957–9; WEL(G) 1956
Hall, Elaine Mary: WDB 1980
Halliday, Glenice: FLH 1955; FLH(R) 1956
Hamilton, Mary: WLT(W) 1986
Harbutt, Elisabeth: SWL 1948
Harford, Francis: FAF 1908–9; HUN 1909
Harper, Heather: GTR 1965, 1967–8, 1970
Harrhy, Eiddwen: WEL 1976, 1978; WEL(R) 1974–5
Harries, Kathryn: GTR 1986, 1991; SGL 1986
Harris, John: MM 1986
Harshaw, Margaret: BRH 1954–6, 1960; BRH(W) 1953
Hatchard, Caroline: NN2, WEL 1908–9, 1924; GEH, WDB 1908–9
Haugland, Aage: HUN 1975–6, 1978
Hayward, Marie: GEH 1966
Haywood, Lorna: HLW 1976, 1980
Heaton, Maud: GRG 1934–5, 1938–9
Hedmont, E.C[harles]: LG 1908; SGM 1895
Heidersbach, Käte: GTR 1934
Held, Alan: GUN 1995–6
Helian, Christine: RSW 1902
Helgers, Otto: FAS 1926–8, 1930–33; FAF(S) 1926–8; HAG 1926–8, 1930, 1932–3; HUN 1925–6, 1928, 1931
Heming, Percy: ALB(S) 1935
Hemsing, Jan: ALB(G) 1914
Henderson, Roy: DON 1928, 1929
Henschel, Jane: FRK 1994, 1996; WLT(G) 1995–6
Hensel, Heinrich: LG 1911–13; SGF, SGM 1911–12; SGF(G) 1913
Herincx, Raymond: DON 1975–6
Hering, Karl-Josef: SGF 1968, 1970; SGF(G) 1966
Hertzer-Deppe, Marie: FLH, NN, SWL 1903
Hesse, Ruth: FRK, WLT(G) 1971
Hiedler, Ida: SGL 1907
Hieser, Helene: SGR, WEL 1898, 1900
Hilliard, Kathryn: WEL 1927
Hinckley, Allen [C.]: FAF(S), FAS, HAG 1905; HUN 1905, 1907
Hine, Clytie: FRE, OTL, WEL(G) 1911
Hitchin, Booth: DON 1921
Hoesslin von, Erna: WLT(W) 1927
Höffgen, Marga: ED 1959–60; ED(S), NN1 1964

Hoffman, Grace: FRK(W) 1962, 1964–5
Hofmann, Anna: SGR 1910
Hofmann, Ludwig: FAS, HAG 1955; WAN, WOT(R) 1932
Hofmann, Peter: SGM 1976, 1978, 1980
Hölle, Matthias: FAF 1996; HUN 1994, 1996
Holm, Richard: LG 1958–60, 1964–6
Holt, Barbara: WGL(G) 1963; WDB 1962
Homer, Louise: SWL 1899, 1900
Hooke, Emelie: GEH 1953
Hooper, Barrington: FR 1926
Horsman, Leslie: FAF(S) 1933
Hotter, Hans: GUN 1949, 1958; WAN 1948–9, 1951, 1953, 1955–60, 1965; WOT 1949–51, 1955, 1965; WOT(R) 1967; WOT(W) 1948, 1953, 1960–62
Houston, Eleanor: FRE 1954
Howard, Ann: WLT(W) 1965
Howard, Kathleen: ED, FRK(W), WLT 1913
Howarth, Judith: WDB 1990; WGL(R) 1988, 1991, 1994; WGL(G)1991, 1995–6
Howe, Janet: RSW 1955; WLT(W) 1954
Howell, Gwynne: FAS 1991, 1994
Howells, Anne: WEL 1970
Howitt, Barbara: GRG 1957; NN2 1951; RSW 1953
Hübner, Franz: HAG, HUN 1980, 1982
Huffstodt, Karen: SGL 1996
Hunold, Erich: DON, GUN 1911
Hunter, Rita: NN3 1963, 1965, 1968
Hüpeden, George: DON 1906
Hyde, Walter: FR 1908; LG 1909, 1922–3; SGM 1908–9, 1922–4

I

Iacopi, Valetta: SWL 1948, 1954–6
Illiard, Ellice: WDB 1934
Ilosvay, Maria von: ED 1957; FRK 1954–6, 1958; NN1, WLT(G) 1954–8
Irwin, Jane: NN2 1995–6; SGR 1996

J

Jackson, Haigh: FR 1911
Jaffary, Nellie: FRE 1924
Janson, Agnes: RSW 1898, 1903
Janssen, Herbert: DON 1938; GUN 1926–39;
Jarred, Mary: ED 1933–4; ED(R) 1938–9; FRK(W) 1933; GRG 1929; NN 1934–9
Jeritza, Maria: SGL 1926
Jerusalem, Siegfried: SGF 1995–6
Joachim, Gabriele: SWL 1931–3
Johnson, Gertrude: NN3, RHD(G), WDB, WGL(R) 1922
Johnson, Patricia: SGR 1954
Joll, Phillip: DON 1982, 1988; WAN, WOT 1986
Jones, Bessie: NN2, WDB, WEL 1914
Jones, Dilys: ED(R) 1913; FLH, NN1 1914; RSW 1908–9, 1911–14
Jones, Gwyneth: BRH 1978, 1980, 1982, 1991; BRH(W) 1989; BRH(S) 1990; GTR 1966; NN3 1964–5; OTL, WEL 1964; SGL 1966, 1968; WEL(G) 1963
Jones, Leah-Marian: FLH 1996; FLH(G) 1995; FLH(R) 1994
Jones, Parry: SGM 1931
Jonsson, Greta: FRE, GEH 1913–14
Jordan, Arthur: SGF 1923; SGF(S) 1922
Jörn, Karl: LG 1906–7
Joshua, Rosemary: WGL, WDB 1996
June, Ava: FRE 1970–71, 1974; GEH 1962, 1967–8, 1970–71, 1974
Jung, Helene: ED, SWL 1924

K

Kacerowska, [Mme]: GEH, NN2, WEL 1912
Kallensee, Olga: HLW, NN3, WDB, WGL 1911
Kalter, Sabine: FRK, WLT(G) 1935
Kamann, Karl: WAN 1938, 1953; WOT 1938; WOT(W) 1953
Kappel, Gertrud: BRH 1924, 1926; BRH(W) 1912–13, 1925; BRH(G) 1912–13
Kasza, Katalina: BRH(W) 1974–6; BRH(S) 1975–6
Keene, May: GRG 1930–33
Kélémen, Zoltán: ALB 1976, 1978; ALB(R) 1970, 1974–5; ALB(S) 1970, 1975
Kelly, David: DON 1958–9
Kennedy, Roderick: FAS 1988
Kenny, Yvonne: WDB 1978
Kern, Adele: WDB 1933
Kerr, Virginia : OTL 1994, 1996
Kiess, August: ALB 1911–14; WOT(W) 1913–14
King, James: SGM 1968, 1970
Kingsley, Margaret: NN3 1970–71; OTL 1965–68, 1970–71, 1974–6
Kingston, Morgan: SGM 1925
Kipnis, Alexander: FAS 1929, 1934–5; HAG 1929; HUN 1929, 1934
Kirchhoff, Walter: LG, SGF(S, Act III only) 1924
Kirkby Lunn, Louise: ED 1903, 1905–6; ED(S) 1907, 1910, 1912–14; FRK 1902, 1907–10, 1912–14; WLT 1903, 1905, 1907–8; WLT(G) 1906, 1910, 1912–14; WLT(W) 1902
Kitchen, Linda: WDB 1995
Klafsky, Katharina: BRH(S, G) 1892
Klein, Peter: MM 1949–51, 1955–9; MM(S) 1948
Klopfer, Victor: FAF 1903; FAF(S), FAS 1900; HUN 1900, 1902–3
Klose, Margarete: FRK, WLT(G) 1937
Knapp, August: GUN 1892
Knight, Gillian: ED(R) 1991; FLH 1976, 1978, 1980, 1982; FLH(R) 1974–5; GRG 1971, 1989, 1991, 1994, 1996; NN2 1971; SGR 1974–6, 1978, 1980, 1982; WEL 1971; WLT(G) 1976
Knote, Heinrich: SGFS) 1901
Knowles, Charles: DON, HAG 1908–9
Knüpfer, Paul: FAS 1906–7, 1914; HUN 1906–8, 1914; HAG 1914
Knüpfer-Egli, Marie: FRE 1905–7, 1912; GEH 1911; GTR 1903, 1905–8, 1911–12; NN2 1906, 1910–11; NN 1903, 1905; OTL 1903, 1908, 1912; SGL 1903, 1906, 1910; WEL 1903, 1910; WEL(G) 1906; WEL(R) 1911
Kollar, Sophie: GEH 1892
Kollo, René: SGF 1991; SGF(S) 1990; SGM 1976, 1989
Kolniak, Angela: FRE, WLT(W) 1934
Konetzni, Anny: BRH 1935, 1938–9; BRH(W) 1951
Konetzni, Hilde: GTR 1955, 1958; SGL 1938–9, 1955
Konrad, Ernst: SGM, SGF 1906
Kovacs, Esther: SGL 1975
Kozub, Ernst: SGM 1962, 1964–7
Krasa, Marcel: ALB 1903
Kraus, Ernst: SGF 1903, 1905, 1907; SGF(G) 1900; SGM 1900, 1902–3, 1907
Kraus, Otakar: ALB 1954–60, 1965, 1968; ALB(R) 1951, 1967; ALB(S) 1951, 1953, 1962, 1964; ALB(G) 1963–4
Kraus-Osborne, Adrienne von: WLT(W) 1907
Kremer, Martin: LG 1934, 1936
Kronen, Franz: DON, GUN 1912
Kuen, Paul: MM 1954; MM(S) 1953
Kühne, Rolf: ALB 1980, 1982
Kurt, Melanie: BRH(W) 1910; SGL 1910, 1914

L

Landwehr, Rosel: WGL, WDB, NN3 1924; HLW 1924–5
Lane, Barbara: WDB 1935
Langdon, Michael: FAF 1954, 1959–60, 1964–6, 1968, 1970; FAF(R) 1971, FAF(S) 1958; HAG 1966, 1968, 1970; HUN 1961–2, 1964–6, 1968, 1970
Langendorff, Frieda: WLT(G) 1911
Langridge, Philip: LG 1996
Lanigan, John: LG 1971; MM 1966–8, 1970; MM(R) 1964–5
Lark, Kingsley: WOT 1921
Larsén-Todsen, Nanny: BRH 1927; BRH(S, G) 1930
Laubenthal, Rudolf: SGF 1927–8; SGF(G) 1926, 1930
Laufkötter, Karl: MM 1938–9
Laurin, Hope: SGL 1921
Lawrence, Helen: WDB 1970
Lawton, Jeffrey: SGF 1986
Leathwood, Gladys: VLK 1923–4
Lee, Kate?: VLK 1895
Leer, Edward: FR 1930–32
Leffler-Burkhardt, Martha: BRH 1903
Leggate, Robin: MM(R) 1994, 1996
Lehmann, Lilli: SGL 1899
Lehmann, Lotte: GTR 1928; SGL 1924, 1926–35
Leider, Frida: BRH 1927–8, 1930, 1932–8; BRH(W, G) 1924, 1926, 1929, 1931
Leigh, Adèle: WDB 1955–6
Lemnitz, Tiana: SGL 1938
Lemon, Doris: NN3, RHD(G), WGL(R) 1923; WDB 1923–4
Lewandowski, Josef: FR 1903
Licette, Miriam: GTR 1929
Lieban, Julius: MM 1892, 1906; MM(S) 1897
Lieban, [Frau]: HLW 1897
Liebl, Karl: SGF(S) 1958 [Acts II and III only]
Lindermeier, Elisabeth: FRE, GTR 1957
Lindholm, Berit: BRH 1976, 1978, 1980, 1982; BRH(W) 1974–5; BRH(S) 1975
Lindsey, Anna: FRE, VLK 1922
Lippe, Juliette: BRH(S, G), SGL 1931
Lisowska, Hanna: GTR 1976
Lissmann, Friedrich Heinrich: ALB 1892
List, Emanuel: HAG 1934–6; HUN 1925, 1935–6
Litter, Ferdinand; FAF(R) 1892
Litvinne, Félia: BRH 1905; BRH(W) 1899, 1907; BRH(G) 1910
Ljungberg, Göta: GTR, SGL 1924, 1927–8
Lloyd, Robert: FAS 1975–6, 1978, 1980, 1982
Lloyd-Davies, Mary: GEH 1986
Lohse, Magda: SGL 1902
Lonsdale, G.: GRG 1907
Lorent, Mathieu: ALB(S) 1892; FAF(R) 1898
Lorenz, Max: SGF 1937
Ludlam, Winifred: RSW 1905–7
Lugt, Marijke van der: BRH(W) 1965

M

McAfee, Marion: WDB 1928
McArthur, Margaret: SWL 1930
McCulloch, Frances: SGR 1897–9, 1902–3
McCusker, Isa?: VLK 1895
McDougall, Muriel: VLK 1921
McIntyre, Donald: DON 1967–8; WAN 1971, 1975–6, 1978, 1980, 1982; WOT 1970–71, 1974–6, 1978, 1980, 1982
Mackie, William: FAS 1986
Maclennan, Francis: SGM 1909
Madeira, Jean: ED 1955–6

Madin, Viktor: ALB 1929–30; ALB(R, S) 1928; ALB(G) 1931; DON 1926–8, 1931
Magrath, Charles: WAN 1902–3
Malone, Jose: WEL(G) 1936–7
Malone, May: FRE 1921
Maltin, Marie: NN 1927
Malyon, Julia: OTL 1961
Mang, Karl: HAG, HUN 1908
Manners, Charles: FAF(S) 1902
Mantelli, Eugenia: BRH(W) 1896
Markwort, Peter: MM 1949; MM(R) 1954
Marowski, Hermann: FAS, HUN 1924
Martin, Frances: HLW 1934
Martiny, Liane: FRE, HLW 1927
Mason, Anne: WEL(G) 1991; WEL(R) 1988; WLT(W) 1989
Masterson, Valerie: WGL 1976; WGL(R) 1974–5
Matters, Arnold: DON 1935, 1939
Maude, Frances: SGR 1931
Mauro, Ermanno: FR 1970
Maxwell, Donald: DON 1991; GUN 1991, 1996
Meisslinger, Louise: ED(S) 1897; FLH(G), NN, WLT(W) 1898; FRK 1893, 1898; GRG 1903; SWL 1892–3, 1897
Melchior, Lauritz: SGF 1929–39; SGF(S) 1926–8; SGM 1924, 1926–32, 1935–6, 1938–9
Metcalf, Suzanne: OTL 1905
Metzger, Ottilie: ED(S) 1902
Meux, Thomas: ALB 1908–9; ALB(G) 1910
Michael, Beth: OTL 1996
Michael, William: ALB 1922–3; ALB(S) 1924; DON 1932
Milde, Rudolf von: DON, GUN 1898
Milinkovič, Georgine von: FRK 1957
Mill, Arnold van: FAS 1965
Milner, Augustus: WAN, WOT 1921
Milton, Irene: VLK 1924
Minton, Yvonne: FRK 1980, 1982; NN2, WEL, WLT(W) 1966–8; SWL 1965; WLT 1976, 1978
Miranda, Beatrice: BRH(G) 1922; SGL 1922–3
Modenos, John: ALB(G) 1970
Mödl, Martha: BRH 1959
Mohwinkel, Hans: DON, WOT(W) 1903; WAN 1901
Moika-Kellogg, ?: GRG 1899
Montague, Diana: WEL 1982
Moody, Fanny: BRH(S) 1902–3
Moody, Lily: ED(S) 1902
Mora, Barry: DON 1980, 1986; GUN 1982
Moran-Olden, Fanny: BRH(W, S) 1893
Morden, Irene: GEH 1934
Morena, Berta: BRH(W) 1914
Moresta, [Miss]: SWL 1909
Morris, James: WAN 1990–91; WOT 1991; WOT(R) 1988; WOT(W) 1989
Morton, Richard: FR 1986
Mott, Charles: DON, GUN 1914
Moxon, Alice: GEH 1927
Mühlmann, Adolph: DON, GUN 1900
Müller, Edmund: GUN, WOT(R) 1903
Müller, Maria: SGL 1937
Mullings, Frank: SGF(G) 1922
Murray, Ann: WLT(G) 1996
Mutch, Alys: SWL 1910–12

N

Napier, Marita: SGL 1974, 1976
Nebe, Karl: ALB 1898
Neidlinger, Gustav: ALB 1965–6
Neilson, Maude: WDB 1921
Newton, Joyce: SGR 1935–6
Nezadal, Maria: GTR 1935–7, 1939
Nicholls, Agnes: BRH(S) 1908, 1922; HLW 1905–7; NN3, WGL 1906–7; NN 1905; SGL 1907–8, 1922, 1923–4; WDB 1906–7, 1922?; WGL(G) 1905
Nietan, Hanns: FR 1906–7
Nilsson, Birgit: BRH 1957; BRH(S) 1960, 1962; BRH(G) 1960, 1963
Nimsgern, Siegmund: GUN 1976
Nissen, Hans Hermann: WAN 1928, 1934; WOT 1934; WOT(R, S) 1928
Nordica, Lillian: BRH(W, S) 1899, 1902; BRH(G) 1898
Nowakowski, Marian: FAF(R) 1950; FAS 1949, 1951

O

Oberländer, Anita: OTL 1938–9
Oberstetter, Edgar: FAS, HAG 1903
Ohms, Elisabeth: BRH 1928; BRH(S) 1929
Olczewska, Maria: ED(S) 1926–8; FRK 1924–33; WLT 1924; WLT(G) 1926–33
Olitzka, Rosa: ED(S) 1893, 1901; FLH 1900; FRK 1895, 1899–1900, 1907; NN 1900; VLK 1895; WLT(W) 1899–1900, 1907;
Oliver, Alexander: MM(R) 1991; MM(S) 1990
Onegin, Sigrid: ED(S), FRK(W), WLT(G) 1927
Osten, Eva von der: SGL 1914
Owens, Anne-Marie: RSW 1989, 1991

P

Paalen, Bella: FRK(W), WLT(W) 1925
Packer, Ruth: HLW 1939
Palmer, Gladys: ED(R) 1927; FLH 1928–33; FLH(R) 1926–7; NN, SGR 1927–33; WLT(W) 1926
Pandar, Elisabeth von: VLK 1914
Parker, Gladys: VLK 1921
Parker, Robert: WAN 1923, 1935; WOT 1923; WOT(R) 1914; WOT(W) 1924, 1931
Parly, Ticho: SGF 1967; SGF(S) 1966
Parr, Gladys: FLH(R) 1921
Parry, Marjorie: GEH 1931
Paul, Willy: ALB(R) 1924
Payne, Patricia: ED 1975, 1978, 1980; ED(S) 1976; NN1 1976, 1978, 1980; SWL 1974–6, 1978, 1980; WLT 1986
Pease, James: WAN 1955–6; WOT 1956; WOT(W) 1955
Pennarini, Aloys: SGF, SGM 1902
Perard-Petzl, Luise: GTR 1913
Perry, John: SGF(S) 1921, 1923
Philips, Thea: HLW 1931–3; NN, WGL(G) 1930–33; SGR 1930
Pierce, Judith: HLW 1958–62, 1964
Pike, Simon: WBD 1986
Plowright, Rosalind: OTL 1980
Pohl, Carla: BRH(S) 1996
Polaski, Deborah: BRH 1996; BRH(W) 1994; BRH(G) 1995
Porte, Betsy de la: SGR 1934; WEL(R) 1929, 1934–6; WLT(W) 1935–6
Pring, Sarah: WEL 1996
Pringle, Lemprière: FAF(R) 1898, 1900; HUN 1897–9
Prowse, Alice: HLW, NN, WGL 1909
Puchmayer, Annie: GEH 1914
Purcell, Patricia: GRG 1967–8; WLT(W) 1970–71

R

Rabke, Henry: ALB(S) 1921
Raboth, Wilhelm: FAF, HAG 1906–7; FAF(R) 1905
Radford, Robert: FAS, HUN 1908–9, 1922–3; HAG 1922–3
Rae, Muriel: OTL 1948–9; WGL(R) 1949
Raisbeck, Rosina: GEH 1954, 1960; NN2 1949–50; RSW 1948–51; WEL(R) 1949–51, 1956
Ralph, Paula: WEL, OTL 1892
Rappé, Jadwiga: ED(R) 1988
Rea, Sean: FAF(R) 1986
Recoschwitz, I.: FRK(W) 1895
Reichmann, Theodor: WAN, WOT(W) 1892
Reinfeld, Nicolai: SGF(S) 1924
Reinhardt, Delia: FRE 1927; GTR 1926–7, 1929; SGL 1925
Reinl, Josephine: BRH(W) 1906; FRK 1905–6
Reiss, Albert: MM 1903, 1905, 1924, 1926–9; MM(S) 1901–2
Remedios, Alberto: FR 1971; SGF 1980, 1982
Renard, Alice: WLT(W) 1906, 1908
Renner, Karl: DON, GUN 1924
Reszke, Edouard de: HAG 1898; WAN 1897–8;
Reszke, Jean de: SGF 1898; SGF(S) 1897
Rethberg, Elisabeth: SGL 1936
Reuss-Belce, Luise: FRK(R), GTR 1900
Révy, Aurelie: HLW 1900
Reynolds, Anna: SGR 1966
Ridderbusch, Karl: FAS, HAG, HUN 1971
Riedel, Deborah: FRE 1991
Riegel, Kenneth: LG 1988, 1991
Rintzler, Marius: ALB 1971
Ripley, Gladys: SWL 1934–8
Roberts, Gwladys: ED(R) 1912; GRG 1909, 1912
Robinson, Forbes: DON 1960; FAS 1964–7
Robson, Elizabeth: OTL 1982; WEL 1965; WGL 1966–8, 1970–71, 1980, 1982
Rode, Wilhelm: WAN, WOT 1928
Rooy, Anton van: WAN 1898, 1900–03, 1905–7, 1910–13; WOT 1898, 1900, 1903, 1906–7, 1910–13; WOT(R) 1905; WOT(W) 1902, 1908
Rose, Peter: FAS 1996
Roth, Max: WAN 1936
Rothmüller, Marko: GUN 1951, 1955
Roudez, Maud: GEH 1897–9
Rouleau, Joseph: FAF 1962
Rourke, Josephine: WGL, WDB 1913
Rundgren, Bengt: HAG 1976, 1978
Rünger, Gertrude: FRK, NN, WLT(G) 1934
Rüsche-Endorf, Cäcilie: BRH 1911; BRH(W) 1914; SGL 1908
Russell, Ella: VLK 1895
Russell, Francis: SGM 1931
Russell, Shirley: WDB 1948–9
Russell, Sydney: FR 1910; MM 1922–3; MM(S) 1924
Rydl, Kurt: HAG 1995–6
Rysanek, Leonie: SGL 1955

S

Sales, Regina de: HLW 1897–8
Salminen, Matti: FAF 1975–6, 1978, 1980; FAS 1974
Saltzmann-Stevens, Minnie: BRH 1909–11; BRH(S), SGL 1912–13; BRH(G) 1913
Santley, Maud: FRK 1908; RSW 1907; WLT(W) 1908
Saville, Frances: GTR 1898; WDB 1897
Schaeffer, [Mlle]: NN1, FLH, GRG 1913
Schech, Marianne: SGL 1957–8
Scheff, Fritzi: WDB 1900
Schirp, Wilhelm: HUN, HAG 1938
Schipper, Emil: WAN 1926, WOT(W) 1925–6, 1928
Schirach, Rosalind von: GTR 1935
Schlembach, Josef: FAS 1910
Schnaut, Gabriele: SGL 1989

Schoeffler, Paul: DON 1934, 1936–7; GUN 1935, 1949–50; WOT 1939, 1955
Schon, Kenneth: WOT 1949
Schorr, Friedrich: GUN 1924, 1933; WAN 1924, 1927, 1929, 1930–33; WOT 1924, 1927, 1929, 1930–31, 1933; WOT(W) 1925, 1932
Schumann-Heink, Ernestine: ED 1892, 1898, 1900; ED(S) 1897; FLH, NN 1898; FLH(R) 1892, 1900; FRK 1892, 1897–8, 1900; WLT 1898, 1900; WLT(G) 1892; WLT(W) 1897
Schützendorf, Alfons: DON, GUN 1910; WOT(W) 1909–10
Schwarz, Hanna: WLT(G) 1980, 1982, 1991
Sedlmair, Sophie: BRH(S) 1897
Seinemeyer, Meta: SGL 1929
Selig, Franz-Josef: FAF 1991
Sembach, Johannes: LG 1910, 1914; SGM 1910
Serena, Clara: ED(R), FLH(G), NN 1927
Seymour, Linda: FLH(G) 1937; WLT(W) 1937
Shacklock, Constance: ED 1954; FLH(G) 1949–51; FRK 1950; GRG 1948–51, 1953–6; NN1 1949–51; NN2 1954–7, 1960
Shanks, Andrew: GUN 1922–3
Shanks, Donald: FAF(R) 1974
Sharp, Martha: WGL(R) 1991
Shaw, John: DON 1970–71; GUN 1965, 1966–8, 1970–71
Shearer, Clare: SGR 1994
Shelby, Karen: SGR 1991
Shirley, George: LG 1974–6, 1978
Shuard, Amy: BRH 1965–8, 1970–71; BRH(S) 1962, 1964; BRH(G) 1964; FRE 1955; GEH 1955–8; GTR 1959–60; NN3 1955, 1957–9; SGL 1959–60
Sidhom, Peter: DON 1994, 1996
Siewert, Rut: ED 1958; ED(S) 1962
Simon, Hugo: FR 1892
Simon, ?: GRG 1892
Sinclair, Jeanette: WDB 1957, 1959
Sinclair, Monica: FLH(R) 1949–51; NN1 1963; NN2 1959–60; SGR 1950–51, 1953; SWL 1960, 1962, 1964, 1966–7
Sinico, Clarice: VLK 1895
Skrobisch, Jean: FR 1914
Slezak, Leo: FR 1900
Sobrino, Louise: GEH 1900, 1902–3, 1905; HLW 1899; WDB 1901–2; WGL 1900
Soomer, Walter: DON 1905
Soot, Fritz: SGF 1924; SGM 1924–5
Sotin, Hans: HUN 1974
Souez, Ina: WEL(G) 1929; WGL(R) 1932
Sparkes, Leonora: HLW, NN3, WGL 1908
Stabell, Carsten: FAF(R) 1994; FAF(S) 1995
Stenning, Elsa: HLW 1936–8
Stern, Jean: ALB 1939
Sterneck, Berthold: FAF(R) 1934
Stevens, Horace: WOT(W) 1923, 1931
Stewart, Thomas: GUN 1963–4
Stockhausen, [Herr]: DON, GUN 1907
Stolze, Gerhard: LG 1965; MM 1960; MM(S) 1962, 1964–6
Storm, Erika: WLT(W) 1938
Stosch, Anny von: FRE, GTR 1938
Strätz, Carl: LG, SGF(G) 1910
Street, Molly: RSW 1931
Strienz, Wilhelm: FAF(S) 1938
Strong, Susan: BRH(W) 1897; FRE 1900; SGL 1895, 1897, 1899
Stuart-Roberts, Deborah: WEL 1986
Sucher, Rosa: BRH(S) 1892
Sutherland, Joan: HLW 1953–6; WDB 1954, 1958; WGL 1954–8
Svanholm, Set: LG 1949–51; SGF 1949–51, 1954–5; SGF(S) 1948, 1953; SGF(G) 1957; SGM 1948–51, 1954
Svendén, Birgitta: ED(R) 1994; ED(S) 1990, 1995
Szantho, Enid: ED, FRK(W) 1936
Szirmay, Marta: ED, NN1, SWL 1982

T

Taggart, Jenny: OTL 1908
Talvela, Martti: FAS, HAG, HUN 1970
Tatham, Emmie: GRG 1907
Tay, Evelyn: SWL 1931; VLK 1921
Tear, Robert: FR 1974–6, 1978; LG 1980, 1982, 1994
Teare, Christine: HLW, NN3 1986, 1991; OTL 1989
Temperley, Jean: GRG 1970
Ternina, Milka: BRH 1900, 1903; BRH(W) 1898, 1906; BRH(S) 1901; BRH(G) 1898; SGL 1898, 1900, 1906
Tessmer, Heinrich: MM 1930–32
Thomas, Marjorie: FLH 1954, 1957–60; FLH(G) 1956; NN1 1959–60; NN2 1958; RSW 1956–8
Thompson, Betty: WEL 1930–33; WEL(G), 1934–5, 1938–9
Thorborg, Kerstin: FRK 1936–9; WLT(G) 1936, 1938–9
Thornton, Edna: ED, FLH, NN1 1908–10; ED(R) 1907; ED(S) 1922–4; FRK 1922–3; FRK(W) 1924; NN 1905; SGR 1905–8; WLT(G) 1908–9, 1922–3; WLT(W) 1910
Tibell, Anna: ED 1930; ED(R) 1931; WLT(W) 1930–31
Tierney, Vivian: GTR 1995–6
Tinley, Colin: MM(S) 1921
Tinsley, Pauline: HLW 1974, 1978; NN3 1976, 1978
Tolli, Cilla: FLH, NN1, SWL 1907
Tomlinson, John: HAG, WOT(R) 1991; HUN 1989, 1991; WAN 1991, 1995–6; WOT 1994, 1996
Toros, Hella: OTL 1954–5
Townend, Olive: VLK 1922
Townley, Vivien: HLW 1967–8
Townson, Freda: FLH(G) 1938–9; SWL 1939
Tranter, John: FAF(S) 1986, 1990; HAG, HUN 1986
Traubmann, Sophie: HLW, WDB, WGL 1892
Tree, Lillian: BRH(W) 1895
Trefelyn, [Mme]: VLK 1895
Treleaven, John: FR 1980, 1982
Treptow, Günther: SGF(S) 1953
Treskow, Emil: WAN, WOT(W) 1939
Treweek, Elsy: FRE, GTR, VLK 1923
Triguez, Eugénia: WDB 1933
Turner, Blanche: FRE 1949–51; OTL 1950–51, 1953
Turner, Eva: BRH(W), FRK(R) 1921; BRH(S) 1921, 1935; SGL 1930
Turner, Jane: FLH(G) 1991; FLH(R) 1988; SGR 1989, 1991
Turner, [Miss]: SWL 1902
Twemlow, [Miss]: SWL 1909

U

Uhde, Hermann: GUN 1954, 1956–7, 1959–60; WOT(R) 1960
Ulfung, Ragnar: MM 1975–6; MM(R) 1974
Unkel, Peter: FR 1913
Upleger, ?: RSW 1892
Urlus, Jacques: SGM 1914, 1924

V

Välkki, Anita: BRH(W) 1961, 1964
Vane, Sybil: NN3, WGL 1914
Varnay, Astrid: BRH 1958–9; BRH(W) 1951; BRH(S) 1948, 1951, 1953
Vaughan, Elizabeth: FRE, WDB 1965–8; NN3 1982
Veasey, Josephine: FRK 1965–8, 1970, 1974–6, 1978; FRK(R) 1964; RSW 1959–62; WEL 1959–60; WLT 1964; WLT(G) 1963, 1965–8, 1970
Verco, Wendy: RSW 1986
Vickers, Jon: SGM 1958, 1961
Vigne, Jane de: RSW 1897
Vinay, Ramón: SGM 1953, 1955–7, 1959
Vincent, Horace: MM(R) 1921
Viviani, Ludovico: FAF(S) 1897
Vogel, Adolf: ALB 1938
Völker, Franz: SGM 1934, 1937

W

Wadia, Marie: GRG 1910
Waldmann, [Herr]: FAF(S) 1893
Walker, Edyth: BRH(W) 1908; ED, FRK(W), RSW, WLT(G) 1900
Walker, Norman: FAF 1949; FAF(S) 1939, 1948, 1950–51, 1953
Walker, Penelope: FRK 1986; RSW 1994, 1996
Ward, David: FAS 1960, 1975; HUN 1960; WAN 1962, 1964–6, 1968, 1970–71, 1975; WOT 1964–6, 1970–71; WOT(R) 1968, 1975
Wareham, Edwin: SGM 1895
Warner, Monica: BRH(W) 1931; RSW 1938
Wasserthal, Elfriede: GTR 1954
Watson, Claire: SGL 1961–2, 1964–5
Watson, Jean: ED 1950–51; ED(S) 1949, 1953; FLH(R) 1949; SWL 1949–51, 1953, 1957–9
Watson, Lillian: WDB 1982
Watts, Helen: ED 1967–8, 1970–71; NN1 1965–8, 1970–71
Webb Ware, Constance: SWL 1907
Weber, Ludwig: FAS 1936–9, 1949–50; HAG, HUN 1936–9, 1950
Webster, Gillian: WEL 1996; WEL(R) 1994; WGL 1991
Weed, Marion: FRE, GRG 1898
Wendon, Henry: FR 1927–9, 1934–9
Wenkel, Ortrun: WLT(G) 1978
Wenkoff, Spas: SGF(G) 1991
Wenner, [Frl.]: SWL 1906
Westhoven, Ada von: SGL 1907
White, Willard: FAF(R) 1988; FAF(S) 1990
Whitehill, Clarence: GUN 1905–6, 1908; WAN 1905–9, 1914, 1922; WOT 1905, 1907–9, 1922; WOT(W) 1906, 1914
Wickham, Florence: NN1, FLH(G), SWL 1908
Wicks, Dennis: FAF(S) 1971
Widdop, Walter: SGF(S) 1924, 1935; SGM 1929, 1932
Wiegand, Heinrich: FAF(S), FAS, HUN 1892; WOT(W), WAN 1893
Wildbrunn, Karl: FR 1905
Wilkens, Anne: GRG 1974; WLT(W) 1975–6, 1978, 1994, 1996
Willer, Luise: ED(R), FRK(W) 1926; ED(S), FRK, WLT(G) 1931
Williams, Ben: FR 1933
Williams-King, Anne: FRE 1986
Willis, Constance: FLH 1935; FRK(W) 1930; NN 1935–8; SWL 1929
Willis, Helen: SGR 1986
Wilna, Alice: WDB 1911

Wilmor, [Mlle]: RSW 1893
Windgassen, Wolfgang: SGF 1956–60, 1964–5; SGF(S) 1962; SGF(G) 1963; SGM 1960
Witte, Erich: LG 1954–7
Wittekopf, Rudolf: HUN, FAF(S), FAS 1898
Wittich, Marie: BRH 1905; BRH(S, G) 1906; SGL 1905–6
Wittkowska, Marta: BRH(W) 1914
Wlaschiha, Ekkehard: ALB 1996; ALB(R) 1988, 1994; ALB(S) 1990, 1995; ALB(G) 1995
Wolff, Fritz: LG 1930–33, 1937–8; SGM 1933
Woodall, Doris: ED, FRK(W), WEL(R) 1921
Woodland, Rae: HLW 1965–6
Worthington, Samuel: DON 1933
Wray, Josephine: FRE 1929–33, 1935–7, 1939; SGL 1931; OTL 1930–33
Wyn-Rogers, Catherine: ED 1996; NN1 1995, 1996; SWL 1989, 1991, 1994, 1996

Y

Yakar, Rachel: FRE 1978
Yelland, Maria: SWL 1908–9

Z

Zador, Desider: ALB 1905–7, 1910; ALB(G) 1908
Zec, Nicola: FAF, HAG, HUN 1924
Zimmermann, Erich: MM 1934, 1937–8, 1950
Zimmermann, Marie: FRE, GTR 1903